KU-636-100

Contents

Acknowledgements

I would like to thank, from the bottom of my heart, all the staff of the National Association of Therapeutic Parents (NATP) who support me in our mission to provide effective support to all therapeutic parents and change lives for children who have suffered trauma.

I would also like to thank the parents who contribute every day to our Facebook group, and give us all such great inspiration and ideas. I would particularly like to thank all the moderators and volunteers who help to empathically support therapeutic parents in their journey through the NATP, and our workshops, training and online for all the wise words and encouragement they share so selflessly and voluntarily every day.

Most of all, I would like to thank my husband, who became one of the most patient, resourceful therapeutic parents I have ever met, and my children, who are the joy of my life, for teaching me more about therapeutic parenting than any expert ever could.

Introduction

I am a therapeutic parent and I make no apologies for this. I am doing what my children need me to do to help them become functioning members of society, to be able to show kindness, build relationships and become effective parents themselves one day.

I first started fostering in 1987. Things were a little different then and foster carers were not very well supported. Moving three children from fostering to adoption inspired me to begin a career in social work. In 1992 I qualified as a social worker and began working with children and families, as well as fostering and adoption.

After adopting my five children, who are all siblings, in 1998 and 1999, I became aware that my social work training had not equipped me to deal with the issues presented to me on a daily basis by my traumatised children. I had all my old 'nursery nursing' skills, such as establishing boundaries and routines, but my children quickly taught me that my standard parenting strategies were now redundant!

I also realised that I had, inadvertently, often given inaccurate advice to parents caring for traumatised children, and that there appeared to be a gap between what social workers are trained to do and the expectation of adopters and foster carers about their knowledge.

In 2007 I took on the management (and later ownership) of a fostering agency that was struggling to obtain good outcomes. I implemented a whole therapeutic parenting approach using the TRUE model which I devised in 2010. This model is explained fully in my first book on therapeutic parenting, *Therapeutic Parenting in a Nutshell* (Naish 2016). Staff were fully trained in therapeutic parenting strategies, and understood the correct way to support foster carers, and the children in their care, using the TRUE model and associated techniques. The agency obtained an Ofsted 'Outstanding' grading in 2014 in recognition of our excellent outcomes, and family stability.

In 2015 I left the agency to move full time into training and established Inspire Training Group, part of Fostering Attachments Ltd. I had become more concerned about the distance between supporting professionals and parents. I went all over the country delivering training and was often told by carers and parents that they felt disillusioned, isolated and blamed. I frequently heard that the system we were all working in was much harder to deal with than the children's behaviours. Although this was a sentiment I shared, I had not realised the problem was so widespread.

As I was not able to find any research that was relevant to what I was seeing, I commissioned, and supported (through Fostering Attachments Ltd), the first comprehensive research into compassion fatigue in foster care in the UK, with the University of Bristol's Hadley Centre for Adoption and Foster Care Studies. This resulted in the final report 'No One Told Us It Would Be Like This: Compassion Fatigue and Foster Care' (Ottoway and Selwyn 2016). The findings are referred to throughout this book.

My eldest daughter, Rosie who was now an adult, began delivering training and working alongside me. Parents frequently expressed the view that they found it invaluable to have Rosie's viewpoint to help them to adapt their parenting style. We were often asked if we could write a children's book from the perspective of a child who had experienced trauma. We decided to write a series of true stories based on our own family experiences, which would also help parents and children to understand where the behaviours were coming from and the best way to respond to these behaviours. My five children are represented in the books as Rosie Rudey, Katie Careful, William Wobbly, Sophie Spikey and Charley Chatty. Throughout this book I have referred to strategies within these stories, which parents and carers may well find a useful complement. I also sometimes refer to my children by their 'book name', which helps to identify different characteristics more easily.

Following the success of *Therapeutic Parenting in a Nutshell*, many therapeutic parents and supporting professionals told me how much they also needed a quick, practical reference guide covering all the day-to-day issues and challenges we face. I thought I would write a concise, jargon-free, behaviour-based A–Z, which was easy to navigate and solution focused. I anticipated having about 25 topics but after looking closely at all the subjects I am asked about, and asking other therapeutic parents what they needed, this quickly increased to over 60!

I need to just get one thing clear though. I am *not* a perfect therapeutic parent! I spent several years making lots of mistakes, and even on good days I would slip up more times than I care to mention. My children taught me everything I know about therapeutic parenting, as I had to constantly adapt my strategies to find a way to re-parent them effectively.

Although this book encapsulates all the strategies and solutions I have used personally and professionally, I have been given lots of ideas and input from all the thousands of adopters, foster carers and other therapeutic parents in our Therapeutic Parents' Facebook group. In this group, we noticed that we had the same issues and challenges coming up time and time again. Over the last three years, the site has accumulated a wealth of knowledge and essential strategies which parents have found hugely beneficial. All of that experience has now been funnelled, sieved and discussed to provide you with the concise and relevant information you need…often in a hurry!

Some of the strategies and advice in this book do not fit in at all with standard parenting and might be new concepts for some supporting professionals in the field, but I felt it was essential to share strategies that other parents have found to make a fundamental, *positive* difference to the child. After all, at the end of the day, we are all working towards the same outcomes.

Throughout the book, I mainly refer to the 'child' and 'the parent'. This is deliberate on my part as our children are often functioning at a much younger age emotionally. Although our children need to be cared for, what they need most is *parenting* – therapeutic parenting.

How to use this book

Part 1: The Basics

This section gives parents and carers an overview of common behaviours seen in many children who have either suffered trauma or experienced some other kind of maternal or postnatal stress leading to high levels of the hormone cortisol, and/or sensory issues. This section also explains where these behaviours come from. It is a fundamental part of therapeutic parenting that we try our utmost to take on the child's perspective, and understand where the behaviour is coming from, otherwise we cannot meet the challenges with the correct therapeutic response.

Part 1 also gives an explanation of the most commonly used therapeutic parenting strategies, including the step-by-step P.A.R.E.N.T.S. model, which can be adapted to most situations. If you familiarise yourself with the explanations of behaviours and the overview of common therapeutic parenting strategies, including 'Strategies to Avoid', this will easily be understood when moving on to the references in Part 2.

I have also included information on avoiding and resolving compassion fatigue, which is a debilitating condition and frequently a major factor in family (placement) breakdown.

Part 2: The A–Z

Ideally, most parents will use this section to quickly look up the issue they are most concerned about. If you have an electronic version on your phone as an ebook, you can also quickly get to the subject you need, even in the middle of an incident.

This section contains a list of common issues we face, listed as an A–Z. You will see that some topics are signposted to an overview. For example, 'Manic Laughter' is included in 'Overreacting'. Each section explains what the behaviour or issue looks like, why it might happen and the related strategies and points for consideration. Part 2 includes tried and tested therapeutic parenting methods for all the presenting problems I am asked about most frequently.

What is therapeutic parenting and who is it for?

Therapeutic parenting is a term commonly used for foster carers, adopters, special guardians and kinship carers who are looking after children who may have suffered trauma. This may be through early life neglect and/or abuse. Therapeutic parenting is also used for biological parents, particularly where there may have been pre-birth trauma, separation, illness or any other factor affecting the child's functioning and understanding of the world, or affecting their attachment. Many biological parents find therapeutic parenting styles useful to use with children who are on the autism spectrum or have high cortisol levels and/or attention deficit hyperactivity disorder (ADHD).

In fact, therapeutic parenting is beneficial for *all* children due to its reliance on firm boundaries and structure with a strong empathic and nurturing approach.

Definitions

In our research with The Hadley Centre, University of Bristol (Ottoway and Selwyn 2016), I wrote the following definition in the Executive Summary (p.4):

> Therapeutic parenting is a deeply nurturing parenting style, with a foundation of self-awareness and a central core of mentalization, developed from consistent, empathic, insightful responses to a child's distress and behaviours; allowing the child to begin to self-regulate, develop an understanding of their own behaviours and ultimately form secure attachments.

The aim of therapeutic parenting is to enable the child to recover from the trauma they have experienced. This is done by developing new pathways in the child's brain to help them to link cause and effect, reduce their levels of fear and shame, and to help them start to make sense of their world.

Therapeutic parenting in practice

Therapeutic parenting is a different way of life. Carers need to *live* as therapeutic *parents* with *all* their children. Luckily, therapeutic parenting is also extremely effective for securely attached children. It just works more quickly.

Therapeutic parents are *not* therapists. They don't *do* formal therapy. They are simply parents who need to parent differently to help their children's brains to grow and make new connections.

So, our parenting looks different. We help our children to feel calmer when they are frightened and behaving badly from that fear. We use empathy to help our children to recognise their feelings. We have very clear boundaries and routines so our children can predict what might happen next. We always try to think about our children's emotional age, and not their chronological age, as, to be honest, their chronological age is not very relevant.

Being a therapeutic parent is a very tough job!

Therapeutic parents live a life that is well structured with strict routines and boundaries. There are no surprises or spontaneous outings and there is no room for doubt. This can be dull at times and frustrating for everyone. The strict routines may be misinterpreted as inflexibility by extended family or supporting professionals. Therapeutic parents often *long* for spontaneity and a change to routine, but have learned, to their cost, that there is always a price to pay for these deviations!

We can't always be therapeutic, no matter how hard we try, but we just need to be as therapeutic as we can, whenever we can. After all, we are only human!

How long will it take to see a difference?

Therapeutically re-parenting a traumatised child is a very long job. It won't be 'done' in a couple of years. We can see some small improvements quite quickly, but they are external changes. The big change is the one where there are fundamental shifts in the child's internal working model. This is all about how the child sees themselves and their relationship with the world. Some of the indicators of progress are when we see that the child feels safe and can:

- demonstrate empathy
- link cause and effect
- think before acting

- trust adults to meet their needs
- maintain a healthy reciprocal friendship for more than six months
- admit when they have made a mistake, without experiencing toxic shame
- feel and demonstrate remorse when they have made a mistake.

All that will take a very long time, probably more than ten years. In the meantime though, we do see other improvements and steps along the way towards these goals. Many parents feel frustrated and desperate as the years go by with seemingly no change. Don't underestimate how the small steps all add up to the total length of the journey. When my children were growing up, I found the following analogy useful to keep in mind.

The Trauma Lake

Let's imagine we are standing on a shoreline with a still, flat lake in front of us. It's called Trauma Lake. Every time I tried an intervention, or resolved a difficult day, I was throwing a rock in that lake. It made a few ripples, but after a few moments, nothing had changed and I felt as if I was back where we all started.

With the benefit of hindsight, I now realise that every therapeutic parenting intervention I did – every phrase, every resolved, horrendous challenge – was a solid rock, a building block being put in place. But my children's trauma lake was deep. Sure enough, over the years, the rocks started to break the surface of the water, and we saw a different child in a different landscape.

They couldn't have surfaced above the trauma without the blocks I had first put in there. All that time...and I thought nothing was changing.

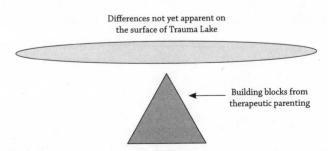

Differences not yet apparent on the surface of Trauma Lake

Building blocks from therapeutic parenting

PART 1

THE BASICS

CHAPTER 1

Why Our Children Do the Things They Do

Often, we can be frustrated by our children's actions. Even more frequently, people around us do not understand how we live and what we are trying to deal with. When we think of our child moving forwards in life, and having been given the wrong signals and equipment to start off with, it's much easier to understand *why* our children do the things they do.

In her book *Everyday Parenting with Security and Love*, Kim Golding (2017) explains in great detail the reasons some children have attachment difficulties, and the relationship these have to trauma and other causational factors.

If you are re-parenting a child who has been subjected to abuse and/or neglect, it's useful to think of their actions in this way:

The child 'car driver'

Someone put my child in the driver's seat of a car!

Even worse, it was someone who should have been looking after my child. Even worse, the steering wheel was tampered with to make the car turn left when the child turned right.

To make it harder, someone cut the brakes. Then, this person started the ignition and fixed the accelerator pedal down to the floor to make it speed off!

My child was in the driver's seat of a car that couldn't stop, went the wrong way, and was moving fast.

Now, people keep blaming my child for crashing into things, for going too fast, for being afraid, for damaging things, or for hurting people.

The social worker put me in the passenger seat and asked me to help my child. Sadly, she suggested doing a theory test first, but that's way down our list of priorities.

Gradually, I am teaching my child to use the handbrake and to manage the steering. They are less fearful just because I am sitting next to them. Always sitting next to them.

All we need now is for people to stop telling us that my child needs to pass a driving test. This therapeutic parent driving instructor is just trying to get us all to our destination in one piece.

Common behaviours and underlying factors

Many of the behaviours we see in our children are fear-based responses, but they may not appear to us in that way. Indeed, our child may present as rude, defiant and attention seeking. If we bear in mind the 'car driver', and start from the basis that a child who has suffered some kind of trauma in their early life often feels out of control and experiences the world very differently, some of their behaviours start to make sense.

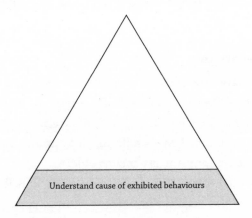

Understand cause of exhibited behaviours

Fear

Our children are often terrified of everyday objects, changes in routine, any type of transition, the dark, food... In fact, the traumatised child's overriding emotion is nearly always one of fear. The fear is masked though, and we may experience it as anger or controlling behaviours. This is why we might see an escalation of defiance when there is an approaching transition.

It's also very disconcerting to realise that, often, what our children are most scared of are *adults*. This is upsetting for parents and something they may not have considered. If your child appears to be rejecting everything, is unable to ask for help and follows you around, seemingly ever watchful, consider that *you may be the source of fear as well as comfort*.

My friend, Sarah Dillon, grew up in care and is now an attachment therapist. She describes the fear of adults in this way:

> If you are scared of something, really scared, what do you do? Say you have a phobia of spiders and one suddenly appears. What happens? You might freeze, feel panicky. You may try to run away, or even kill it. You can't think straight. You might keep a very close eye on that spider so you know where it is at all times. Well, I felt that way about adults. Adults were the source of my trauma and phobia, and every time I was moved I had a new spider to get used to. (Sarah Dillon)

Unable to re-attune

As our children are often fearful of adults and may have had negative experiences, it is almost impossible for them to 're-attune' to the parent following an incident. If we think of a securely attached young child who has committed some mild misdemeanour, the parent may well withdraw their approval as a means of letting the child know they are not happy with them. A securely attached child will usually move quickly to repair the relationship and re-attune, perhaps by seeking comfort or testing out the parent's response. A child who is fearful of adults, or overwhelmed with shame, is entirely unable to make the first move and will remain stuck, defensive and sad.

Blocked trust

If the child has not learned that the parent or carer is reliable and trustworthy then they are unable to rely on them to meet even their basic needs. Our children are often mistrustful of our intentions and find it difficult to interpret our actions, even to read facial expressions. The term 'blocked trust' is also used to describe the child not feeling 'good enough about themselves' in Dan Hughes and Jonathan Baylin's book, *The Neurobiology of Attachment-Focused Therapy* (2016). I have expanded on this later on in the sections, 'sense of self and impact of shame', and 'a compulsion to break a forming attachment'.

Impulsivity

Our children often have high cortisol levels and are hardwired to respond to stress and risk very quickly. They lack the usual impulse controls and can often blurt out what they are thinking, or act without thinking at all. These actions are more reminiscent of a very young toddler or baby as it is possible the child has missed out important developmental stages. Sometimes these behaviours look like ADHD. The child may have lived in an environment where they always needed to be alert and ready for action, or they may have experienced other trauma that has affected their brain development.

Lack of cause-and-effect thinking

Where our children have suffered some kind of trauma in their lives, nothing is predictable. Their early lives may have made no sense. My children did not know the difference between night and day. If even the basics of human existence make no sense, then it is much harder for the more complex layers to be ordered into a fathomable structure by these children. As the children tend to act quickly on impulse, without forward planning, they often suffer as a direct result of their own actions. This is because many of our own inhibitors stem from the fact that we don't want to feel bad later. For example, we might not steal £10 from the kitchen table because we know we might get in trouble, or we don't want to feel bad. Our children cannot project forward and think about how they might feel later. In effect, they lack empathy for their future self.

Control and power issues (see also Part 2, Controlling Behaviours)

It's really useful to turn this particular behaviour on its head. We see it as their need to control, but our children are behaving in this way just to keep themselves safe. The antidote to the all-consuming fear that the child feels is to be in control. After all, if you are powerful you are more likely to survive. Control is a fear-based behaviour and their behaviour is saying, 'I can't trust adults to be in charge yet.'

Our children need to feel powerful but at the same time are deeply conflicted as, ultimately, most of them have a profound unmet need for the adult to be in charge, safe and nurturing.

Lack of empathy

Empathy is usually one of the last skills to develop. Our children need to have all their basic needs met before they can build on those and develop the more profound human characteristics such as empathy, gratitude and remorse. I have found that in general, children who have suffered trauma in early life need to have been responded to empathically, as in 'modelled empathy', for about seven to ten years before they can start to genuinely experience and demonstrate it.

Lack of remorse

Parents often panic a little that their child might be 'evil' because they show no remorse or empathy. Remorse is also a sophisticated emotion which our children may not yet be able to access. This doesn't make them evil.

In securely attached children, we see remorse being established around the age of six or seven. If the child spent a lot of their early life dealing with a stressful environment, then there will not have been time to lay down the foundations for remorse to be established. Once the secure attachments have been made, the child begins to demonstrate some empathy, or the ability to take on the perspective of another, and remorse will follow. My children did not develop remorse until they were aged between 13 and 22.

Hypervigilance

Our children's very existence may have depended on the need for them to be hypervigilant. Until she was 26 years old, my eldest daughter could not sleep unless she was facing the door, and even then this needed some therapeutic intervention. Our children often don't know if the parent is going to disappear completely. Perhaps they have in the past. For this reason, they often have very good visual skills. Hypervigilance does not leave very much room for other things. If you have to remember where everyone is in the class, what they are wearing and what they are doing, there is not much space left for learning.

Sadness, grief and loss

It is sometimes easier to put to one side the enormous losses our children may have suffered. With loss comes sadness and grief. Children are moved between different foster carers to whom they may have formed attachments, then expected to show joy on placement with their adopters. They may be grieving for an absent parent, even if they were abusive. That is what the child knows, and the child may be feeling it is all somehow their fault. Most parents and carers are naturally very empathetic and understanding about this and give the child permission and space to grieve. Grief can be expressed as anger, defensiveness and controlling behaviours. The child does not want to lose anything else in their life. With fostering and adoption, there is often a direct conflict between the positive anticipation of the parent/carer and the sadness and grief of the child who feels compelled to keep themselves safe by attempting to meet the expectations of the new parent (see Honeymoon Period in the A–Z).

Fear of invisibility

When a child has suffered from unreliable parenting, neglect or abuse, they may have a deep-rooted fear of being forgotten or invisible. They will certainly have felt invisible at times. If you are dependent on powerful adults to feed you and keep you safe, but you appear to be invisible, *you might die*. When our children are scared of being forgotten we see some of the most powerful behaviours, such as nonsense chatter, anxiety-based behaviours, following and aggressive or rude behaviours, designed to press the parent's buttons and forcibly remind them that the child is there!

Anger

We often see anger as a constant visible emotion in our children. Anger can be a defensive mechanism to avoid showing sadness. In order to be sad, our children need to display their vulnerability and this is something they don't feel safe enough to do, so they use their anger like a protective shell. The shell is made up of rudeness, defiance and hostility, which seems to ooze from the child. The angry message is, 'Don't touch me. Don't help me. Don't come near me.' See more details on this in 'Aggression'. In our series of therapeutic parenting children's stories, we show the shell on Rosie Rudey in her first book (Naish and Jefferies 2016).

The child's internal working model

Recreating a familiar environment

Some behaviours that appear quite bizarre to parents may be completely familiar and normal for the child. Where there is bedwetting, for example, the smell of urine might have been very much part of the child's early environment, especially in cases of neglect. For the child, therefore, this is not an offensive smell. They don't notice it. The smell of urine is a manifestation of the child's internal working model. Similarly, parents sometimes express dismay when their adopted teenagers seem to suddenly gravitate towards families where there may be drug or alcohol abuse, a lack of routine and maybe even violence. This can be because the child recognises the currency of the interactions and relationships. While it may not feel safe, it does feel familiar, and maybe even as if they belong. Sometimes this is also referred to as 'stimulating the environment' as the child stimulates their new environment to try to recreate familiar relationship patterns. This happens on a very deep level and is instinctive. The child does not think consciously and plan for this to happen.

Sense of self and impact of shame

If a child has not had their early, most basic needs met, they are consumed with a toxic form of shame. Our children work hard to stay out of this shame because it is truly devastating and all consuming. Some of the behaviours we see that relate to shame avoidance are:

- lying
- an inability to take responsibility
- self-sabotage.

The child gets their sense of self from the actions of the people around them. If they are ignored or abused, their sense of self is one of worthlessness and 'badness'. Guilt can be described as 'I did something bad'. Shame is more like 'I *am* bad' (Brown 2012). This feeling of 'badness' is internalised, so the child's internal working model might be, 'I am bad, I am unimportant, I am unlovable.' It is not a decision they have made, it is the way their brain has been wired. The hapless parent who tries to tell this child they are wonderful will likely be viewed at best as unreliable or easy to trick, or at worst as a liar by the child.

A compulsion to break a forming attachment (with the parent) (see also Part 2, Sabotaging)

At the very time when it looks like we might have a breakthrough moment and be forming some meaningful connections, the child appears to 'up the ante'. We have a good day and then it is ruined. We get the child a much sought-after gift and they destroy it. We must bear in mind the conflict that exists within the child. If their internal working model is one of 'badness' and we do something that makes them feel that they might be 'good', they are unable to reconcile these difficult feelings. This is when we see the child at their most destructive or hurtful. They are compelled, through survival instincts, to create emotional distance and pull away. Where there are loyalties to previous carers or parents this compulsion to break a newly forming attachment is even more pronounced. This is not thought through or planned in any way. Even securely attached adults may unknowingly sabotage or end a promising relationship if they have been hurt in the past and wish to safeguard themselves emotionally. With traumatised children this is much more pronounced and much harder to unpick.

Sensory issues

Many of the children who benefit from therapeutic parenting have sensory issues. This can be for a number of reasons. They may have been exposed to high levels of cortisol or stress, or they may have experienced danger, risk and a frightening environment, leading to changes in the brain. Some children are diagnosed (or misdiagnosed) with sensory processing disorder, where everything is magnified and it can be really difficult for the child not to feel overwhelmed and to go into fight, flight, freeze or defensive rage when overstimulated. All of these responses come from the base brain and are instinctual. This is why we often see the worst behaviours if we take children to a supermarket or holiday park. The wealth and intensity of sensory input is simply too difficult to manage and the child experiences a sensory collapse, which we may experience as a tantrum.

Sensory issues may be indicated if you see that the child:

- has sensitive hearing
- jumps or flinches at loud noises or movements
- overreacts
- exhibits challenging behaviour when there are certain types of high wattage overhead or flashing lights
- needs sensory oral stimulation and/or is orally oversensitive
- cannot tolerate certain sensations on their skin (such as labels on clothing).

Throughout this book, I give examples of strategies to help with sensory issues, relating to topic headings. Some children benefit from using fiddle toys, vibrating cushions and even lying on a chair and hanging their head upside down!

Interoception

Interoception is a difficulty in interpreting the body's internal signals. Children who have not had their physical needs met have often not developed the correct pathways in their brain that carry signals around pain, temperature, thirst, hunger and satiety. This is the reason that we see our children either overreacting to small injuries or appearing not to notice more serious injuries. By the same token, they may eat a large meal and then say they are still hungry. The child is not lying. They can't feel that they are full up. The child may get very cold or very hot and be unaware of this. We frequently see our children inappropriately clothed, despite our best efforts!

Cortisol levels

Our children are addicted to sugar almost like a drug and this is fuelled by high levels of cortisol. A child may have high cortisol levels for a number of reasons, many not associated with abuse. High levels of cortisol drive us to act. Normally we would experience a rush of cortisol in response to a stressful situation. It compels us to move or to reach for the biscuit tin! If those levels of cortisol are high for a lot of the time we see our children being restless, fidgety, unable to concentrate, and craving sugar. If the sugar craving or need for movement can't be satisfied then the child goes into fight, flight or defensive rage. It's not much to do with them 'being in control', it's about them *being* controlled by sugar and cortisol. Taking high sugar foods is *driven* by high cortisol levels and is outside our children's control.

Literalness

As the more advanced human skills such as empathy and remorse develop later on in our children, often the capacity for humour is also absent. We have to be very careful as our children may lack creative thinking and can be very literal. Sometimes our children can appear to 'pour cold water' on the lovely imaginative games of other children. I also remember the gasps of horror when I told my children to 'keep their eyes peeled'.

CHAPTER 2

A Word About Developmental Trauma and Related Disorders

The term developmental trauma disorder (DTD) really encompasses all of what we see in our traumatised children and more!

There has been a huge campaign by Dr Bessel Van der Kolk and his colleagues in the USA (2015) to get DTD recognised and included in the mental health diagnostics manual, the *Diagnostic and Statistical Manual of Mental Disorders (DSM-V)*. Sadly, however, despite his research evidencing the existence of DTD, it is still not included as an official diagnosis. Attachment disorder or reactive attachment disorder (RAD) is a serious symptom but a watered-down version, and even that is often not diagnosed at all.

As far as diagnoses are concerned, the experience of many therapeutic parents is that it is very rare for a thorough quality assessment to be undertaken that separates out the different diagnoses (or rather symptoms of an underlying disorder) in a child who has suffered early life trauma. Most of the behaviours and 'disorders' we see are really symptoms of developmental trauma disorder, and once Van der Kolk manages to get that recognised, we might all finally get the support our children need.

You may notice that in this book I don't mention too much about attachment, nor all the other diagnoses our children may have. There is a reason for this. Typically, developmental trauma will result in whole range of associated disorders such as:

- post-traumatic stress disorder
- attachment disorder (or reactive attachment disorder)
- sensory processing disorder
- ADHD
- oppositional defiance disorder
- pathological demand avoidance
- autism
- dyspraxia.

Birth parents who use therapeutic parenting are often doing so because of pre-birth/early trauma and resulting high cortisol levels. This frequently mimics many of the conditions and symptoms that we see above.

Foetal Alcohol Spectrum Disorder (FASD) is often present and sometimes diagnosed in children who have suffered pre-birth trauma due to the effects of alcohol during pregnancy. The presenting behaviours and characteristics may appear very similar to attachment difficulties and are difficult to distinguish. I found that therapeutic parenting techniques were equally effective when parenting children with FASD as this was rarely a 'stand-alone' condition.

The majority of therapeutic parents I have contact with who are caring for children suffering from the effects of early life trauma and abuse, report that their children display many of the characteristics of the above conditions. Sometimes diagnoses may help to unlock resources, funding and assistance. Often the diagnoses are contradictory and confusing.

Furthermore, we also find that when we look at different insecure attachment styles (ambivalent, anxious, avoidant, disorganised), our children are too quickly pigeonholed into one particular style. Our children are rarely consistently functioning within the descriptors of one attachment style, but instead shift between the attachment styles depending on who they are with, how safe they feel, and where they are in their emotional development. For example, for the first four years Rosie was with me she would have been described as ambivalent attachment. She was rejecting, rude, defensive, angry and aggressive. The reality was that she was also avoidant, not wanting to ask for or accept help, as well as ambivalent, in that she did not expect me to meet her needs. To me, she was Rosie, and we just took each day, or hour, as it came.

I found it much easier to take a holistic view. I avoided over-analysing different diagnoses and attachment styles but took on board useful information about them, such as the similarities and helpful strategies linked to dyspraxia with regard to my children's clumsiness and disorganisation.

CHAPTER 3

The Essential Foundations
of Therapeutic Parenting

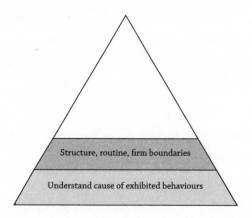

Therapeutic parenting is founded primarily on boundaries and structure. It is not possible to use the more effective strands to therapeutic parenting without this essential foundation. Our children often come from a place where they were lacking the structure of routine, boundaries and safety, so the first way we can help them to feel safe enough to learn and grow is by making their lives predictable. We do this through:

- routine
- being the 'unassailable safe base'
- being honest
- having strong, clear boundaries

- allowing natural consequences
- accessing *appropriate* therapy.

Now let's look at each of these areas in turn.

Establish a strong routine

Routine enables the child to predict important events such as when they will eat, go to sleep or go to school. We need to ensure that snacks and meals are provided at the same time every day. Any slight change in routine can lead to the child becoming dysregulated and distressed. This routine will need to be kept for many years, and it can be frustrating and disheartening. The parents would often like more spontaneity in their lives but learn quickly that they pay the price for deviating from the established routine. On top of this, parents may be judged harshly by others (who do not understand the importance of the routine) as inflexible.

Establish yourself as the 'unassailable safe base'

As the parent, if we begin by establishing ourselves as the 'unassailable safe base', it gives the child a safe space to start to test boundaries.

Being the unassailable safe base does not mean that we are not approachable, warm and nurturing. Quite the opposite. It does, however, mean that the child can rely on us to be very consistent, to say what we mean and do what we say. We move forward to *our* timetable, without being distracted by the child's attempt to control us. The skilled therapeutic parent knows that the child needs us to be in control, even though we are establishing control through empathic and nurturing methods.

I used to envisage myself as a steam train. Behind me I was dragging five little carriages. Unfortunately, there was a parallel track, and very often – several times a day in fact – one of my little 'carriages' would attempt to jump tracks and take me off in a different direction. Well, I knew that I was heading to 'Secure Attachment Station,' and nothing was going to turn me from that. So, in the morning when we were trying to leave the house, and one of my children decided they were not going to put their shoes on, the steam train would pick up the shoes and walk out the door anyway. A little carriage then jumped back on the track behind the steam train and continued towards our ultimate destination.

If we jump tracks and follow our children to their destination we will all end up in the wrong place.

Our children can only bully or control us if we allow them to. Below, the carer is being controlled by the child. As the child demands something, or adjusts their behaviour to provoke a response, the carer rewards the child with their emotional response. The child feels unsafe in this situation and negative behaviour will increase. The stress levels in the carer will also increase and the relationship is unlikely to flourish while maintaining this pattern. Later in this book, I will give you lots of strategies you can use to avoid reacting emotionally and getting caught up in this negative cycle.

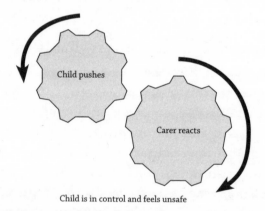

Child is in control and feels unsafe

On the following page, we can see how the carer is not reacting to the child's demands *emotionally*. This does not mean that they are not responding to the child. So, for example, the child might be demanding to have a biscuit, and the carer may be responding with, 'I can see you are hungry'.

The carer remains consistent and present, and is not being controlled by the child. Although it may look like the carer is being harsh, they are actually enabling the child to feel safe.

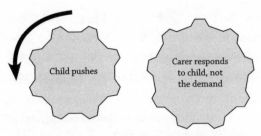

Carer is not controlled and remains the unassailable safe base

Be Honest!

It is vital to say what you mean and mean what you say. Our children can spot dishonesty at a hundred paces! This does not mean that we blatantly offer up information that the child does not need or will not benefit from. For example, we don't have to tell them that we are going on holiday in six months' time! We also avoid talking about an event which *might* happen. If I thought I might take them to the park later, and there was any doubt *whatsoever*, I did not share this information with the child. The words 'might' and 'perhaps' did not exist in our house.

Part of being the unassailable safe base is honesty in relation to anything in the child's life story, contact, and all the other confusing issues our children have to contend with. As the unassailable safe base you need to make sure that you are honest in order to preserve and nurture the relationship. Naturally, we are very focused on promoting positive parts of traumatic early life histories as we want our children to have good self-esteem and to feel loved. We have to exercise caution about going too far down that path. Helen Oakwater's book *Bubble Wrapped Children* (2012) explains the consequences of sugar-coating unpalatable trauma-filled early life histories, especially relating to the risks of social media and related later discoveries.

Here are two statements from children (now adults) who were removed from very abusive birth parents:

Beatrice: When I was in foster care I used to have to have contact with my birth parents. It was a very distressing time for me as I was taken somewhere safe and then had to go and see the people that I feared most in the world. My (adoptive) mum never lied about how my birth parents cared for us; she never bad mouthed them either or said anything about her own feelings. She always spoke factually about them, answering any questions we had. As we grew and had more questions she would go into more detail, being extremely sensitive. Sometimes I would find some of the very abusive things hard and would get upset and Mum would explain how it made her very sad too that these things happened to us. She never used negativity, just facts. I am so glad she never told us that our birth parents loved us, because I know for a fact they did not. I remembered a lot of things. If I had been told that was love, I would not have understood what love meant, and I would have known my mum was lying to me.

A few years ago, I asked my mum for every detail she had on my birth parents as I felt there was always this open box of worries and questions. Now, by knowing my history and everything that happened, it has helped me to get to a point where I am no longer angry about what my birth parents did, but I never want to seek them out to find out why or how. Sometimes I do feel sad as some of the things I know are hard to get over, but I am glad I have the truth.

Donna: I'm a child of abusive and neglectful parents. As I sort through the very last shred of unexposed trauma now in therapy, I am aware that some of the most memorable, hurtful, demeaning, and lonely-making conversations of my young life were when people with good intentions were telling me that my parents loved me. I can't forgive them for it – it doubled, tripled the harm.

What hurt so much about these conversations was that they were overridden by this social convention that things should be nice, things should be okay, so I was supposed to take care of this adult by pretending to them that things were okay. And they weren't, and we wouldn't have been having the conversation unless the adult had known that to some extent, because I never wilfully disclosed to anyone. So, I would resent having to make them feel better (before they went home to their safe houses where people cared about them), and it would feel like a door closing. This is one less safe adult. This is one more person I know won't help me, who I can't tell the truth to, because they can't handle it. And surprise, surprise, I had a great distrust of authority and still an overriding need to handle things myself. It was just this wave of distrust that would come over me – nobody would save me but me. And indeed, no one ever did. And that makes me so sad when I think back to them and I want to yell, 'You were an adult!'

What people didn't realise is that it isn't like I just concluded that they never loved me and then never thought of it again. Of course, the question would be with me my whole life. And (as an adult), I would be able to see that probably, in their version of history, they did love me and did their best and blah blah. But that doesn't mean it was okay. Now I can see that both of those things can coexist. But as a child, I could *not* understand that and I needed one thing to be true so that I could sort myself out on that basis. Them supposedly loving me wasn't freeing. It was a prison. But them being abusive garbage *was* freeing! But it didn't help me as a kid, especially since I didn't ask those people if my parents loved me. They just came in telling me that to make themselves feel better because they were saying something positive. Take what you will from my experience. Stay honest, don't patronise, don't sugar-coat. You build strong adults that way. If they don't ask you, don't get into that aspect. If they ask you, talk about how complicated and dark the truth is, talk about generational abuse and how you and they are breaking the cycle. Talk about how much it hurts you to not know what to say. Just be completely real. You're doing an incredibly beautiful thing for them.

Establish strong, clear boundaries

Therapeutic parents are clear about keeping very firm boundaries that may not be breached. This is all part of the structure that our children require, as they need us to be exact about where the boundaries are, and what our expectations are too.

I gave my children instructions rather than making a request. A request can be interpreted as an option or choice so it is confusing to children who have communication difficulties. So instead of 'Please can you lay the table?' I might say, 'It's time to lay the table now.'

Sometimes, people who are unfamiliar with the whole range of therapeutic parenting strategies and models seemed to believe that we must never show anger or disappointment with the child for breaking a boundary. There is a fine line between being controlled by the child and *feeling* disempowered and angry, and *showing* appropriate anger and disappointment when a boundary is broken. For example, if your child punches a younger sibling in the face, the therapeutic parent may well initially shout at the child and say, 'No, that is not okay!' while moving the child away quickly. Some parents think this is not therapeutic parenting, but it is! If a child breaks a boundary it is fine to let them know, in no uncertain terms, that this is not acceptable.

Often, a parent will say to me, 'I really messed up today. I wasn't therapeutic at all. I shouted at my child.' The parent feels that they should respond in an empathic manner at all times, but this is not realistic, nor does it prepare our children for real life. If the child has broken the boundary you need to let them know that they have broken that boundary and it is unacceptable. Although we can empathise with the underlying issues later on, children need to know when they are going down the wrong path.

Don't be afraid to show when behaviour has crossed the line, but be careful about revealing personal hurt and sadness, in case this is used as a 'new button to press'.

Use natural (or life) consequences

In early life, our children's lives may have made little sense to them. They may not have realised that night followed day, or that food came when they were hungry, for example. Because of this, the child's brain has developed in such a way that cause and effect are not linked very well and many of our children have an internal frame of reference that basically says, 'I have no impact on the world. I am invisible'.

Natural consequences are the life consequences that follow, usually when a boundary is broken or the child has made a bad choice. We set our boundaries and then, when they are breached – usually through immaturity and the lack of cause-and-effect thinking – we show our children that they have made an impact on the world, through natural consequences with nurture. If we fail to do that we are setting us *all* up to fail in the long run. We are reinforcing the message that the child's actions are of no consequence.

I used natural consequences to build synapses in my child's brain, which linked cause and effect, and the world started to make sense to them.

Natural consequences *must* be used with nurture. It is sometimes too tempting to over-punish the child through manipulating consequences and calling them natural consequences. The natural consequence of the child going out without a coat on is that the child gets cold and we help them to realise this. Once we show that they are cold by perhaps helping them to touch their skin with their hand, we might offer them something nurturing or warming. A natural consequence would not be that the coat is removed as a punishment for a week.

With my children, I also extended and linked natural consequences where necessary. So, for example, if the child was rude to me and said I was stupid, later on I might say, 'Unfortunately I am too stupid to drive, I seem to have forgotten how to do it. I won't be able to drive you to football.' (Pause for screeches of horror, etc.) I would offer nurture, wonder aloud and empathise about how sad it is the child couldn't go, but I didn't want them to feel unsafe and as if I had definitely forgotten how to drive for now (see Rudeness in Part 2 for more examples).

Throughout the A–Z part of this book there are lots of examples of natural consequences related to specific challenges.

Access therapy that complements therapeutic parenting

Generally, therapeutic parents find that therapy that includes the parent is the most effective for children who have suffered early life trauma. Therapeutic parents tend to prefer therapeutic models of intervention, where the therapist is a skilled facilitator, the parent is included as the attachment figure and the parent and child are able to build understanding. This helps the child to feel safe and for effective communication to be had where the child may be confused about traumatic events and their timeline.

As the main goal is to promote secure attachments with the main carers, therapists must be knowledgeable about the effects of child trauma and the role of the therapeutic parent and be open to the possibilities of triangulation, sometimes referred to as 'splitting'. This is when the child presents differently with the therapist (or another adult), and can lead to confusion and miscommunication (I explain this further in Part 2 under Triangulation).

Therapeutic parents have found that the model of dyadic developmental psychotherapy developed by Dan Hughes (2016), and also called attachment-focused family therapy, to be an extremely supportive method of intervention along with:

- Theraplay®
- attachment therapy
- filial therapy
- family therapy.

CHAPTER 4

The P.A.R.E.N.T.S. Model of Intervention for Therapeutic Parents

Now that we have the foundations of understanding about where our children are coming from and have established a safe structure, we need a process to help us tackle all the incidents that occur on a day-by-day basis. There are several models of therapeutic parenting, the best known one is PACE (Playfulness, Acceptance, Curiosity, Empathy), described in Dan Hughes and Kim Golding's book (2012). I always struggled, however, with the fact that none of the models seemed to give me a *process* to work through. So, I stopped and thought about the ideal way to progress through an incident. It's so easy to forget the basics sometimes.

When our children are in crisis, an incident can seem to come from nowhere and catch us unawares. The frequency and intensity are exhausting and debilitating. The next time you find yourself in this situation it might be useful to run this checklist in your head for a more structured approach:

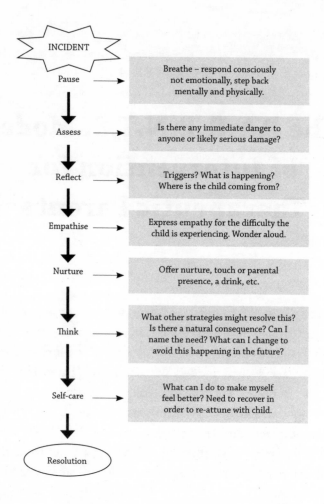

Now let's break it down a little and consider each stage.

P – Pause

As we need to remain the 'unassailable safe base' we need to *try* to respond calmly and consciously to our children. This is our biggest challenge, and is much easier said than done! Keeping your cool is the *absolute number one most important response to learn as a therapeutic parent*. It is so much the essence of it, yet it is also the most difficult to achieve. It takes years of practice to 'act calm' when feeling pretty enraged. I would pretend I was being filmed to make training guides, so I could act the empathy if I didn't feel it. Sometimes I would even actually keep a video running in the background or a voice memo on my phone so I could watch it back to improve my 'performance'. A good way of creating a pause is to consciously take a few deep breaths. If possible, simply say you need the loo, go in and take ten deep breaths. This changes the stress hormones fogging the brain and allows you to think more clearly. If you do manage to 'go to the toilet', try to maintain a calm dialogue to prevent an escalation. You can also:

- Turn away to pretend to do something else so the child cannot see your facial expression.
- Take a breath then remember an urgent task in a different part of the house. If you have been angered by the opening argument statement, this will help to lower your own stress response.
- Use a general 'holding' statement such as, 'That's an interesting point of view.'

Another way I now build in a natural pause is setting my child's profile picture on my phone at a much younger age. Then when they phone me, the first thing I see is them as a baby or toddler!

To access strategic thinking, we need to engage our higher brain to solve the complex issues we are faced with. When we respond instinctively from our lower brain there is rarely a good outcome! If we can take a moment to mentally step back, this can hugely change the outcome. We may even need to physically step back or step away, depending on what is happening. Just bear in mind that if you withdraw completely, and remove all contact, your child is likely to become more dysregulated.

A – Assess

Often, there is an immediate and obvious danger, such as a child attempting to jump out of a high window (or pretending they will)! Obviously, at these times we are not going to move onto reflection and empathising as we have to take immediate action. It is important, however, to consider *outside the moment* what constitutes danger or potential serious damage to an item. For example, if a child is threatening to smash a plate, or is actually smashing it, personally I would not have reacted to that as an immediate danger or potential serious damage. You need to be clear about your own boundaries and differentiate between what you can tolerate and what is truly dangerous. Think about what has happened in the past and what the outcome was. Sometimes a child will feign an intention to commit serious damage, in order to press your button. Ask yourself these questions:

- Look at what the child is doing. Is the risk actual or threatened?
- Does any immediate action need to be taken to protect the child, you or others?
- Are there others who are in danger from the child?
- Is the child in danger from their own actions?
- Can you remove the audience, especially where they are at risk, for example pick up younger children or remove pets?

R – Reflect

Although we tend to reflect on an incident when it is over, I find it useful to do a 'mini-reflection' right near the start. Often by trying quickly to identify possible triggers or antecedents, it is much easier to resolve the incident positively. If we try quickly to gauge where the child is coming from, it's more natural to then 'wonder aloud' and express empathy in the next stage. For example, if my child came in from school and was very rude and angry, instead of thinking about the rude words she was saying to me I might have been thinking about how she managed transitions, or if something had happened at school. Think about the following issues:

- Is there an obvious immediate trigger for the incident?
- Has there been, or is there about to be, a transition which may be provoking anxiety?
- Does the child's body language match their words and actions?
- Is this an attachment-seeking behaviour?
- Does what the child is saying make sense? Does it contradict what they are doing?
- What is the child trying to achieve?

E – Empathise

Dr Brene Brown is a research professor at Houston University and has spent many years researching the impact of shame and empathy. She has spoken at specialist conferences called TED Talks which are all available on YouTube. In her TED Talk 'Listening to Shame' (2012) she said:

> Shame is a focus on self, guilt is a focus on behavior. Shame is 'I am bad'. Guilt is 'I did something bad'. How many of you, if you did something that was hurtful to me, would be willing to say, 'I'm sorry. I made a mistake'? How many of you would be willing to say that? Guilt: I'm sorry. I made a mistake. Shame: I'm sorry. I am a mistake. Empathy is the antidote to shame.

As our children are often consumed and overwhelmed by toxic shame, it is our *empathy* that can be their antidote.

Empathic commentary

We use empathic commentary to give the child dialogue about their internal feelings. We pass the presenting behaviours and respond instead to the presenting *feelings*. This can be confusing for onlookers as we appear not to be challenging the presenting behaviours in the moment. What we are doing is tackling the more deep-seated underlying issues. It does not mean that there will not be some kind of consequence to the behaviour when the child is regulated. For example, the child is being very rude and calling the parent 'a bitch'. Empathic commentary would simply be saying, 'It must be really tough to feel that way about your mum. I can see you are really angry.'

It's important to use empathy to show the child that you are alongside them. Useful phrases might be:

- I can see you are finding this difficult.
- Wow, you are really angry!
- It must be so hard to feel this sad.
- It must be tough to feel that way about your mum.

Wondering aloud also helps us to say out loud what we think may be going on in an empathic way:

- I wonder if something happened at school to make you feel so worried.
- I wonder if you are shouting because you are scared I didn't notice you.
- I wonder if you are angry because the TV programme finished.

Empathic commentary is much more effective to use than asking questions. We *tell* our children what we know and maintain our honest relationship. For example, I would say, 'I noticed that you have had a difficult situation with X. If you need to talk to me I am right here.' Rather than, 'Did X upset you?'

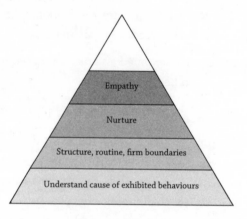

N – Nurture

A nurturing environment always underpins our empathic response, but after we have empathised we can also offer practical nurture. Offering nurture in a timely manner can help to de-escalate a challenging situation. Often my children would flip from furious rage to tears when nurture was offered in place of reciprocal anger or demands of, 'Why did you do that?'

Nurture can be offered physically or suggested, for example:

- It looks as if you could do with a hug.
- Would you like a hot chocolate?
- I was thinking about you earlier when I washed your fluffy blanket.

A simple touch on the shoulder can help the child to feel more grounded. It is important, however, to assess how dysregulated the child is, as touch may also inflame a situation if the child has sensory issues and misinterprets the touch (see 'Use touch and parental presence to regulate', in the next chapter).

T – Think

When thinking of consequences to the behaviour, we need to separate:

- how you feel about what the child did
- what the child *actually* did
- how the child was feeling.

As the situation begins to calm, it's a good idea to think about the next action to take. You might be speaking to the child and helping them to regulate. Where empathy and nurture alone have not resolved the incident, you need to think about (and then apply) the best strategies. You may be thinking there needs to be a natural consequence for what has happened. You might want to plan how you will share your thoughts with the child about why you think they behaved the way they did. You may start to think this through, but might not come to a conclusion for a few hours or even days. That's okay, as sometimes it's best to share those thoughts retrospectively on joint reflection.

We also need to think about what we can change to try to minimise this event or prevent it happening in the future. Think about how much structure there was, was supervision adequate? Has the child been set up to fail? How were *you* feeling? Did you respond appropriately? Be honest with yourself.

This kind of reflection and analysis (mentalisation) really runs through the whole of our parenting, but it is particularly useful immediately following an incident or when there are patterns of entrenched behaviours. Sometimes it is best to think things through and reflect when we are away from the child, especially if we are exhausted and struggling.

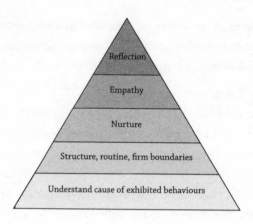

S – Self-care

The last action is to look after yourself. You need to be proactive about this and treat the self-care aspect as an integral part of therapeutic parenting. If you do not look after yourself, you cannot meet the needs of others. There is a separate section on this at the end of Part 1.

Application of P.A.R.E.N.T.S. – anatomy of an incident

The child is watching TV, but breaks a recognised, understood boundary by jumping around on furniture, not watching the programme. After a warning, the parent switches off the TV. The child immediately escalates into a screaming rage, refusing to move on to bath time.

PAUSE – The parent is already feeling annoyed so she says, 'I am just going to get my phone.' She steps away for five seconds, takes deep breaths, listens to what the child is saying in the screaming.

ASSESS – The parent can see that although the child is very angry and throwing his chair about, it is a small, light chair, there is no one else in the room and the danger is minimal.

REFLECT – The parent thinks that switching off the TV was a trigger, but then realises that the child was already dysregulated before this happened. Normally he can sit and watch the programme, but today he was unable to. The parent is also mindful that transitions are a flashpoint and this is always the last programme before bedtime, so maybe there is a worry about going to bed.

EMPATHISE – The parent says to the child, 'Wow, you are really angry. I am sorry you are feeling so cross.' The parent says this loudly enough to be heard. The child continues screaming, demanding that the TV is switched back on. The parent says, 'I wonder if you are cross the TV is switched off because that means it's time for bed. Maybe bedtime is feeling a bit worrying right now.' The child throws himself on the floor face down, screams insults and demands, but his body language suggests the parent has it right. The parent might also say how she was also sad to miss the end of the programme.

NURTURE – The parent strokes the child's back continuing to say out loud how difficult this is. The parent suggests ways that the child might feel better. One suggestion is that the parent tells a bedtime story about the character from the TV programme.

THINK – While continuing to stroke the child's back, the parent thinks that there would be no benefit in adding in a natural consequence for this situation. The parent decides that the best strategy here is to continue to use parental presence and wait it out, then, when the child is more regulated (perhaps when reading the bedtime story), they will be able to revisit the strong feelings expressed together in a safe way. The parent realises that she was quite absent during the programme today, whereas normally she sits with the child and watches it, thereby offering higher levels of structure. She decides she will state this to the child and name the need around 'missing Mummy'. She will wonder aloud about the child finding it difficult to concentrate on the programme due to wondering where Mummy was. If the child is regulated enough and can hear her, she might do some of this now.

SELF-CARE – Before going to read the child a bedtime story, the parent goes to her own 'treat box' and decides what she will have for her reward afterwards. She decides on a bar of chocolate. She plans to eat the chocolate in complete silence, alone. Later on, she manages to do this, although it takes her longer than planned to achieve it.

While she eats the chocolate, she thinks about other incidents that happened during the day, and plans some alternative strategies for the following day.

Sometimes we get it wrong! That's okay, it's impossible to be totally therapeutic all of the time. Just start again next time.

CHAPTER 5

Summary and Explanation of Other Therapeutic Parenting Strategies

In Part 2, I will explain the specific strategies and how to apply them to particular situations. In order for you to be able to quickly reference the strategies, this section contains an explanation of the majority of those we use for many different challenges.

Identify your triggers

Sometimes children's behaviours can trigger us into an overreaction. One of the most useful self-reflection tools we can use is to think about *why* this particular behaviour upsets us so much. Often, we can relate this to something in our own past or relationships. By doing this, the trigger loses its power to some degree. The next time the child behaves in this way, we can at least consciously remind ourselves that our reaction does not belong to the child. Reallocate triggers through reflection after an incident. If you have a partner and have identified that a particular behaviour is very triggering for you, simply decide that the other person will be 'front line' in dealing with this next time if possible.

Set your expectations so they are consistent with the child's capabilities and emotional age

It is unhelpful to think about a traumatised child's chronological age, and what they 'should' be doing. We often come under pressure from external family, friends and supporting professionals in relation to this. If we expect the child to be able to function emotionally and developmentally at their chronological age, we are most likely setting everyone up to fail, including ourselves. When setting boundaries, set them for the *emotional* age. For example, placing a tempting object in reach of the child and telling them not to touch it would be unreasonable with a two- or three-year-old child. In the same way, our children, even at a much older chronological age, would also be unlikely to resist their impulse control. Therefore, we do not put the tempting object in reach in the first place. If we do, it does not mean that the child is naughty and has breached the boundary; it means that we had an unreasonable expectation which could not be met and we need to adjust that.

Responding to the emotional age also makes it much easier for us to empathise; for example, if a child is banging, think about at what developmental stage a toddler may have exhibited this behaviour and respond accordingly.

Time-in

As our children find it difficult to regulate themselves we can help them to regulate by using time-in. Time-in means keeping the child close. We can do this by asking them to help us with something, including helping us to put things right. We can say things like, 'I can see you're feeling a bit wobbly at the moment. I think you need to stay close to me for a little while.' In this way, we are replicating the early life nurture given from parent to child when a baby is dysregulated and trying to manage their emotions. Using time-in as a preventative measure can often stop a small situation from escalating. As the parent, you will be very aware of small changes in your child's behaviour so you can intervene quickly.

Accept the child (separate out from behaviour)

The 'A' in the PACE model of therapeutic parenting (Hughes and Golding 2012) is all about acceptance. Although our children can challenge and frustrate us, we need to make sure that we are accepting the child as a whole even though we do not accept their behaviour. We do this internally and externally through our empathic response to the child's inner world, separating out what they have *done* from who they *are*. We might say helpful things such as, 'It's a shame that you decided to break your car because now you don't have it anymore, and I know that you are feeling really sad about that.'

Using silliness or playfulness

Some of the easiest methods we can use to stop the child in their tracks is to be a bit silly or playful. We do need to be a little unselfconscious to do this, especially if we are out in public, although it can also be quite cathartic. Sometimes I would do things like start a silly dance or a song about what was going on. My children found it difficult not to laugh. As our children cannot experience joy and fear simultaneously, by helping them to experience joy, the fear is reduced and the fight, flight or anger response diminishes significantly.

Use touch and parental presence to regulate

When we think about how very young babies and toddlers can be soothed merely by the presence of a parent or caregiver it is not difficult to see how using that same technique can also help to soothe and regulate our children. It can be very powerful merely to stay nearby. We do not need to say anything at all unless we feel it will help the child to feel calm. If the child is trying to work something out for themselves, and is very angry and frustrated, just sitting near them and asking if they would like us to help can help them to regulate. Sometimes, if one of my children was very angry, went off to their room and started throwing things about, I might just sit down outside their bedroom door and say, 'I am here if you need me, just outside.' Alternatively,

I might remember some 'urgent hoovering' that needed doing nearby. Even this small action can help the child to feel supported and to de-escalate their behaviours more quickly. If the parent is in danger from the child I would be as close as I could be without being at risk or provoking the child.

Remove the audience

If the child is acting out and generally taking the attention of everyone in the room, it's a good idea simply to remove the audience. Sometimes the audience is just the parent. If it's not safe to actually leave and you feel it would further distress or dysregulate the child, you can stay present but remove your attention. You can do this by being suddenly very busy and distracted, you may look at your phone, or even take a pretend phone call (see the phone strategy later in this section). Children are less inclined to perform if there is no one to perform to.

Use curiosity

The C in PACE (Hughes and Golding 2012) is for curiosity. I used to call it 'being a detective' – something therapeutic parents seem to be very good at! Wondering aloud about what may be the cause of the behaviour is a good empathic strategy, using curiosity to try to help *everyone* work out what is going on. We might say, 'I wonder if you are making lots of noise because you are worried I will forget about you?' You can adapt this type of curiosity for lots of different situations.

We may also be curious about behaviour internally, without stating our thoughts. By thinking about where our children's behaviour comes from, we are more likely to give the correct response. If we stop using curiosity and simply take everything at face value we are more likely to misinterpret the child's actions.

Curiosity is a very valuable tool when we 'name the need'. We need to be curious about our children's early lives and experiences, their internal beliefs and concepts in order to properly place presenting behaviours.

An example of this is a conversation I had during training:

Parent: One behaviour I find really annoying is that my child hides when it's time to pick him up from school.

Me: Why do you think he does this?

Parent: To annoy me.

Me: So, you think your child is thinking, 'I am going to wind Mum up. I am going to hide so she gets cross?'

Parent: Yes, he does it to make me look bad in front of all the other mums.

Me: That's really sophisticated thinking for a five-year-old. Can you think of another reason he might hide? Was there ever a time in his early life when he was not sure about how adults might react to him, or if they might suddenly change for no reason?

Parent: Yes, his birth mother was an alcoholic and was very changeable, sometimes very dangerous.

Me: Is it likely then that your child is hiding at transition times to check how *you* are, maybe to see if you are safe?

The parent realised that this did indeed explain the behaviour and went on to address this by simply showing the child that she was safe while he hid. She realised this behaviour had become a trigger for her as she had assumed it was a planned manipulative behaviour, designed to 'make her look bad' as a parent. Once she used curiosity to work out the real root of the behaviour, she was able to respond to her child empathically, and the behaviour diminished.

Showing sorry

Our children are very unlikely to be able to feel remorse and give any kind of meaningful apology. Instead, we help our children to 'show sorry'. Our children usually *do* want to put right what they have done wrong, but they don't know how to. We might say, 'Oh I see you have tipped your sister's juice on the floor. Here is a cloth so you can help me clear it up.' Then afterwards give positive reinforcement.

Distraction

We know that distraction techniques can be very effective with young children. In just the same way they are also effective with our children. One of the most useful strategies I used was simply to suddenly appear distracted myself, looking out the window or just past the child. The child invariably interrupted the downward spiral of behaviour to see what I was looking at. We can also distract them in other ways by suddenly remembering something or asking them if they would like a snack.

The phone strategy

This is a good way of removing the audience and delivering empathic commentary at the same time. You can use it in a variety of situations. It's particularly effective when you need to be somewhere and the child is using delaying tactics. You simply make yourself comfortable, get your phone out and phone your mysterious friend whom the child never meets. You express delight you have an unexpected few minutes to make this rewarding phone call. Within seconds the child has normally abandoned whichever delaying tactic they had employed and superglued themselves to your side. If you *do* actually make the call you can express to your friend how your child is struggling with something at the moment. Be careful not to stray into punitive territory. If you feel the delaying tactics stem from an approaching transition, you can also state out loud in the phone call what is going to happen next.

Watch what the child is *doing*

Avoid always reacting to what the child is *saying*, if they are actually conforming to your boundary. There are often two different things happening. If the child is screaming at you that they are not going to do what you say, while doing what you have said, adjust your response accordingly. Avoid pointing out in the moment that the child is conforming as there may be a sudden reversal!

Use paid back time

If you end up having to do something that takes time away from you, you can get the child to pay back the time later. This is useful for those occasions when incidents feel outside your control. I might use this if I had to spend time looking for a child who had decided not to come home in time. That might mean that I had not done a job that I would have done, and I would expect the child to do that job to pay me back the time. If you are concerned that this might create further conflict and the child would not agree to do the job, simply take back the time in a way which *is* in your control. For example, you may not have time to carry out a task you would normally do for the child as you now have to catch up.

Name the need

This is used to explain the behaviour to the child. It is a skilled, intuitive extension of using curiosity and wondering aloud. We relate the expressed emotions (behaviours) back to an earlier unmet need. I would not do this every time there was an incident, but if there was a pattern of difficult behaviours. 'Naming the need' is used to help the child make sense of their own behaviours and to understand why they do the things they do. It's okay if the child strongly disagrees or shouts back at you that you are wrong. Watch the behaviour that follows to see if you were right or not. Some parents worry that they may do harm by guessing wrong. This is unlikely to be the case because our children need to know that we are thinking about them and wondering why they might do the things they do, from an empathic start point.

An example of 'naming the need' was when my daughter, Rosie, was eating lots of chocolate, stealing it and getting it from wherever she could. Although we tried all the usual strategies, nothing seemed to work. Eventually I speculated that she might be taking and eating lots of chocolate in order to fill an empty space inside her. I stated that I thought the empty space had been created when she was very little and had not had her needs met, but unfortunately no matter how many bars of chocolate she ate this would not fill the gap inside. We spoke about other ways that it might be filled. This really helped my daughter to get a handle on her behaviour and to understand why she was doing the things she did. She explained that the next time she went to take chocolate it was as if there was a little voice in her ear reminding her of why she was doing it.

If our children cannot make sense of their own behaviour they can't begin to try to control it. If you are worried about using 'naming the need' and making wrong assumptions, then use third-party stories. Your instincts are usually right! Our series of therapeutic parenting children's books all use 'naming the need' within the story. Alternatively, you can say that you are thinking about another child you used to know.

Repair mistakes

Remember that there is no such thing as a perfect therapeutic parent. We all have our bad days, some more than others. Some parents have far too high expectations of themselves. There are days, however, when it all becomes too much for us and we say and do things we regret. When emotions overwhelm us, we must try to do no harm and certainly avoid physically harming our children. Walking away fast is sometimes the best plan.

It's important that we repair as painlessly and quickly as we can with the child. We must also strike the right balance between making a repair and appearing to lack confidence. Some parents go too far over the top in their apologies, and this in itself can make the child feel unsafe. If you have lost your temper and shouted at the child, maybe said something unkind to them, apologise to the child for what you said and the tone you used. Say that you will try not to do this again. You can also explain how you were feeling at the time, and what led to you feeling this way. In this way, we are modelling healthy emotional analysis. Then close the subject and move on. Do not be tempted to give the child lots of treats to make up for it. Repair without overcompensating. Remember to keep your structure intact as far as possible and this in itself will help to re-establish harmony (such as it is).

CHAPTER 6

Responses and Strategies to Avoid

Standard parenting strategies teach our securely attached 'birds' to fly. Therapeutic parenting strategies teach our 'penguins' to swim. They are all birds, but they need to learn to survive in different ways. Please don't throw your penguin off a cliff to try to force them to fly.

Smacking and hitting

There is no place in therapeutic parenting for smacking and hitting our children. There are two main reasons for this. First, our children may have experienced physical abuse and therefore we will increase their fear of us, or they may be entirely indifferent to being hit where violence was commonplace. This will only increase feelings of disempowerment and loss of control *for the parent*, leading to the risk of increased physical violence in an attempt to control the situation.

Second, our children may interpret pain differently, especially where they have high levels of cortisol and/or have sensory issues. The merest touch may feel very intense or they may not feel pain at all. Simply the action of striking our children is likely to lead to a breach of trust and damage the attachment relationship that is so fundamental.

Hitting a child says, 'I am not in control. You are unsafe.'

Forcing compliance

We do not grab hold of our children and force them to move to where we want them to be. We must not do this because the fear response in our children is too great and we must not abuse our power. The only time you should physically move the child is if they are in danger.

The exception to this is with a very young child who lacks understanding and may need to be picked up.

Blaming and shaming

There is no point using blame and shame tactics. If someone has put the child in a car without a steering wheel or brakes, we can't then blame the child for crashing into us. I know we may not have put them in the car, but the child will feel pretty helpless in all of this, so the idea of blaming them and pointing out the error of their ways is at best misguided. This is a tragic situation for all concerned and blame has no place here. Blame induces shame, and we already know that our children are often overwhelmed with toxic shame.

As we are trying to help our children stay out of shame, it is better to use a problem-solving learning approach.

Insisting on the truth

We don't insist the child tells us the truth! Some parents think that this is a very radical idea, but let's stop and think about who is the loser here. If we spend two hours having an intense argument and stand-off with the child to try to force them to admit a lie, we have wasted two hours of our life and placed the child in shame. Instead we just let them know that we know the truth, so they don't spiral down into toxic shame.

Sometimes parents think that this means there are no consequences for telling a lie and that the child will 'never learn'. As we know, our children struggle to tell the truth because they often don't know what the truth *is*.

Instead of insisting on the truth, we might say something like, 'Well, I have decided that you did do X and the consequence of that is Y.' You have the same outcome without all the shame, blame and wasted time. For more strategies see Part 2, Lying.

Asking why

Avoid this at all costs! Asking the child why they behaved in a certain way is the same as saying, 'I have no idea why you do what you do. I am no longer a safe adult.' The child is unable to provide the answers for us and may feel more fearful if they are asked to provide explanations to the parent, as well as feeling anxious about the fact that the parent does not understand their behaviour either.

Imagine you have always driven a manual car. There are three pedals: accelerator on the right, brake in the middle and clutch on the left. You then change your car to an automatic car. Now there are only two pedals – accelerator on the right and brake on the left. Despite your best efforts you keep slamming on the brake thinking that you are pressing the clutch. You don't want to do this, and it's causing quite a lot of inconvenience to you and your passengers. How useful is it for your passenger to ask you why you are doing it?

Although in this case you can give them a rational explanation, it doesn't mean it will stop your behaviour. It is hardwired into muscle memory, it is not a conscious choice you are making. Asking why doesn't help, it just reinforces the mistake, hints at blame and increases shame.

Reward charts

We don't use standard reward charts with children who have a background of trauma. There are several reasons for this:

- They can cause conflict with the child's internal working model – the child then chooses to stay on the 'bad side' to prove they are not worthy, or that they do not care.

- The child believes they are 'bad' in any case, so seeing other children succeeding reinforces their sense of failure and 'badness'.
- The child quickly learns to exploit reward charts, making them redundant. The child learns really fast how to manipulate the reward system to get the reward they need with minimum effort.
- Basic reward charts don't tackle most of the underlying entrenched behaviours and cannot take account of impulsivity and lack of cause-and-effect thinking.

Once or twice I did design a reward system that worked for a short time with some of my children, but they were fairly sophisticated, tailor-made strategies, not standard ones. Social workers and teachers tend to have an over reliance on, or simplified view of, the effectiveness of reward charts and this invariably undermines the parent. The example below is written by a teacher:

> I'm a teacher and here's what I know. Reward charts and the like (clip charts, card changes) are junk. The essential question in creating a classroom community for a teacher is this: Do I value compliance or engagement? Compliance is all about manipulating behaviour and punishing. Compliance seeks to change behaviour through punishment, ignoring the real reason for the behaviour. Engagement seeks to understand why behaviours occur and then equip students with the skills needed to succeed. Skills like empathy, optimism, resilience and flexibility. Engagement creates community, and within that community students can feel that, regardless of what they do, they are valued and accepted. Even though a teacher may have that heart and belief, systems based on compliance tell students a different story.

Avoid surprises and spontaneity

Part of maintaining good structure is also the need to avoid spontaneity and surprises. Although this can make life very dull at times, what seems like a surprise to us usually just equates to fear of the unknown for the child. Sometimes it's difficult to separate out the need to keep structure while giving joy to our children, with the need to avoid them spiralling out of control through fear and difficulty managing transitions. So, although we plan surprises, we will let the child know about them very close to the time. In this way, our children benefit from the nicer things in life without high levels of associated anxiety. This also lessens the opportunity for sabotage.

Over-praising

If we know that our children have missed out on a lot early on in their life, it can be tempting to try to over-compensate. We might do this by taking them on wonderful holidays, which they cannot appreciate, or simply by giving them lots of praise in the mistaken belief that we are building their self-esteem. In fact, we are creating a similar conflict to the reward chart. If the child shows us a picture that is fairly average and we give them boundless praise, we appear disingenuous. The child knows that this picture is not 'wonderful' but it's okay. Furthermore, if the picture *is* wonderful and we give ceaseless praise the child is likely to destroy the picture. They cannot internalise the conflict between *how they feel* about themselves and *what you are saying* about them. It is better to give muted praise and base it on fact, for example, 'That is an interesting picture. Tell me who is in it.'

Over-punishing and unrelated consequences

When we lose our temper and cannot think of the right thing to say or do, we sometimes end up taking more and more away from the child in order to try to provoke the response we want (need) to see. This type of over-punishing is futile. We do it because we think:

- it will make us feel better
- the child will finally 'get it'.

Invariably we feel worse and achieve nothing. If you are in a situation where you have forgotten about natural consequences, have already taken away items and this has had no effect at all on the child's response or behaviour, it's time for a different tactic. In the moment, it is much better to say, 'If you choose to do X there will be consequences. I will let you know what they are later on.' In this way, you buy yourself some time and avoid giving a punishment that is inappropriate and damaging to both of you. If, for example, you say you will 'ground the child for a month', who is going to suffer, and how can you enforce it?

It is also at these times parents make the mistake of creating unrelated consequences. If I had used unrelated punishments, instead of natural consequences, I would have inadvertently made the behaviours worse. When our children hurt us, our emotional instinctive response is to 'hurt back'. An unrelated consequence might be telling the child they have to write lines to make up for not doing the washing up. Unrelated consequences do not help our children to link cause and effect but they certainly breed resentment!

Also see Sabotaging in Part 2 to learn more about how we can avoid removing important treats in our children's lives, and how and why our children may lead us to do this.

Following the child

If the child needs space we give them space. If they are dysregulated and choose to move away from the adult in order to try to calm themselves, we need to help them have this space. Although we might want to use parental presence to reassure them, we may need to do this at a distance. Therefore, if a child walked away in the middle of an argument and went into their room, I would not follow the child into that room unless I felt there was a risk of significant injury. This applied even if I heard the child breaking things. (Note: the way we had set the bedrooms up meant there was always minimal possibility for serious damage.) Damage can be looked at and sorted out later on. I would never enter my child's room if they had run away to get away from me. This would have been provoking an incident when they were in fight, flight or defensive rage, and it would have been unfair of me.

During my time working in fostering, I saw many incidents where a child was blamed for attacking the carer, but the carer had followed the child and cornered them when they were dysregulated.

This is setting the child up to fail. Step away, unless there is a high risk of injury.

Time-out

We don't send children alone to 'time-out'. That would be like leaving a crying baby to 'sort themselves out'. Instead, we keep them close and try to work out what their behaviour is telling us, just like we do with a very young child. Time-out is excluding the child and isolates them in their shame. It is unrealistic to expect our children to be able to calm themselves down and to self-regulate.

Time-out also replicates neglect and it is important to remember that children from this background may have spent many hours or days alone. If they are left alone without the comfort of a nurturing adult we cannot hold them responsible for the consequences of our actions.

Planned ignoring and withdrawal

In a similar way to 'time-out,' planned ignoring or withdrawal of parental *emotional* availability is ineffective, and possibly harmful, if the parent is doing this in order to encourage the child to 'make the first move' to put things right. The child is unable to re-attune so remains 'stuck'. This can cause an escalation of an already tense situation. The therapeutic parent must always take the lead by reassuring the child that they are safe and that life continues. It can be difficult to take the first step in re-attunement if you have been very upset or hurt by the child. However, it is not a matter of accepting the behaviour, but rather handing the child a spade to begin to dig themselves out. You might do this by simply referring to a neutral everyday topic, thereby reassuring the child that you are safe and approachable.

Discussions about behaviour

Long, dull lectures and discussions about the child's behaviours will not change the situation fast. Our children find it difficult to concentrate, they will often smile, nod and agree with what we are saying. We can finish a long (one-sided) discussion about unwanted behaviours, feeling pleased that the child seems to have agreed to everything we have said and appears to want to change. Promises and assurances may have been given. We may be very surprised the next day when the behaviour is repeated again. This is because the child was merely nodding, smiling and agreeing to make us be quiet and to stop the noise. I know this to be true because my son was kind enough to confide this in me. Our children also carefully watch our facial expressions and take clues from us. They are keen to say what we want to hear, to keep themselves safe.

Making a child say sorry

Forcing a traumatised child to apologise merely heightens their sense of shame and there will likely be an escalation into a difficult stand-off. You cannot 'win' and it's a dangerous mindset to get into. We don't insist our children *say* sorry for these reasons:

- The child is already overwhelmed with fear and shame so is likely to fight hard to avoid further intensity.
- The child is unlikely to have developed empathy and remorse so an apology is meaningless.
- The child may say sorry in a meaningless way, making us feel manipulated.

Instead we use 'showing sorry,' as explained in Chapter 5.

The 'sympathetic face'

We need to be really careful about the expression we use when speaking to the child. An empathic expression, either verbally stated or mirrored, is quite different to the 'sympathetic face'. This is particularly important for supporting professionals to understand. Our children are hardwired to survive, therefore they are constantly analysing our faces to check how we are feeling about them and how safe they are. When we present a sympathetic face to the child where there is little need for sympathy, it is likely that whatever the child is talking about may escalate into a scenario designed to elicit further nurture or action. With a parent or carer who knows the child well, this is not a huge problem as we can simply decide whether or not it is appropriate to respond in a nurturing manner. It is a problem, however, where this might lead to the child making false allegations.

By alerting school and others working with the child to this, we can help them to spot when facts might need to be checked at an early stage. An example of this is given in False Allegations in Part 2.

Using food removal as a punishment

As our children may often have been hungry and have issues around food, we cannot use food as a punishment mechanism. For example, we cannot tell them they will go to bed with no dinner if they are late in. It is too triggering and we need to use alternative methods in order to avoid being considered a source of further abuse by the child and others.

The more controlling you become in response to issues that you cannot control, the more likely it is that the child will go on to develop more severe, entrenched behaviours. Removing food, for example, would likely result in an escalation of stealing food.

CHAPTER 7

Managing Our Own Feelings – Compassion Fatigue and Self-Care

Naturally, the relentlessness of the task can take its toll on carers and parents. Self-care is vital to enable you to stay mentally and physically well and to see the child through to reach their full potential, whatever that might be.

A carer suffering from compassion fatigue feels disconnected and guilty. The child may become a source of dread or fear. The parent or carer cannot access strategies or an empathic response. The compassion fatigue might relate to one child only, and the carer may present as depressed, cynical, angry and withdrawn.

Secondary trauma and compassion fatigue (also sometimes called blocked care) are not the same, although this is a commonly held misconception. Secondary trauma is where the carer feels traumatised by the child's *experiences*. For example, they might have nightmares about what the child has been through, and may feel high levels of anger about this. Compassion fatigue is when the carer becomes so drained and exhausted by the child's behaviours and needs that there are real physiological changes in the brain, rendering the carer unable to connect with the child or access empathy and higher thinking. You can read more about this in Dan Hughes and Jonathan Baylin's book *Brain-Based Parenting* (2012).

Dr Heather Ottoway and Professor Julie Selwyn (2016) found that over 75 per cent of foster carers showed signs of compassion fatigue and burnout, which was higher than other helping professions. If we bear in mind that foster carers may receive higher levels of support than other types of therapeutic parents, such as adopters and special guardians, the conclusions are deeply concerning. So, if you have ever felt resentment, disconnection or fear relating to the children in your care, you are not alone!

An element of compassion fatigue is burnout, which is described as, 'feelings of physical and emotional exhaustion. Symptoms include anger, frustration, hopelessness, depression and feeling inefficient in your job' (Ottoway and Selwyn 2016, p.9). The research clearly links provision of appropriate support, including access to respite, to an increased ability to parent in a compassionate, empathic manner.

Blame and compassion fatigue

This research demonstrated that it is common for carers to have feelings of isolation, and become detached emotionally 'just to get through each day', leading to an inability to manage more than the child's most basic needs. Foster carers also reported that they felt many social workers had little or no understanding of the reality of the challenges faced on a day-to-day basis, and that blaming and judgemental stances adopted by supporting professionals were further isolating the parent.

As a former social worker, I know that there is a lack of training and preparation generally in the sector to assist social workers in getting to grips with the effects of child trauma, including the effects on the parent and carer generally. If we add to this the fact that this sector is underfunded and under-resourced, the outlook is bleak.

Social workers do not become social workers in order to make people's lives difficult. When I trained to become a social worker, it was because I wanted to make a difference and help people. We are now in a society that undervalues social work and does not invest in the training, so we are working within a sector where social work is underfunded and underskilled. In addition, there are also high levels of compassion fatigue in social work. Social workers are expected to manage very high and complex caseloads, with an emphasis on risk avoidance.

A common mistake made by helping professionals is to bombard a carer who is suffering from compassion fatigue with strategies. Unfortunately, the strategies cannot be heard or acted on while the carer is in blocked care. There is often a toxic interaction when the already stressed, overworked social worker comes into contact with a carer who has compassion fatigue who is looking after a traumatised child. There is a breakdown in communication and a tendency to withdraw and blame. This leads to family disruption. I call it *family* disruption rather than *placement* disruption as placement disruption implies that this only affects the actual placement, with the emphasis on the need to *change placement*.

'Placement disruption' is a neat, clinical description that deftly circumnavigates the unpleasant, traumatic reality for *all* involved. If an adoption disrupts, or a placement 'breaks down', the entire family (including the child who is moving) is affected, usually for life.

The relationship between blame, compassion fatigue and family breakdown is one of the most pressing challenges we face in social work.

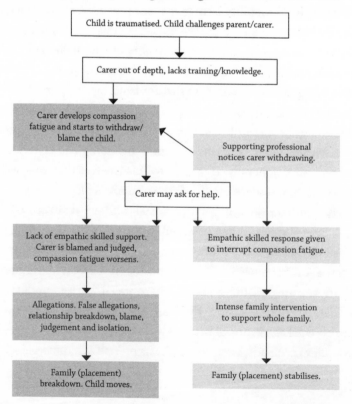

Grief, guilt and anger

At times, caring for our children brings up all sorts of difficult emotions for us. Most debilitating of these are grief, guilt and anger. We may feel all of these emotions in relation to the past care of our children, and even if we were in no way responsible, we still hold on to feelings of responsibility at times.

The anger and indignation we sometimes feel on the child's behalf can at times seem overwhelming. This may also be compounded by the ongoing treatment of the child if there are issues with school or social care, such as a lack of planning or understanding of their needs.

We might also experience grief because the child is not the child we thought we would have and we are not living the family life we imagined. It's important to work through these feelings openly, with an empathic supporter. Someone who has 'walked in your shoes' and really understands what you are experiencing.

Managing bereavements

One of the main challenges that threatens family stability is when there is a close family bereavement. Parents often find it difficult to manage their own grief alongside the apparent lack of empathy or increased challenges from the traumatised child.

The only way you can deal with this is to understand that your own grief is a separate entity to your child's non-empathy. When you have been devastated by a close loss, do not look to your child to make you feel better as they will be feeling panicky and fearful about the loss and also the changes in you. They will test you to check you are still the same. When I lost my father, I placed my husband firmly in the firing line for dealing with the children's issues, and I got on with dealing with my grief.

Ameliorating the effects of compassion fatigue
Empathic listener

One of the best strategies to make us feel better is to enlist the support of an empathic listener. This means identifying somebody at an early stage who has had similar experiences to you, and who will simply listen and empathise without bombarding you with solutions and strategies.

A fellow therapeutic parent in a similar situation, facing comparable challenges, can be a stalwart ally. This is so helpful because when we are able to speak about our feelings freely, without blame or judgement, not only do we begin to work out the solutions ourselves, but this interaction also changes the brain chemistry and 'unblocks' the brain. This allows us, over time, to access our empathic connection to the child again.

Respite (brain break)

When we are in compassion fatigue we often need to be able to remove ourselves from the child in order to access our higher thinking. This is why sometimes we get our best ideas when we are separated temporarily. I call this a 'brain break'. A mini brain break might be as short as ten minutes or maybe as long as two weeks. Many carers avoid using brain breaks because their level of guilt is too high or the stress from the child is so great. There is a build up to respite where the child's behaviour deteriorates through stress and anxiety, and then there is fallout afterwards.

One of the ways this can be mitigated is to ensure that the respite carer comes into the home and the parent(s) leave. In this way, the child does not feel rejected and can stay in their routine. I found using this model led to an increase in parents being able to access respite and, therefore, family stability.

If you are feeling guilty about taking a brain break, do bear in mind that our children often need a break from us as well! They may not know this but it is hard work attaching to a parent and managing your feelings. If managed carefully, brain breaks should be a positive way for the child to experience that there are other adults who are also safe and can be relied on.

Self-care

It is not indulgent, selfish or reckless to build in self-care, support and respite as part of your daily or weekly routine. It is an essential, fundamental requirement. Self-care helps therapeutic parents to avoid compassion fatigue and continue to be able to look after their children. *Self-care prevents family disruption and further trauma for all concerned.* Considering that as an alternative reality, it is clear to see that denying self-care, ironically, is a selfish act.

The foundations of therapeutic parenting rely on empathic, skilled support and self-care.

Ways to build in self-care

- Deciding you will spend an hour on the phone later with a cup of tea, venting to a supportive friend.
- Having an indulgent, lengthy bath.
- Saving a sweet treat and magazine for a planned quiet moment.
- In a two-parent household, dividing up part of the weekend or holiday so each parent has 'time off'.
- Taking regular, planned brain breaks as a priority, not an afterthought.
- Making some time-out for a period of quiet reflection and planning. This might be phoning a friend to talk things through, or sitting in the garden with a drink.
- During stressful moments, focusing on something distant, like a bird flying outside the window, and engaging with that thought to take you out of the moment.

- Keeping some headphones in the toilet, so you can pop in and enter a different headspace for five minutes if it all gets too much!
- Using mindfulness and meditation techniques.
- Attending support groups such as the National Association of Therapeutic Parents' Listening Circles, designed to interrupt compassion fatigue.

PART 2

A–Z OF BEHAVIOURS AND CHALLENGES WITH SOLUTIONS

In this section, I have included reference to the majority of issues I am frequently asked about. It may well be that your child demonstrates a behaviour that is not listed here, so that may be a less usual behaviour, and one I have not come across very often.

For very complex areas, such as sexualised behaviour and self-harm, I have covered some of the relevant factors relating to therapeutic parenting and then signposted parents towards resources I have found useful myself in these areas in the past.

The purpose of this part of the book is to give you a quick overview regarding the challenges you are facing. *What it looks like* describes the behaviours or issues I am tackling in this section. *Why this might happen* gives indicators of some of the underlying issues that cause these difficulties. This is not exhaustive.

Some sections have a *Reality check*. This gives parents some quick and helpful facts as an overview.

Most sections are divided into *Preventative strategies*, *Strategies during* and *Strategies after*, for ease of reference. Other topics, which do not lend themselves well to this structure (School Issues, for example), have a slightly different format.

ABSCONDING *(see also Defiance)*

What it looks like

- The child may sneak out, fail to return home at the expected time or walk out openly. The parent may be able to guess where the child is or may be completely at a loss as to the child's whereabouts. The child may be missing for a few minutes, hours or days.

Why this might happen

- The need to feel in control – absenting themselves may be the best way of gaining temporary control over a situation or their own feelings.
- Lack of cause-and-effect thinking.
- Dysregulation/impulsivity – acting in the heat of the moment.
- Shame – avoidance.
- Feelings of hostility towards the parent.
- A desire to break a forming attachment (with the parent).
- Fear or fearful anticipation of a negative response from the parent.
- Attraction to peer-group activities.
- Blocked trust – unable to rely on caregivers to meet needs.
- Loyalty to birth parents/former carers (returning there).

Preventative strategies

- Think about placement of child's bedroom. How easy is it for the child to leave unnoticed?
- Look at your boundaries and rules. Have they changed as the child has got older? Are they age appropriate? Think about the emotional age of the child in particular. Is the absconding reminiscent of a toddler wandering off?
- Increase visibility and supervision by minimising exits to and from the house (so you can see exits and returns). Make the main entrance/exit noisy through the use of doorbell mats.
- Ensure you always have the child's latest mobile number!
- Identify a friend or other therapeutic parent who can be the 'searcher'.

Strategies during

- Ask yourself – what was the child's state of mind before leaving? Are they in distress? Are they likely to self-harm or harm others? If so, contact emergency services.
- Often it is *not* useful to immediately leave the house yourself and go looking for the child. My children were frequently lurking in nearby bushes and I learned fast that the harder I looked the better they got at hiding. Instead, I made sure they would be able to see me going about my business and that I appeared calm and relaxed.
- Make sure you have good visibility of the immediate surrounding area. The more action and drama they see, the more likely it is that they will move further away.
- Use phone apps and software that track the child's phone, such as 'Find My Friends'. This can help you to see where the child is.
- Sometimes there is not a lot you *can* do once you have informed those who need to be alerted. Make time to have a cup of tea or take a quiet moment to breathe deeply and gather your thoughts, so that you are thinking rationally and are able to think the incident through and plan for the child's return.
- Reflect on the immediate triggers that caused the child to leave, if you can identify them. You then have some phrases and actions

to use later or to put into a message for the child – for example, 'I think you got really angry when I said you couldn't go out later.'

- Keep an open dialogue through texts if the child has a phone. Not a constant stream but just gentle reminders about what you are doing, and that you are thinking of them. Adopt a warm empathic tone, even though this might be difficult to do! It's useful to use empathic words in texts, or in messages via others who may be in contact with the child. ('I know you are very angry. I hope you feel okay soon.') Avoid phrases such as, 'I'm so worried about you' and similar statements as this can make it harder for the child to return, due to feelings of shame. These phrases may also intensify feelings of powerfulness and therefore increase the time they are missing.

Strategies after

- Do not be tempted to get into a long drawn out 'why' conversation when the child returns. Meet them with empathy and openness ('I am so glad you are back, you look a bit cold', etc.). I know this is very difficult when you are worried and angry, but using this approach makes it less likely that they will abscond again. More importantly, if they do, this attitude will help them to return more easily.
- Notify the 'searcher', who can then discreetly look for the child in known places without alerting the child to the fact that they are searching for them. My friend often 'accidentally' bumped into my child and helped her to return without invoking shame ('Oh, fancy seeing you here! I was just popping round your Mum's with some nice cakes. Would you like a lift?').
- When the child returns, offer them something to eat or drink. This has the immediate effect of helping to reduce their stress levels and removes the fear/shame barrier.
- Use some 'naming the need' and reflection strategies to think about why your child absconded. In particular, see if you can relate this back to a time in their life when they were restricted and unable to move about freely. This can lead to an overwhelming compulsion to leave the home, especially during adolescence.

- Use natural consequences where appropriate, for example you may be late doing something they would like you to do, as you have been busy looking for them. Be careful with this, however, as it can easily trigger a fresh absconding episode!
- The following day, or during a period of 'repair' in your relationship, casually establish where the child went by talking about where they went. This can help enormously in future absconding episodes as our children tend to repeat patterns.
- Use *Rosie Rudey and the Very Annoying Parent* (Naish and Jefferies 2016) with your child, as it is a story about running away to maintain control.

ABSENCES *(trauma-related/dissociative seizures, non-epileptic seizures)*

One of my children was misdiagnosed with epilepsy due to trauma-based seizures. I am not saying for one minute, however, that all children who have suffered trauma can't also have epilepsy. This is just a brief overview as a word of caution, and a suggestion to ask more searching questions where there is a history of trauma and your child appears to dissociate or have absences.

What it looks like

- Daydreaming.
- Epilepsy.
- Not responding.
- The child reports headaches following absence.
- The child appears mentally absent with a fixed stare.
- The child doesn't remember what happened.
- The child reports being able to hear but not respond.
- The child uses the wrong words.
- Loss of control over bodily functions.
- Yawning.
- Panic attacks.

Why it might happen

Explanation from Sarah Dillon, an attachment therapist:

> The child's body is externalising his internal stress. When we don't have the words to express our inner distress or pent up emotion, our body can manifest the trauma in some very strange ways. Floating sensations, etc. are associated with dissociation arising from a fragmented sense of self and very deep-rooted trauma. It's a bit like his whole body has inhaled stress for a long period of time and is now feeling safe enough to exhale. Talking to and soothing the child through this process of healing will make it less worrisome for him.

Strategies

- Be aware that anti-epileptic medication will not be effective.
- During a seizure, use the same first-aid response as for an epileptic seizure.
- Increase stress-relieving activities such as colouring or arts and crafts where possible.
- You are already likely to be in a strong routine, but this is very important where there may be non-epileptic seizures.

For more specific help, visit the website of the Functional Neurological Disorder (non-epileptic seizures) support and information group (see the list of websites at the end of the book).

ADDICTION *(see Drugs and Alcohol, Obsessions, Smoking)*

AGGRESSION *(see also Biting, Controlling Behaviours, Rudeness, Sibling Rivalry, Spitting)*

What it looks like

- Hitting.
- Kicking.
- Punching.
- Threatening behaviour/words.
- Using objects as weapons.

- Throwing objects.
- Damaging objects.
- Premeditated violence.

Why it might happen

- The need to be in control – the child may threaten aggression or be aggressive in order to regain/gain control.
- Fear response, especially if the child feels cornered.
- Sensory issues – if the child is overloaded with sensory information, particularly during transitions, this can lead to an outburst of aggression.
- Dysregulation, anger – acting in the heat of the moment.
- Shame.
- Feelings of hostility or momentary hatred towards the parent.
- A desire to break a forming attachment (with the parent).
- Fear of invisibility – the child might be aggressive towards another child to remind the parent they are there.
- Recreating a familiar environment – violence may have been commonplace in the child's earlier life.
- Lack of empathy.
- Blocked trust – the child may be unable to trust the responses of adults.
- Impulsivity.

Reality check

Aggression covers a whole range of issues. It may be hitting a sibling or full-blown attacks on others. It is essential that parents seek appropriate training and support such as non-violent resistance (NVR), management of actual or potential aggression (MAPA) or safe handling and de-escalation strategies (S.H.A.D.E.S.) training, when dealing with a child who is unable to stop themselves from behaving in a dangerously violent way. It is equally important to tackle this issue early on. I have worked with many parents who did not work to mitigate violence in children as young as two or three and paid the price when those children reached their teens. It is, of course, exceptionally difficult when an older child joins the family who is already showing signs of aggression, as there is a great deal of remedial work to be done first.

Preventative strategies

- Look for training – detailed above – around de-escalation and safe holding. This can help to build your confidence, leading to a real reduction in these types of incidents as the child feels safer, realising that you are not scared.
- Build in strategies with the child that help to avoid future episodes. You can use simple explanations about base-brain fear responses to help the child begin to get a handle on their own responses, for example, 'Maybe the small, scared, part of your brain is stopping your big thinking part from being calm.'
- Use phrases like, 'I know you have a good heart'. Then explain that one of the ways to help their thinking brain get back in charge is for them to run around or jump up and down. Decide together something that they could do. This is guiding the child towards the 'flight' path, rather than the 'fight' one. Choose trigger words to help the child do that in the moment.
- You may also use the story *William Wobbly and the Very Bad Day* (Naish and Jefferies 2016) as a way of exploring feelings that turn into violence.
- Carry a small 'bum bag' containing keys, phone and money. If you need to leave quickly you can do so with all essentials already on your person.

Strategies during

- Is there an escape route you can offer the child? Ensure that you are not blocking their exit. Flight is better than fight!
- Use distraction techniques. If the child is just beginning to be aggressive, suddenly look past the child in a distracted way, as if you have just noticed something fascinating. The child will often stop mid-flow and turn to see what you are looking at. Depending on the unfolding situation you can then either turn this into a playful moment or prolong the distraction, buying you valuable thinking time.

- Look carefully at what the child is actually doing. Sometimes our children are threatening violence while moving away.
- Remember at times of maximum dysregulation, no amount of talking to your child about their behaviour and explaining consequences will help them to calm down as their base brain is in fight or flight.
- Relate empathic commentary to what you think the child is angry about; for example, 'Wow I can see you are really angry about not being able to have extra TV time today.'
- Use phrases such as, 'I know the good heart part of you doesn't like hurting people.' This gives the child a way out.
- Put yourself in the child's shoes, and comment from their perspective, whether or not you agree with it.
- If the child is shouting things like, 'I hate you', empathise with that feeling, 'It must be really hard to feel like you hate your Mum.'
- Use parental presence – stay close to the child (if safe) and adopt a calm and reassuring tone of voice. Where the child is out of control, seeing the parent still appearing to be in control can lower the fear that is feeding the anger.
- You know your child best. Sometimes you can hug the child with reassuring words. Bringing the child close can limit their ability to continue hitting and kicking. Make sure you read their body language well, as a hug at the wrong moment can trigger aggression due to feelings of restriction and claustrophobia in the child.
- A gentle touch to reassure may be safer than a hug, and more easily accepted. So, with the empathy demonstrated, a touch on the child's shoulder can help them to regulate.
- I found that if I suddenly 'noticed' a small injury on the child (which might or might not be there in truth), this could cut straight through the aggression. 'Oh stop! Wait! You have hurt your ear, let me see...' The child's overriding need for a nurture link, combined with concern for themselves, can stop the aggression dead in its tracks.

- I use a technique called 'matching the affect', which Dan Hughes refers to in many of his talks, books and articles (see, for example, Hughes and Baylin 2012, p.52). For example, I may shout or raise my voice, if appropriate, to match the dysregulation of the child. The crucial difference, however, is that I would be completely in control of myself and demonstrate that. For example, my child is shouting and screaming that she knows I don't love her. If I speak quietly with nurture, and say, 'I can see you are struggling with this', it may make her angrier, as she might feel that I am not listening. So instead I use nurturing words but with a stronger, louder tone, 'Well, I am your mum and you are stuck with me and I have to love you forever!'

Strategies after

- Once the aggressive outburst is over, everyone may need a little space, or sometimes the child will draw close. Go with whatever feels right instinctively.
- 'Naming the need' might be used to explore the overwhelming feelings that led to the aggression. 'I wonder if when you were very little, scary things were happening a lot around you, so you used to fight hard to protect yourself? I am sorry you had to be so scared, but now...'
- Natural consequences – if there is an actual injury, you might add in a painfully long and boring healing process for yourself, such as rubbing in cream, which may also effectively involve the child so that they can 'show sorry'. This also helps re-attunement. The important thing to bear in mind with any consequence is that the child feels unsafe, hits from fear, and then spirals out of control without really understanding where their feelings came from. They do not understand why they are aggressive and it will be frightening for them and reinforcing their view of themselves as 'bad'. Piling unrelated consequences on top of these feelings will only lead to a negative downward spiral of repeated episodes.
- At a suitable moment, make it clear that physical violence is never acceptable. It's important to state this.

A note about self-care

- Being the target of aggression is one of the hardest challenges to recover from and one of the major risk factors relating to compassion fatigue.
- Be aware of your own injuries and anxiety levels and seek emotional support to talk through the incident.
- If needed, take some time out, leaving the child with an adult who was not involved. Make sure your time out is focused on healing and relaxation for *you*.
- Keep a diary of violent incidents and ensure the information is shared with supportive professionals.

ALCOHOL *(see Drugs and Alcohol)*

ANGER *(see Aggression, Arguing, Sleep Issues, Rudeness, and Part 1, Chapter 1)*

ANXIETY *(see also Part 1, Chapter 1, and Charming, Chewing, Nonsense Chatter, Obsessions, Separation Anxiety)*

N.B. Anxiety is a central core emotion, which manifests through many different behaviours, so check the behaviour related to the anxiety for fuller strategies.

What it looks like

- Clinginess – see Separation Anxiety.
- Close monitoring of parent or others.
- Following.
- Repetitive behaviours.
- Strong connections to inanimate objects to self-soothe.
- May appear obsessive, checking obsessively – see Obsessions.
- Chewing clothing – see Chewing.
- Biting nails, picking sores and so on – see Self-Harming.
- Inability to settle or be alone.

Why it might happen

- Fear of parent/carer or other adults – inability to trust others to keep them safe. Adults are the source of terror.
- Fear of abandonment, especially where there are traumatic separations and unresolved grief and loss.
- Fear of starvation.
- Fear of invisibility.
- A need to try to predict the environment.
- Fear of change/transitions, especially related to past unreliable caregivers who may have changed in personality or who disappeared frequently.
- Separation anxiety.
- Blocked trust – unable to trust reassurances or interpret actions of others.

Preventative strategies

- Make life predictable and safe. Strong routines and boundaries are a must. Use visible wall charts and planners, so the child can easily see what is going to happen and when.
- It's also important to think about when you share information. You may think it appropriate to tell a child about a change or event a few weeks in advance. A traumatised child with high anxiety levels will have much more time to worry!
- Use a 'deep pressure vest' – often recommended by occupational therapists. The child feels as though they are being hugged tight and it can help them to regulate. There is also a version that can be pumped up by the child, but these are much more expensive.
- Make sure you hand your child over to a known, safe adult, especially at school.
- Think carefully about invitations and events you attend. Parties can be exciting but overwhelming.
- Magic spray – this is water or lavender water in a bottle. It can be sprayed round the room or under beds and other places to make monsters and other fears disappear.
- Fiddle toys can help the child to focus on an object and can help to prevent picking, nail biting and so on.

Ongoing strategies

- When the household is busy, a simple touch can help to reassure your anxious child that they are not forgotten.
- Using empathic commentary can help your child to recognise when their anxiety levels are rising.
- Give lots of reassurance. This sounds obvious but our children need *a lot* more cues and pointers than other children. It may be obvious to us that the wind is moving that tree, but an anxious child sees a scary, moving tree.
- You can use *Katie Careful and the Very Sad Smile* (Naish and Jefferies 2017) to help the child name and deal with anxious feelings.

ARGUING *(child vs parent) (see also Competitiveness, Controlling Behaviours, Rudeness, Shouting and Screaming, Sibling Rivalry)*

What it looks like

- The child questions/disagrees with everything the parent says.
- The child provokes an argument.
- The child says 'no' to everything.

Why it might happen

- The child needs to be in control in order to feel safe.
- Testing the parent's boundaries.
- 'Automatic arguing' – entrenched behaviour with no real thought.
- Fear of invisibility – arguing engages the other person.
- Fear of adults.
- Unable to manage transitions.
- Rewards the child with a reaction (trigger for the parent).
- Recreating a familiar environment – the child may be familiar with a lot of arguing and disagreements.
- Comfortable to be 'in the wrong' – the child may provoke an argument if they feel conflicted, for example after having had a good day or a reward.

- A desire to break a forming attachment (with the parent).
- Lack of empathy – unable to appreciate the viewpoint of another.
- Blocked trust – the child is mistrustful of adults' intentions.
- Loyalty to birth parents/former carers.

Reality check

It is only possible to have an argument if you join in. Many parents ask me how they can avoid arguing with their child, or reduce arguing, and I simply say, 'Do not argue!'

As the unassailable safe base, your position is far too secure to demean yourself by arguing with the child. You simply state your expectations clearly. Avoid straying into areas this behaviour is trying to take you.

Preventative strategies

- Remember – it takes two to argue. Think of yourself as an absorbent sponge, rather than a tennis racket.
- Is a response actually required? The child may be muttering argumentatively but this may not need to escalate into an argument at all. Step away mentally.
- Simple statements such as, 'You are probably right' or 'That's an interesting perspective', allow you to disengage from the argument without ignoring the child. This is easier said than done I know, but with practice, arguments can become an issue of the past.
- Try saying 'yes' instead of 'no.' This can work really well, as our children seem to be on red alert for the word 'no!' So, you might say, 'Yes, you can have a biscuit later; however, we just have to pop out first.'

Strategies during

- Empathise with the underlying need, for example, 'I expect you are grumpy because you are hungry. I am hungry too and dinner will be very soon.'

- You may not agree with your child. Let's face it, often they make claims that are, at best, unreasonable. You can, however, imagine what the situation would look like from the perspective of life not 'being fair', 'It seems so unfair, doesn't it, when we have to do jobs we don't like?'
- Speculate on the child's fear of invisibility, 'I wonder if you want to argue with me because you were worried I had forgotten about you?'
- Although parental presence can help your child to feel calmer, be careful not to be drawn into the argument. You can stay close without speaking about the actual topic the child is arguing about.
- Simply state what is required in a calm manner, 'You know what you need to do' or, 'I have every confidence that you can work this out. Let me know if you need a hand.' For example: Child: 'Why can't I wear my pink shoes? You are so mean!' Parent: 'That's okay, you can rest for a while until you are ready to make the right choice.'
- Make it clear that you cannot be controlled. You need to remain the unassailable safe base. For example, 'I know you are very angry that I won't let you eat the whole packet of biscuits.'

Strategies after

- Think about your own body language. If you get a chance, look in the mirror.
- Tell the child why you think they were trying to start an argument and where this may have come from. For example, 'I think you got angry earlier when I told you to tidy your room and then you had some cross words left over for a little argument.'

AVOIDANT BEHAVIOURS *(see Choosing, Controlling Behaviours, Defiance, Rejection, and Part 1, Chapter 1)*

B

BABY VOICE *(see Immaturity)*

BANGING *(see also Anxiety, Headbanging, Sleep Issues)*

What it looks like

- The child makes banging noises, usually when away from carer or parent (in the bathroom, bedroom, etc.).

Why it might happen

- Fear of invisibility – banging reminds the parent of the child's presence.
- Emotional age – this behaviour may be reminiscent of a younger aged child and can be a developmental stage the child needs to progress through.
- Early habit-forming behaviours if the child was left alone/distressed for long periods.
- Rewards child with response if parent or carer overreacts or reacts strongly.
- Sensory processing issues – the child may be overwhelmed with sensory overload.
- Nurture-seeking behaviour.

Preventative strategies

- Think about when the banging happens and what you can do to lessen the anxiety around this. It may be as simple as changing or extending a bedtime routine or using some strategies relating to anxiety.
- Consider padding walls or objects and removing items used to bang. Replace with a soft, noise-free alternative.
- Introduce other sensory items that can help the child to regulate, such as trampolines, rocking horse, rocking chair.
- Look objectively at your response. Are you giving a strong emotional response to the banging?

Strategies during

- If the banging often happens and you know the cause, consider if you need to physically go to the child or can use a different intervention. If you do need to go to the child, approach slowly and without urgency, taking deep breaths on the way. If you feel you do not need to go, set a time limit of two or three minutes to make a reassessment. Be warned though, you will need to adhere to boundaries and also be mindful if there was early neglect, so that you are not inadvertently making the problem worse.
- It's a good idea to state, 'I see you needed my attention.' You can also comment on the noise level, 'Wow, that is a very loud noise!'
- Wonder aloud about the child's fear of invisibility.
- Parental presence may be sufficient to help your child to regulate and stop banging. You can just go and sit near the child.
- If you need to remove an object the child is using to bang you can say that you don't want them to hurt themselves. Removing an item being used to bang is also a natural consequence.
- If appropriate you can offer a drink or a hug if you think this will help your child to regulate. You need to be careful that you don't get into a cycle that rewards the banging.
- Think of the child as a much younger child, a toddler banging the bars of their cot. How might you respond to that?

- Ask a completely random question, unrelated to the banging, such as, 'Did you see where I left my phone?' This helps the child to see that you are not angry. You have connected to them, but it appears to be unrelated to the banging. It also shifts the child's brain quickly and helps them to be more aware of their own behaviour.
- If the banging is against the door of a room you are in, for example your bedroom or the toilet, state that you need an extra five minutes uninterrupted by banging. This often helps the child to stop, just because they become aware of their own actions if they are on 'auto pilot'.
- If this is a very entrenched behaviour, and you have tried all the usual empathic nurturing responses, you can simply put headphones on and appear really pleased that you have the time to listen to your favourite tunes instead. Headphones can help you take yourself out of the moment if the noise is causing you to feel stressed.
- If possible, walk into the garden to enable you to listen to a different audio.

Strategies after

- You can state, 'It seems as if you wanted my attention. Shall we think of a better way?' You can then agree on the 'better way'.
- You may also name the need behind the banging, 'I think you may have felt lonely and that's why you were banging. Perhaps you felt lonely a lot when you were little because...'
- Speak to an empathic listener about how you feel about this issue and how it affects you.

BATH TIME ISSUES (including showering) (see also Defiance)

What it looks like

- The child refuses to bath or shower.
- The child pretends to have a bath or shower but does not.

- The child becomes very oppositional and defiant around bath time.
- The child appears fearful of the bath.
- The child makes strange noises or lots of mess in shower/bath.

Why it might happen

- Fear of invisibility – the child cannot be seen when in shower/bath.
- Separation anxiety – if bath or shower time is a time when the child is alone.
- Inability to manage transitions, especially as bath time may be leading towards bedtime.
- Dysregulation, acting in the heat of the moment.
- Fear or fearful anticipation of negative interaction.
- Fear of abandonment.
- Rewards the child with a reaction (a trigger for the parent).
- The bathroom may have been a place where traumatic events occurred in the past.
- Need to be in control and feel powerful.
- Internal working model (self-sabotage) – the child does not wish to feel clean.
- Emotional age, especially in relation to making lots of noise and playing as a younger child.
- Lack of cause-and-effect thinking.
- Recreating a familiar environment, especially where there is a fear response and traumatic situations have occurred in the bathroom previously.
- Blocked trust – bath/shower time is a vulnerable time for the child.

Preventative strategies

- Reframe your thinking. What can you control? What is not possible to control?
- Is this something that frequently happens? Is it a simple case of changing the timing of the bath?

- Keep bath time at exactly the same time each day. Ensure activities do not overrun.
- Installing a treat that only happens in the bathroom can work wonders. This might be Bluetooth speakers, LED colour-changing lights, novelty bath bombs, or a favourite drink.
- Structure the routine so that there is always a nice thing happening after the bath. Maybe a favourite programme, a weekly takeaway or a story. If bath time is immediately followed by bed, this is a double transition, so expect double resistance!
- Set alarms. These can be fun songs or upbeat songs, relevant to the activity. It is less triggering for a child to have an alarm that informs them it is time for an activity change, than a parent telling them!
- Taking a child swimming or to a water park is a good way to make sure they actually do get in a shower! Consider building this into a weekly routine. This is very useful if you have an older child who goes into the bathroom but does not appear to be actually getting clean.

Strategies during

- Avoid getting into an upward spiral of control. Remember an 'urgent task' you need to do elsewhere to give yourself time to think. You could also use 'the phone strategy' in Part 1, Chapter 5.
- What is the child actually saying/doing? Sometimes they are actually conforming and having a bath or moving towards the bathroom while saying they will not.
- With an older child who has privacy for bathing/showering, wonder aloud about the child's fear of invisibility while in the bath/shower, and reassure them with an activity you are preparing for them while they are in the bath.
- It's common for our children to make noises when in the bath or shower. This is to remind us where they are. Sometimes it's just the younger emotional age behaviours similar to a toddler playing with water. Make sure you comment on the noises you hear to lessen their fear of invisibility and 'disappearing'.

Over time, this lessens the noise. Providing toys designed for a younger aged child can help.

- With older children, you can directly relate wi-fi time to bath time. For example, two minutes in the shower/bath = five minutes wi-fi/internet time. Make sure you place an upper limit!

Strategies after

- Follow through with the post bath-time treat. Ideally this will be a nurturing time.
- Name the need, where appropriate, about when bath times may have been frightening.
- Keep praise about actually having the bath low key. We don't want the child to form the mindset that the simple act of having a bath is remarkable; instead, we need to normalise this.
- Where bath-time stresses are everyday occurrences and are exhausting for all, consider building into your routine one or two days a week when there is no bath time. However, it is important not to replace the timeslot with something more rewarding as this will increase your child's resistance!

BEDTIME ISSUES *(see also Sleep Issues)*

What it looks like

- The child refuses to go to bed.
- The child gets up repeatedly.
- The child becomes very oppositional and defiant around bedtime.
- The child appears fearful of being left alone.
- The child escalates banging and aggression and is generally dysregulated.

Why it might happen

- Separation anxiety – bedtime means that there will be a prolonged separation.
- Fear of invisibility – when the child is in bed sometimes they fear they will 'disappear' or be forgotten about if they go to sleep.

- Fear of being alone (with traumatic thoughts).
- Unable to manage change/transitions.
- Rewards the child with a reaction (trigger for the parent).
- Need to feel in control and powerful, as frightening things may have happened in the past.
- Recreating a familiar environment – bedtimes may have been non-existent.
- Fear of the parent/carer and other adults – the child is unable to monitor them if they are in their bedroom.
- Boredom, especially where high levels of cortisol make it difficult to sleep.
- Fear of abandonment.

Preventative strategies

- A strong routine is a very important preventative strategy. Bedtimes can be at different times at the weekend from weekdays, but they must be adhered to.
- Be mindful of environmental factors. If you are expecting an uneventful bedtime around the times of Christmas, birthdays, contact or any other similar occasion, you are going to be disappointed!
- The consistent message to the child must be that bedtimes mean going to bed! This sounds obvious, but if a child is allowed to continually leave the room and wander about then this continues to be usual, or becomes the new norm.
- Using mindfulness and meditation techniques with the child once they are in their room as part of the routine has helped many therapeutic parents to enjoy a relaxed evening. There are free bedtime-based sessions, including breathing regulation, available on the internet.
- Think carefully about bedtime stories. Reassuring stories that remind the child of being safe, loved and thought about are reassuring as end-of-day thoughts. Our series of children's books were written with this in mind (see Naish and Jefferies 2016, 2017). I also like *The Invisible String* (Karst 2000), which is particularly appropriate for our children.

- Melatonin levels, which enhance sleep, can be increased through strategic placing of milk and bananas into the child's diet. There are also brands of milk available (Lullaby Milk, for example) that have increased melatonin in their milk. If you boil some bananas up for about ten minutes and add some cinnamon, this makes a delicious bedtime drink with high levels of natural melatonin.
- Using lavender oil in the child's bath, or using a diffuser with that scent, also promotes feelings of relaxation.

Strategies during

- Where a child is upset and resisting bedtime, it can really help to regulate them by stroking them, and singing softly. This is something we do automatically with younger children and babies. Our children may have missed out on this. Stroking the face and shoulders in particular increases delta waves, which assist sleep.
- Where a child is fearful of all the traumatic thoughts that crowd in once you have gone, it's useful to stay with the child until they fall asleep. I know this is hard work, but again, we have to think what emotional and developmental stage they are at. If they have not been helped to self-soothe and to get themselves to sleep as young infants, then they need to learn that now. So, it's back to basics. It will be worth it in the long run.
- When we need to start withdrawing, it is a good idea to do this in stages. You may spend the first week actually right next to the child. The following week you might just be sitting quietly nearby. When I did this with my daughter, I gradually moved nearer and nearer the door over a two-week period. I then left my shoes peeping round the door and stepped out of them.
- Using a one- or two-way baby monitor is also useful if you can bear this! It keeps a thread of communication and reassurance going and can be used in a time-limited way. You can also use one on the silent setting only so the child can see you and you can see them.

- Try to avoid using TV or a phone or tablet to help the child sleep (unless there is a meditation exercise or similar on it). This is more likely to overstimulate them and lead to more problems later on.
- Music, especially classical music playing quietly, can help the child feel less alone.
- I made tapes and CDs for my children with me singing and reading stories. They played these on a loop to help them to self-soothe.
- You may also provide a torch for children to use to read or look at pictures. This has the added advantage of reassuring them when they can shine it into dark places.
- If the child leaves the room you need to return them to the room and *stay with them* until they are settled. There is no quick fix for this. We don't do 'super nanny' and leave them to cry it out.

Strategies after

- You can revisit the anxiety or fear around bedtimes through 'naming the need'. It's best to do this during the day, and not near to the actual bedtime.
- If bedtimes are difficult every day, ensure you enrol the help of another therapeutic parent or empathic friend to support you at times in this task. Make certain you build in regular brain breaks (respite) for yourself so that you are able to tackle this challenge.
- Speak positively about the day when a 'sleepover' might be possible, once bedtimes are easier for everyone to manage.

BEDWETTING *(see also Messy Bedrooms, Urinating)*

What it looks like

- The child wets the bed and alerts you.
- The child wets the bed and appears unaware.
- The child wets the bed and is aware, but remains in the bed.
- The child wets the bed, is aware and conceals bedding.

Why it might happen

- Fear response – the child may wet themselves in fear or may be frightened to ask to go to the toilet, or frightened of the toilet.
- The child may enjoy the sensation of warmth from the urine.
- Sensory issues – the child may lack feeling and be unaware of the usual impulses.
- Immaturity/emotional age – the child is simply at a much younger developmental stage than they are at chronologically.
- Trauma-related issues, particularly around neglect and/or sexual abuse.
- Rewards the child with a reaction (trigger for the parent).
- Recreating a familiar environment – it may be normal past entrenched behaviour. The smell of urine is a familiar babyhood smell. This is subconscious.
- Comfortable to be in the wrong – the internal working model of the child means they are comfortable and at ease with being seen to be 'dirty' or 'smelly'.
- Medical issues, particularly in relation to sensation and bladder control.
- The need to feel in control and powerful – the child at least has ultimate control over bodily functions.
- Lack of cause-and-effect thinking – the child is unlikely to link the thought 'I will wet the bed' to 'I will be wet'.
- Fear of invisibility/being forgotten – seeking a response.
- Fear of the parent/carer and other adults.
- Fear of change/transitions.
- Separation anxiety.
- Dissociation, especially where it appears the child is unaware (see also Absences).
- Overwhelming need to keep the parent close – seeking a nurture response, especially as wetting the bed is almost guaranteed to gain interaction with the parent, whatever form that interaction takes.

Reality check

It's really important to step away from the notion that they are doing it 'to you' or that it's all about control. It is nothing at all to do with how close the bathroom is. This is not a logical problem, it is a very deep-seated, emotional, trauma-based issue that will require all your tolerance, insight and patience. Often parents of traumatised children spend years tackling this issue from a medical perspective (I know I did). Sadly, the answer is almost never that straightforward.

Some children describe the sensation of wetting themselves or wetting the bed as 'feeling a warm hug'. This is a stark reminder that the sensation of warm urine may have been the only comforting sensation some of our children experienced in very neglectful situations.

Useful strategies

- If your child appears unaware of the sensations of being wet, try looking into sensory integration therapy.
- If using pull-ups or night nappies, try putting normal pants on underneath so the child feels the sensation of wetness, if you think they are able to.
- Have a regular toileting routine that is linked in to mealtimes, drinks and so on.
- You may want to look into standard strategies, just because supporting professionals will expect you to have tried them – for example, limiting fluids one hour before bedtime, lifting the child for the toilet. These methods have very limited success with traumatised children. Don't be tempted to strictly limit fluids, but it's a good idea to avoid them in the hour before bedtime.
- It is likely that you will become aware of the wet bed either in the morning or when you are lifting the child to go to the toilet. This is one issue that is virtually impossible to interrupt just before it happens.
- Provide a torch for the child to use to go to the toilet.

- It is essential that you limit the stress that this causes you, otherwise you can quickly enter into a power struggle that you *cannot* win. These issues are often very long term, but they *do* resolve. Look at minimising the impact on you, the child and the household.
- Don't be worried about using pull-ups or night nappies far beyond the chronological age of the child.
- Check carefully your child's reactions around leaving their room to visit the toilet. Think about reintroducing a potty in the room if you think fear is a contributing factor.
- Where wetting is happening every night despite the fact that you are lifting the child to go to the toilet, stop lifting them and make a future plan to try again. If we think of our babies and toddlers, we may change them in the night but we don't put them on the toilet.
- Consciously step away from punitive consequences without nurture. I have read many horror stories of desperate, exhausted parents making their children wash the sheets in the bath. It is highly unlikely this will resolve the behaviour – it will simply increase shame and damage your relationship.
- As children get older, it's important to help them to deal with the aftermath themselves. This must not be done in a shaming way. Be matter of fact, show them how to strip the bed and use the washing machine. Offer to help. They may have this issue to deal with as young adults so they need to be able to manage it.
- Where the child remains lying in the bed after they have urinated, as stated, sometimes children do this as it may have been the only experience they had of feeling warmth if they have lived in neglectful or physically abusive homes. You can name the need around this and explore it with the child.

Footnote: My son wet the bed every night for 14 years. It was one of the most relentless, frustrating challenges we faced. A real step forward was when we realised how he was recreating his familiar babyhood environment and completely lacked awareness around sensations. This helped us to stop feeling angry as parents and to tackle the situation from a place of empathy.

BIRTHDAYS, CHRISTMAS AND OTHER CELEBRATIONS *(see also Obsessions, Rejection, Sabotaging, Ungratefulness)*

What it looks like

- The child talks endlessly about their birthday or Christmas, sometimes months in advance.
- The child completely sabotages the birthday and or birthday surprises.
- The child is entirely unable to self-regulate before, during and after their birthday or leading up to the special day.
- The child disrupts the birthdays or special celebrations of others.
- The child exhibits rejecting behaviours on special days such as Mother's Day.

Why it might happen

- Comfortable to be 'in the wrong' – their internal working model makes the child believe they do not deserve nice things. May create huge conflict within the child.
- Blocked trust – the child does not trust the honesty or motivation of the person giving a gift.
- Loyalty to birth parents and former carers – resisting attachment to new carers/parents, especially in relation to Mother's Day or parents' celebrations, which can be particularly difficult.
- Recreating a familiar environment – the child is uncomfortable with receiving nice things and being given special time and/or has witnessed a disregard for property and personal appearance.
- Lack of cause-and-effect thinking – not able to remember that if something is broken, it stays broken.
- Dysregulation – acting in the heat of the moment.
- Shame – relating to feelings of unworthiness.
- Feelings of hostility or momentary hatred towards the parent.
- A need to try to predict the environment – the child needs to keep everything the same, avoid surprises and so on.
- Fear of change/transitions – any kind of celebration event means there will be a change in routine.

- Fear of drawing attention to self, especially relating to birthdays.
- Sensory issues, unaware of 'heavy-handedness'. May be clumsy and break gifts unintentionally.
- Emotional age – the child may be experiencing the event as a much younger child would.

Preventative strategies

- Where the child is unable to acknowledge or manage the birthdays or special events of others, it's a good idea to plan well in advance. For example, help the child to choose a card or small gift. This is also useful at Christmas.
- If the child is unable to manage this, then get the gift on their behalf and clearly state that you know they would have bought or made this had they been able to.
- Keep everything low key. The bigger the event, the more *you* will pay!
- Where a child is talking incessantly about their own birthday or Christmas, this may be misinterpreted as excitement, when actually it is often stress and anxiety. What happened at Christmas in the past?
- Be mindful of what birthdays/Christmas/Mother's Day and Father's Day may have meant in the past, especially the birthdays of unsafe adults, and where there is the loss of the maternal/ paternal figure.
- Be very clear about what will happen on the actual day. Do *not* be tempted to plan surprises. If possible, stick to a 'routine' for special days so the child can learn to predict what happens at Christmas, for example.
- For Christmas, do not be tempted to go off visiting extended family with the child. This can be much too difficult for our children and needs to be very carefully planned and thought through. If you do decide to do this, make sure you have one adult allocated to the child to help them 'break out' when needed. On a sensory level, it can be very overwhelming.

- If you celebrate Mother's/Father's Day, try to put your own feelings about this to one side. It can be extremely hurtful to work so hard with your traumatised child and then find that you feel unappreciated, or worse, the child completely sabotages the day. Many therapeutic parents have found that calling it 'Family Day' generally produces a much nicer time for everyone and minimises feelings of torn loyalties. As our children get older they are usually more able to appreciate us. I have found my own children more than made up for any 'forgotten' Mother's Days in later life. In the meantime, plan your own birthday or Mother's/Father's Day yourself to ensure you get the time *you* want. I used to celebrate Mother's Day on the previous day by organising a day out shopping for myself with lunch...and that definitely took some work! This way I was refreshed for Mother's Day, had minimum expectations and could support my children through what was a difficult day for them too.
- Where tricky behaviours escalate prior to the day, be mindful that the child's internal working model makes them feel as though they do not deserve treats. State openly that while there may well be (natural) consequences for the demonstrated behaviours, these consequences will *not* include the removal of the birthday treat, as you have decided that they deserve this. Taking away the birthday treat is much more about making ourselves feel better. It will not have any long-term healing effect on the child, in fact quite the opposite.
- Think carefully about gifts that you buy. Ensure you are thinking about the child's emotional age, sensory issues, tendency to destroy/lose objects and so on.
- Be mindful that our children's obsessions are often not about receiving the item they 'really, really need'. See Obsessions.

Strategies during

- On the day, readjust your expectations so you are not feeling excited about how thrilled and grateful your child will be.

The parent's expectations are often the cause of disappointment, leading to shame-fuelled rages.

- Ensure that any birthday party is low key, with other therapeutic parents on hand to help diffuse anxieties and dysregulation. A good model is to invite three 'friends' with parents for tea, or a cinema trip with pizza. Where there are several siblings, try to include little jobs and treats for the others spaced out through the day. This helps everyone to feel included and lessens tension.
- Make sure you use wondering aloud and empathic commentary to help the child understand their own feelings as they arise: 'I wonder if you are trying to get me to say "no birthday" because you think you don't deserve one?'
- Stagger present opening throughout the day, ensuring that the last one happens once the child is in bed at the end of the day. Try to ensure this present is suitable for bedtime!
- Limit sugar! This sounds difficult but at least try providing sugar-free drinks and lots of savoury foods.

Strategies after

- You can use 'naming the need' to explore issues relating to anxiety about the child's birthday, as well as why they may be struggling with other people's birthdays. You may find it useful to talk about a fear of being overlooked or forgotten.
- 'Naming the need' is also very effective for when the celebration days of others have 'gone wrong.' You might say, 'I think you really struggled with Mother's Day because it reminded you of your mum, and maybe you feel as if you are being disloyal?'
- *Callum Kindly and the Very Weird Child* (Naish and Jefferies 2017) also explores feelings of jealousy around birthdays and can be used either before or after the event with siblings.
- Expect an anti-climax of sorts. Some of our children are demonstrably relieved that the change in routine is over with and they can relax back into their familiar patterns. Other children may take some days to 'come down', especially where there has been a sugar overload. Don't be tempted to cram lots of different activities into the following days.

BITING *(see also Aggression)*

What it looks like

- The child bites adults or other children.

Why it might happen

- The need to be in control – the child may threaten biting or bite in order to regain or gain control.
- Fear response, especially if the child feels cornered.
- Sensory issues – if the child is overloaded with sensory information, particularly during transitions, this can lead to biting, especially with a child who has issues with chewing and mouthing.
- Unable to link cause and effect/impulsivity – even though there may have been discussions and explanations about biting, the child is unable to relate the end result to the initial action.
- Dysregulation, anger – acting in the heat of the moment.
- Shame – deflection of shame-inducing incident into biting.
- Feelings of hostility or momentary hatred towards the parent or another.
- Fear of invisibility – the child might be aggressive towards another child to remind the parent that they are there.
- Recreating a familiar environment – biting may have been commonplace in the child's earlier life.

Preventative strategies

- Use 'Chewelry' bracelets or similar and direct the child to bite on the bracelet when you see they may be about to bite. When biting is related to a sensory need, the impulse to bite must be relieved and re-directed. (See Chewing for more information on this.)
- Think about the child's emotional age and consider what you might put in place for a younger child.
- Look for warning signs (if there are any), such as mounting frustration. Use distraction techniques and playfulness to intercept.

- Be aware of triggers such as transitions, ending of activities, toy sharing.
- Tell the child that high sugar levels can cause biting so you will need to limit sweet treats if there is any biting. This can be remarkably effective where the child has some control over the biting.

Strategies during

- Biting can happen very quickly. If the child bites and does not release, holding the back of the child's head in place can prevent serious injury. This action (usually) instinctively makes the child release the bite. You can access training in this through de-escalation courses.
- If child A has bitten child B then your positive attention and empathy must be shown first towards child B.
- Our instinct may be to shout 'No!', swiftly followed by some clear, firm words. This is fine. It's one of those occasions when an immediate reminder of boundaries is needed.
- If the child has already bitten, or you think is likely to bite again, use time-in to keep the child near to you.
- Empathic commentary would be directed mainly towards the victim (or self) but you can add in, 'I think you didn't want X to have your toy.' We condemn the action, not the child.

Strategies after

- One of the best ways to handle biting is to prevent it. We know our children struggle with cause and effect but the use of natural consequences here can really help them to get a handle on this behaviour.
- The child needs to be helped to 'show sorry'. This might be a very long, dull exercise in rubbing cream into the bite area or holding on a compress for some considerable time.
- If you were due to go out but the child bit your arm, tell the child that your arm may not be strong enough to drive or carry your bag.

- With a younger child, you might speculate that it is in fact the teeth that are at fault here. This is particularly helpful when you really want to avoid shame. You may encourage the child to clean their teeth to get all the 'bitey bits' off the teeth to help stop it happening. This can become very boring for the child and can help to build in inhibitors. (Note that we do not clean the child's teeth for them or do this in an abusive or harsh way.)
- Be careful to avoid using punitive consequences and punishments that are not linked to the action. Remember that often these behaviours come from fear and we need to *reduce the fear* to gain control of the behaviours.

BLOCKED CARE *(see Part 1, Chapter 7)*

BLOCKING *(see Controlling Behaviours)*

BOASTING *(see also Lying, Overreacting)*

What it looks like

- Over-exaggerating small achievements.
- Creating a scenario where the child is 'the hero'.
- Paying compliments to themselves.
- Appearing excessively proud.
- Pretending they have won special recognition or prizes.

Why it might happen

- Fear of invisibility – boasting increases visibility and perceived stature.
- Need to feel and demonstrate powerfulness.
- Need to control immediate environment and the opinions of others.
- Need to influence the main carer/parent's view of the child, particularly when they are feeling vulnerable.
- Lack of cause-and-effect thinking – the child usually cannot link the fact that what they are saying will be checked out.

- Emotional age 'magical thinking' – very similar to the fantasies of a younger child.
- Loyalty to birth parents/former carers, especially in relation to claims about their past life.

Preventative strategies

- Be aware that our children's fragile sense of self may be fragmented, so some of the claims they make may be believed by them.
- Be careful not to overreact to the claim and start getting into a 'telling lies' scenario. This will only increase the child's feelings of powerlessness and will not decrease their claims.
- Keep up very good levels of communication between the school and other people caring for your child. This way you will always be clear about the reality of the claims.
- Let your child know that you always check things out. If they have any impulse control around this, over time it will reduce the boasting.
- Allow activities that increase the child's sense of self-worth and powerfulness. This can be something as simple as them choosing the meal once a week.

Strategies during

- When the child starts boasting about something that you know is wildly exaggerated, reply with a neutral response such as, 'That's interesting' or, 'That's an interesting point of view.' This allows the child to know that you have heard what they are saying, but that you are not giving any real credibility to the story. You can also say, 'Tell me more.'
- In order to preserve the child's fragile ego building, you can make positive neutral comments if you wish, such as, 'I always knew you were clever, because of the way you...(give example).' Then disengage or change the subject. Be aware, however, that it is important that the child is not left with an impression that you believe the boasts.

- As you are the 'unassailable safe base', it's really important that the child knows that you 'know everything'. So if, for example, the child claims they were 'top in spellings' and you know this cannot be so, say, 'I am really pleased you have decided you are doing so well. I will wait for confirmation from (teacher) as they haven't informed me of this yet.'
- Playfulness can work really well with boasting. For example, the child says, 'I saved Matthew's life!' The parent says, 'That's amazing! Show me how you did it!' Cue playful interaction.
- You can create a trigger word, as we do with nonsense questions, to alert the child to the fact that you know this boasting is not founded in reality. This helps to build synapses where the boasting is 'automatic'. For example, 'My teacher says she is going to put me forwards for the Olympics!' Parent, 'Well I always knew you were a clever potato.' Potato is the key word that is used in all boasting episodes!

Strategies after

- You can name the need behind the boasting, especially where this is an entrenched, long-term behaviour, 'I wonder if saying these things makes you feel big and strong?'
- *Charley Chatty and the Wiggly Worry Worm* (Naish and Jefferies 2016) helps parents to name the anxious feeling associated with boasting behaviours.
- Be clear about levels of communication and that you do not believe the boasts. You might say, 'I understand you think you saved Matthew's life, but I think it was not quite such a big story as that.'
- Give the child alternative accomplishments to feel proud of; for example, 'I know you didn't really come top in spellings but I think you have done stuff *way* better than that…(give example of kindness or empathy shown, helping or overcoming adversity).'
- Be clear that your admiration and appreciation for the child is not related to, or dependent on, their accomplishments.

BOSSINESS *(see Competitiveness, Controlling Behaviours, Sibling Rivalry)*

BOTTLES *(late use of) (see Immaturity)*

BREAKING THINGS *(see Damaging, Sabotaging)*

BRUSHING TEETH *(see also Bath Time Issues, Defiance)*

What it looks like

- The child refuses to brush their teeth.
- The child says they have brushed their teeth when they have not.
- The child does not brush their teeth properly.

Why it might happen

- Sensory issues – it may actually be painful for the child to brush their teeth.
- Inability to manage transitions – teeth brushing is normally a transition from one phase to another.
- Rewards the child with a reaction (trigger for the parent).
- Need to control.
- Lack of cause-and-effect thinking – the child is unlikely to link the outcome (visits to dentist, tooth decay, etc.) to the action needed today.
- Recreating a familiar environment – the habit of brushing teeth may not have been part of the child's daily routine.
- Comfortable to be in the wrong/self-sabotage – the child may not want 'nice, shiny teeth'.

Preventative strategies

- Reframe your thinking. What can you control? What is not possible to control?
- Keep teeth brushing times at exactly the same time each day.

- Ensure activities do not overrun – combining this with an activity that can only take place afterwards can be effective.
- A useful idea is a novelty chewable toothbrush and teether. This can help with sensory issues too. The child can bite as much as they like and the silicone brush does not splay like normal bristles.
- Avoid using the terms 'cleaning your teeth' or 'brushing your teeth'. Instead, say things like 'Time to visit Tommy Toothbrush'.
- Be sensitive to sensory issues, which may mean that brushing teeth is painful.
- Be aware that it can take up to two years to establish this as part of the child's routine. Even then they will need 'reminding'!
- Some parents find it useful to show their children pictures of tooth decay in order to educate them about what could happen. Occasionally, our children's sense of self-preservation is strong enough to encourage teeth brushing to start or resume.

Strategies during

- Using novelty toothbrushes, toothpaste and timers can be very effective. This might be giving the toothbrush a name and writing notes from the toothbrush. Colgate does 'two-minute stories', which can be used during the time it takes for the child to brush their teeth.
- Avoid getting into an upward spiral of control. Remember an 'urgent task' you need to do elsewhere to give yourself time to think. You could also use 'the phone strategy' (see Part 1, Chapter 5).
- Be aware of sensory issues and go back to basics, as you might with a younger child. This might be using a finger or a baby toothbrush.
- Tell the child you trust them to brush their teeth and move away. It does not matter if they do not brush their teeth! The important thing here is to break the cycle of control. This way, although they may miss a few occasions, once your reaction is no longer rewarding for them they will naturally increase teeth brushing.

- Notice if the child is moving towards the sink to brush their teeth, even if they are saying they are not going to. Sometimes we encounter automatic resistance!
- The use of iPod apps can reward the child with instant reactions, guidance and timers for teeth brushing.
- Some parents use disclosing tablets to great effect (these are chewable tablets that make dental plaque visible). Children like the brighter colours and are fascinated by the results.
- Empathise with the child. For example, 'I know you don't like cleaning your teeth. I don't like it either. Shall we brush each other's?'

Strategies after

- Keep praise about actually brushing their teeth low key. We don't want the child to form the mindset that this is out of the ordinary.
- A natural consequence for not cleaning teeth is severely restricting anything sugary. This can encourage the most resistant of children. Sometimes the consequence can be used immediately. For example, 'I know you would like some cake but you didn't clean your teeth this morning so the sugar will stick to your teeth. Of course, if you were to clean your teeth now...'

C

CAR JOURNEYS *(see Controlling Behaviours, Holidays, Sibling Rivalry)*

CAUSE AND EFFECT *(see Part 1, Chapter 1, Lack of cause-and-effect thinking)*

CHANGES IN BEHAVIOUR *(see Transitions)*

CHARMING *(see also Honeymoon Period, Triangulation)*

What it looks like

- The child is charming towards main carer, especially during early stages of placement (see Honeymoon Period).
- The child smiles in a fake 'rictus' way.
- The child suddenly develops interests in hobbies and activities to ingratiate themselves with others.
- The child changes personality when around new people, for example being very helpful.

Why it might happen

- Fear of invisibility or being forgotten – seeking a response.
- Fear of adults – being charming is a way of ensuring survival.

- Need to control – survival strategy of obtaining food, favours and so on.
- Fear or fearful anticipation of a negative response from the parent.
- The need to feel safe – gauging the personalities and actions of others.
- Shame – instinctively creating a new persona in order to avoid revealing the 'shameful self'.
- Separation anxiety – fear of abandonment.
- Overwhelming need to keep the parent close – needing to observe what the adult is doing at all times in order to feel safe.
- Overwhelming need to feel loved/important.
- Emotional age – the child may be functioning at a much younger age and needing to have those early nurture needs met.

Preventative strategies

- Make others aware of your child's behaviours. This sounds easier than it is! When you have a very charming child, people tend to believe what is in front of them. This is why we need to stay factual and grow a thick skin!
- Where the child is showing a fake smile, due to nervousness, you can practise smiling in the mirror or use photos and be clear with your child about when this signals to you their fear.
- Make sure that you let the child know that you see the 'real' them.
- Be really clear about your boundaries with other adults who have contact with your child. Away from the child, be clear that they must not undermine you and let them know that you are aware of the 'true child'.
- Be aware that this is a survival mechanism, and not a conscious thought-out manipulation. It helps if we respond to it as such.

Strategies during

- Avoid shame – if your child presents their charming persona to a visitor to your house (when only two minutes ago they were screaming at you), do *not* be tempted to call them out on that in front of the visitor. This is likely to result in blame heading your way, and your child escalating the negative behaviours.

- The main issue to deal with during an episode of fake charm is your own feelings about this. Practise remaining neutral. Concentrate on dealing with the person you are speaking to.
- Do not allow the person who is being charmed to undermine your boundaries. You need to give an important message to your child, 'I see what you are doing. I see the real you. You are valuable.' So, for example, Granny arrives with chocolate, but it is dinner time. The child starts a charm offensive, saying they are hungry, complimenting Granny and so on. Get the upper hand by stating, 'What a lovely smile X has! I am just doing dinner, so if you are hungry for Granny's chocolate I am sure she will let you have a bit after dinner.'
- Start using a signal that alerts the child and places a marker for them to use later. Remember they are often unaware they are being charming or fake. So, for example, you might start using a phrase like, 'You are *so* polite with visitors. Well done!'

Strategies after

- If you have managed to 'place a marker' you can revisit this by saying something like, 'Earlier when you were being *so* polite with the visitors, I noticed that your smile looked a bit scared.'
- It's useful to name the behaviours for the child. Use some 'naming the need' around how some children get really good at being polite and helpful around visitors, as when they were small, visitors or adults might have been very frightening.
- Remind yourself that this is a behaviour that naturally diminishes over time as our children start feeling more secure with us.
- Where the child has initiated inappropriate contact, if necessary place clear boundaries around who is hugged. A simple rule such as, 'You can only hug these people (list)' can be very effective.

Footnote: Naturally, many unknowing others will think you are a very harsh parent when you try to warn them about the 'charming child'. When my teenage son moved in with his girlfriend and her mother, I warned the mother that despite his exceptionally helpful, kind presenting persona, he would steal from her at the first opportunity. She decided I was too critical, a harsh parent, and she disregarded my advice, moving quickly on to give my son some 'love and understanding'. Three days later she phoned me in a rage after he stood behind her, memorised her bank card number and emptied her account. I had no sympathy. I may even have smiled a little.

CHEWING *(see also Absences, Damaging)*

What it looks like
- The child chews holes in clothing (usually cuffs and necklines).
- The child chews toys or other items.

Why it might happen
- Sensory issues – the child needs something to chew.
- Early lost nurture – the child may need something in their mouth.
- Dissociating – the child is often unaware of what they are doing.
- Anxiety, especially separation anxiety.

Preventative strategies
- Be aware of the child's developmental (emotional) age. Think about whether this behaviour looks like that of a younger child. Consider if you need to reintroduce dummies or bottles to meet an earlier unmet nurture or sensory need.
- Use 'Chewelry' or similar products such as cuff covers that go over jumper sleeves. Chewelry can be bought from eBay or similar sites, by looking for aids for autism and sensory processing. Chewelry comes in the form of necklaces and wrist bands and provides a more rewarding chewing sensation for the child.

- Provide a piece of cloth with your scent or perfume on. When this is tucked into the child's sleeve, the scent can reduce chewing, or can relocate it to the material.
- Some parents have found using massage around the face, mouth and neck reduces chewing when it is due to sensory issues.

Strategies during

- You can provide 'fiddle toys' if you become aware that your child is chewing. Again, these are usually found along with aids for autism. By handing one of these to your child when you see them chewing, you can interrupt the behaviour.
- Rename the holes made by chewing as 'worry holes' to properly name the cause of the behaviour.
- Interrupt the chewing by providing a crunchy snack, such as breadsticks, as this provides oral stimulation.
- Use distraction as an effective way to interrupt chewing.
- Try letting your child know what they are doing, especially if they are watching TV or seem 'zoned out'. Say, 'I can see you are chewing your jumper. I wonder if you are worried about something?'

Strategies after

- Although it is very frustrating when our children walk through the door with a newly chewed jumper, avoid asking them why or expressing exasperation about the ruined jumper. Instead, say something like, 'Wow, I see you had a lot of worries today.'
- Look at the holes together and speculate what the worry behind them may be.
- Use 'naming the need' to help the child to develop awareness about when they chew and where it comes from. You might speculate on what the child had around them to play with when they were little, especially if there was early neglect and the child was left alone for long periods of time.

- Ensure the child is aware of alternative chewing opportunities, but be aware that 'in the moment' they may be unable to access these alternatives.
- As the child gets older, teach them to sew. In this way, the child learns to repair the damage and it can help to build awareness. (Do not expect the sewing to be very good!)

CHOOSING DIFFICULTIES

What it looks like

- The child is unable to make a choice between a small number of options.
- The child is unable to express an opinion or preference.
- The child is unable to make a decision.

Why it might happen

- Fear of drawing attention to self.
- Fear of adults.
- Fear of revealing true self (note, this is subconscious).
- Rewards the child with a reaction (trigger for the parent).
- Need to control – not wanting to reward the parent with positive choice.
- Blocked trust – unable to read what the parent wishes them to do.

Preventative strategies

- Ensure that choices are limited in number, for example only two choices.
- Space out occasions when the child needs to choose as it is likely they are finding it stressful.
- Where this is an ongoing, entrenched issue, set up a situation where you know a choice will need to be made and you have time to wait it out. This might involve the child choosing the route to or from a destination or which shoes to put on to leave the house.

- Don't avoid situations where choices need to be made. Our children need to practise this.
- Be careful not to simply sideline the issue and make all the choices and decisions for the child. This can lead to real issues later with anxiety and self-esteem.

Strategies during

- When waiting for the choice or decision to be made, appear distracted with another job or conversation.
- Do not insist on the child making a choice.
- Avoid leading the child to the choice you think they should make.
- If the child asks you your opinion say, 'I think your brain is strong enough to choose this.' Or use a similar confidence-building statement.
- Avoid sighing and expressing exasperation (tough, I know!).
- Use empathic commentary, 'I can see you are finding it really hard to choose. I wonder if it makes you feel wobbly inside when you need to make a choice?'
- Help the child to visualise what might happen depending on each choice. Sometimes our children are fearful about making the 'wrong' choice. For example, 'Well if you choose strawberries, you will probably enjoy them as you have eaten them before, and if you choose ice cream you might like the cold feeling.'

Strategies after

- Revisit the choice the child made. Use positive reinforcement to remind the child how well they did in making an actual choice.
- Tell the child that you saw how difficult it was for them to make a choice. Wonder aloud about what your child thought you might think of them if they had made the other choice.
- Use 'naming the need' to explore feelings around staying invisible and 'not being noticed'. See if you can relate this to a time this would have helped the child to avoid making a choice to stay safe, and let them know your thoughts.

CHRISTMAS *(see Birthdays, Christmas and Other Celebrations, Rejection, Sabotage, Transitions, Ungratefulness)*

CLINGING *(see Separation Anxiety)*

COMPASSION FATIGUE *(see Part 1, Chapter 7)*

COMPETITIVENESS *(see also Boasting, Controlling Behaviours, Sibling Rivalry)*

What it looks like

- The child always has to 'be the best'.
- The child cheats in order to ensure they win.
- The child is unable to even consider the possibility of not winning.
- The child is unable to take turns or share.

Why it might happen

- Fear of invisibility, in particular the need for others to notice the child.
- Needing to feel powerful.
- Rewards the child with a reaction (trigger for the parent).
- Needing to control others.
- Recreating a familiar environment – entrenched behaviours around 'being the best' and winning favour with adults.

Preventative strategies

- Create simple rules that make 'winning' less attractive; for example, the first one to the door holds it open for everyone.
- Ensure that mealtimes are structured, with everyone being given a turn to speak. You can pass round 'the talking spoon' if necessary, which the 'speaker' has in front of them while it's their turn.

Strategies during

- It's important to give equal attention to the 'winner' and the 'loser'. This may sound obvious when dealing with competitiveness, but it's easy to fall into the trap of ignoring the victor. This is likely to lead to an increase in undesirable behaviours.
- Step away from attempting to rationalise this and having long logical conversations with the child. Keep in mind that the competitiveness may well feel like a fight for survival for the child.
- Use wondering aloud to let the child know you have seen what is happening and to help to explore alternative outcomes. For example, 'Goodness, I can see you really wanted to get to the table first! I wonder what would have happened if your sister had got there instead?'
- Use empathic commentary to name the uncomfortable feelings for the child, 'I see you really felt as if you needed to win just then. You looked really worried in case you did not.'

Strategies after

- It's useful to ensure there is opportunity for a new attempt or a practice to help the child to experience alternative outcomes. This helps the child to learn that your feelings towards them do not change if they 'lose' and that nothing bad happens. For example, if you are playing a game and the child cheats in order to win, let them know you think they may have made a mistake then experiment with what would have happened, allowing the child to experience the true outcome.
- Be careful about turning a blind eye to cheating and other manipulative behaviours in order to 'keep the peace'. Although this offers us some short-term respite, in the long term it stores up trouble for the child and leaves them ill-prepared for a world that will not allow them always to win.

CONSTANT CHATTER/QUESTIONS
(see Nonsense Chatter)

CONTACT *(see Life Story, Transitions)*

CONTROLLING BEHAVIOURS *(see also*
Defiance, Competitiveness, and and any other specific
behaviours or situations where control issues are
relevant e.g. Transitions, and Part 1, Chapter 1)

What it looks like

- Giving adults instructions.
- Ordering other children around.
- General bossiness and rudeness.
- Blocking (entrances, exits, stairs, etc.).
- Rejection of house rules.
- Rearranging items such as place settings.
- Taking space.

Why it might happen

- Fear of adults, especially in relation to potential negative outcomes if an adult is 'in charge'.
- Unable to manage transitions – the child controls, or attempts to control, timings.
- Rewards the child with a reaction (trigger for the parent).
- Lack of cause-and-effect thinking, especially in relation to being unable to visualise outcomes.
- Recreating a familiar environment – where the child was responsible for others, they may continue in a 'parentified' role.
- A compulsion to break or prevent a forming attachment.
- Lack of empathy.
- The child feels the need to protect the parent from the demands of other children.

- Blocked trust – the child is unable to rely on the adult to be 'in charge'.
- Loyalty to birth parents/former carers.

Reality check

First of all, we need to think about controlling behaviours as fear based. Our perception is, 'This child is too controlling.' The child's is, 'I have to keep myself safe, and I cannot rely on others to do so.'

Imagine you were a passenger in a car. The car was driven very badly, the driver takes silly risks, you crash and you are badly injured. It takes you months to start to recover. Then a few months later another friend (whom you cannot remember whether or not to trust) tells you they are taking you out in the car for a surprise. You say, 'No way!' He says, 'Stop being so controlling...'

Preventative strategies

- Establish a strong routine, which is predictable and under your control.
- Establish yourself as the unassailable safe base (see Part 1, Chapter 3).
- Establish house rules such as 'the parent has the remote control for the TV' and 'the driver chooses the music in the car' to help consolidate your position.
- Create as much of an open-plan environment as is possible. (We physically removed walls and widened stairways, removed 'pinch points' and hidden corners to increase visibility and lower opportunities for controlling behaviours and anxiety.)
- Use visible wall charts and calendars to show what is happening. Make sure this stays under *your* control.
- Where the controlling behaviours centre around ownership, for example the child going into others' rooms, use locking door handles so that free entry is restricted, but the child in the room can always easily leave.
- Have allocated spaces that do not change. Use them for car seats, places at the table and, if necessary, specific chairs in the lounge.

This can also be done in a nurturing way by ensuring that the space is comfortable, welcoming and has something there belonging to the child. This is a very effective preventative strategy as, after all, many issues centring around control are about the child needing to have their own space protected and respected.

Strategies during

- Tell the child they are safe, and that you are in control.
- Do not be tempted to change course under pressure, especially when your instinct is telling you not to; for example, you are driving the child to school and they insist you drive a different way to the route you were intending to take.
- Use wondering aloud to explore the controlling behaviours, 'I wonder if you are telling me which way to drive because you are worried I have forgotten the way?'
- Learn not to show doubt or hesitation, as this makes your child feel unsafe and will increase their urge to take control. You can always 'change your mind' if necessary.
- If you need to make a decision and are unsure what to do, tell the child clearly that you have made a decision and will share your thoughts later. You can also say, 'I am going to discuss this first with...' This helps the child to feel that you are clear and confident and have already made a decision. They will usually want to know what the decision is and may up the ante, but this can be dealt with using strategies from the section Arguing.
- Allow the child to be completely 'in control'! This works well when you know there is an event or situation arising soon where you know they will need your help. It may look something like this: 'I can see you really think you would do a much better job at being Mum than me so I have decided to let you have a turn. Don't forget about the washing up, or dinner tonight. I am off to read my book.' At first the child will revel in their newfound power. Later though, they may need you to drive them somewhere, prepare a meal or fix the computer! The novelty soon wears off.

Be prepared though! Many of our children will do anything rather than ask for help.

- Use empathic commentary to speculate on the feelings around being in control, 'I can see you are definitely trying to be the boss today! I expect you are worried that no one else can sort this out apart from you. It must be exhausting to have that worry all the time!'
- Where the child is taking up space in order to control, announce that we will all soon be playing musical chairs. Then everyone gets up and moves about at the same time. Note that some preparation is a good idea with this one! *Everyone* gets up and moves around, sitting back in more acceptable positions. Keep going until the correct position is used. Use words such as 'helping' and 'practice'. You have to be mentally prepared for this!
- Remove the target; for example, if the child is attempting to control what everyone watches on the TV, the TV gets switched off for a set amount of time.
- If the child starts rolling about on the floor or similar behaviours, playfulness can interrupt the incident. I used to start rolling about on the floor too! My children did not enjoy this and the behaviour soon stopped.

Strategies after

- There is no one specific strategy for dealing with control issues after an incident, as this particular behaviour is likely to be a long-term challenge. Instead we also use ongoing recognition of this difficulty through 'naming the need' to explore early life issues around chaos and needing to stay in control.
- Act out situations where the child was not in control in the past and explore the outcome. For example, if a child felt powerless in an abusive early relationship, help them to think through the alternative scenarios which now occur.
- Use *Rosie Rudey and the Very Annoying Parent* (Naish and Jefferies 2016) or *Sophie Spikey has a Very Big Problem* (Naish and Jefferies 2016) to explore control issues.

Footnote: My eldest child, Rosie, was extremely controlling in every way and always needed to be in charge. One of the factors we identified as a causative factor was her overwhelming sense of responsibility for her younger siblings. She had internalised the idea that she was somehow responsible for allowing them to be harmed in the past and was therefore determined to ensure this did not happen again. She attempted to micro-manage every aspect of their lives.

Once we had identified the cause, we acted out a scenario (using playfulness) where Rosie watched my youngest child, then aged six, attempting to stop my husband from getting past her. Naturally this was impossible. I asked Rosie, 'Why can't Charley stop Ray from getting past her?' Rosie laughed and condescendingly 'explained' that she was only six and Ray was a 'grown man'. I said, 'Exactly, so when you were six, how could you have stopped X from doing what he did?'

This was a very strong reality check and it significantly helped to diminish Rosie's controlling behaviours as she realised that she had not been responsible in any way.

CRUELTY TO ANIMALS *(see also Part 1, Chapter 1*
'Lack of Empathy' and 'Lack of Response')

What it looks like

- The child holds small animal too tightly.
- The child deliberately allows animals to fight and injure each other.
- The child hurts an animal in a calculated, planned way.
- The child neglects an animal or deliberately allows harm to occur.
- The child hurts an animal in the spur of a moment, while dysregulated.
- The child is emotionally abusive to an animal through trapping, holding, frightening or another action.

Why it might happen

- Rewards the child with a reaction (trigger for the parent).
- Lack of empathy.
- Need to feel loved, especially in relation to holding and squeezing animals.
- Need to control the animal.
- Need to feel powerful.
- Need to make the animal 'love' them or appreciate them as a 'saviour' from abuse.
- Lack of cause-and-effect thinking.
- Recreating a familiar environment where animal cruelty was normal.
- A desire to break a forming attachment (with the parent or the animal).
- Lack of remorse.

Preventative strategies

- There is only one really good strategy to totally prevent animal cruelty and that is complete supervision. If you have made a commitment to the animal and the child to care for them, then that is your responsibility. I know that this is very difficult and it often appears impossible to do, but by restructuring and careful thought, it can be done.
- Use stair gates to separate children and animals so that you have good visibility of them both. This also helps each to develop an understanding of the other.
- Practise empathy by wondering aloud about how the animal might be thinking or experiencing life. This should be done at times when there is not an incident of cruelty, and it helps to build understanding. For example, if a child keeps grabbing an animal and holding it too tightly, tell the child they must sit next to you, very close and not move away. As the child begins to feel discomfort, explore if this is how the animal might feel. Discuss what might make the child want to stay close. (They may suggest

it's because you had sweets, for example.) Draw parallels from this regarding the child's relationship with the animal.

- Put in very firm boundaries about what the child can and cannot do. Initially, none of my children was allowed to pick our dogs up at any time. This gradually altered as I became clear about which children began to demonstrate a genuine empathy and interest in the dogs.

- Ensure that animals have an 'escape route' in case of cruelty. Cats may have a high window left open, or a very small space only they can get into.

- Where you cannot ensure the safety of the animal and feel you have exhausted all options, you need to rehome the animal for their safety. In short-term fostering households I know some parents choose to keep the pet and rehome the child. It is important to consider, however, that we can never really know the personality and needs of children coming to live in our homes.

- If there is an incident, be really careful about giving the child a huge 'rewarding' response. A neutral response with natural consequences is far more effective than an emotional reaction in reducing or preventing re-occurrences.

- If children and pets have been allowed to mix as there had been no previous cause for concern, then you may only become aware of an issue by a change in behaviour in your pet, an animal being injured, going missing or dying. Be very careful not to take anything at face value. Follow your instincts.

Strategies during

- Be aware of your own body language and emotional reaction. Animal cruelty may understandably trigger a very big emotional response in us. Walk away, with the animal (if it is safe to do so), to allow yourself some space to get regulated and to check the animal over. Take some deep breaths. Comfort the animal and help yourself to feel calm before responding to the child.

- If you are worried about how you might respond to the child say, 'I can't speak to you at the moment as I need to concentrate to make sure (pet) is okay.'
- It is fine to show controlled anger and let the child know this behaviour is *not* okay. However, we need to be very aware about how far we go with that anger and how much in control we are of our own emotions.
- Think about whether or not this act was deliberate or accidental. Go with your instinct if you are not sure. This will have a strong influence on how you manage the incident.

Strategies after

- If you were very angry when you discovered the cruelty, you may have said things to the child that you regret. You will need to take the first step in the repair as the child will be deep in shame (rather than feeling remorse), and will be unable to take the first step. It is fine to say, 'Earlier when I saw how you had hurt (pet) I was very angry. I said some things which I did not mean. The parts I did not mean were when I said… However, I did mean it when I said that this is completely unacceptable and we now need to look at ways I can help you to avoid doing this in the future, as I know you don't want to feel this bad.'
- Through 'naming the need', explore feelings around powerfulness and a time when the child may have felt powerless.
- Revisit your household rules around pets and children mixing. Do not be lured into a false sense of security that you have 'talked it out' with the child and all is now 'back to normal'. If a child has deliberately hurt an animal it is likely they will do it again.

D

DAMAGING *(see also Chewing, Dirty Clothing, Sabotaging, Sneaky Behaviours)*

What it looks like

- The child deliberately and frequently breaks their own possessions.
- The child damages furniture.
- The child damages the possessions of others.
- The child is unusually 'careless' or heavy-handed.

Why it might happen

- Self-sabotage – feelings of not deserving the item, low self-esteem.
- Lack of cause-and-effect thinking.
- Associated diagnoses of dyspraxia, or dyspraxic tendencies.
- Dysregulation – acting in the heat of the moment.
- Feelings of hostility or momentary hatred towards the parent.
- Fear of invisibility or being forgotten – seeking a response.
- Recreating a familiar environment – material objects may have had no value.
- The need to feel in control and powerful.
- Dissociation – the child may be unaware of breaking the item.
- Sensory issues – heavy-handedness.
- A compulsion to break a forming attachment (with the parent), especially in relation to breaking precious items.

Preventative strategies

- Make sure all valuables are locked away and cannot be accessed. This sounds obvious but I am always amazed by the parents who tell me how their child targeted their 'one precious thing'.
- Ensure that the furniture you buy is hardwearing and easy to replace. We found Ikea furniture ideal. The children did not quite manage to destroy it!
- Supervision is key. Avoid areas where expensive or fragile items are hidden from the adult's view.
- Try to establish a central family zone where ornaments and furniture are cheaply bought, easily replaced and cannot break into sharp objects.
- In the central family zone, try to add in items that suggest nurture. For example, we had an ornament theme of parent and baby animals, furry throws for the children to snuggle in to (or chew) and high levels of visibility.
- Avoid giving high levels of praise, especially where this is 'over the top'. This often leads to the child 'reminding' you that they are not worthy of this praise through damaging or destroying items (see Sabotaging).
- Be careful how you respond to a child obsessing over an item. Remember that the item itself is likely to hold little real value for the child, so when it is damaged it can be disappointing (see Obsessions).

Strategies during

- If you notice your child breaking something, call their attention to it immediately. They may be unaware of what they are doing.
- When you see that damage has occurred, state what you know. Use your instinct here and do not be swayed. For example, 'That's a shame for you that you broke your phone. You don't have a phone to use now.' It is *not* useful to ask why or to remonstrate with the child, explaining how *you* feel about this.
- Use wondering aloud to name the feelings behind the behaviours if you think it is useful. For example, 'I wonder if you scratched your name on the table so I wouldn't forget you were here?'

Strategies after

- Help the child to 'show sorry' through the natural consequence of helping to repair. It does not matter if the repair is very poor. It is the action of helping to put things right that helps the child to link cause and effect. When my son punched a hole in his door in temper, afterwards we showed him how to nail another piece of wood on top to keep his privacy! It did not look nice but he painted it and was proud of his handiwork. As he was proud of it, he did not do this again.
- If the child has broken something of their own, make sure that it is not replaced. This is very difficult and it can be tempting to replace the item but this does not help the child to link cause and effect. At the very least, help the child by suggesting extra jobs to earn money to help to buy a new item. Do not be tempted to replace the item on the basis that the child has 'promised' to repay the money. You are setting everyone up for a fall and this is not fair.

DEFIANCE *(see also Controlling Behaviours, Lateness, Rudeness, Transitions)*

What it looks like

- The child ignores the parent or others.
- The child appears not to hear.
- The child refuses to carry out a task they have been told to do.
- The child continues to do something they have been told to stop doing.
- The child claims to have forgotten (see also Memory Issues and Disorganisation).
- The child refuses to move.
- The child moves very slowly, lags behind or hides (see Lateness).

Why it might happen

- The need to feel in control and powerful.
- Lack of cause-and-effect thinking.
- Dysregulation – acting in the heat of the moment.

- Shame, especially in relation to the avoidance of shame.
- A subconscious compulsion to break a forming attachment (with the parent).
- Fear or fearful anticipation of a negative response from the parent.
- Attraction to peer-group activities.
- Fear response – afraid of the outcome if they comply.
- Feelings of hostility or momentary hatred towards the parent.
- Fear of invisibility and being forgotten – seeking a response.
- Lack of empathy.
- Lack of remorse.
- Fear of parent, carer or other adults.
- A need to try to predict the environment.
- Fear of change/transitions.
- Separation anxiety (for example, when refusing to go to school).
- Fear of drawing attention to self (or being seen to be different).
- Dissociation, especially in relation to not listening.
- Overwhelming need to feel loved/important/noticed.
- Comfortable to be in the wrong/self-sabotage.
- Emotional-age thinking.

Preventative strategies

- Think about where your child is developmentally. Sometimes we expect our children to be able to function at their chronological age rather than their emotional/developmental age. Is your child refusing to use a knife and fork or have they missed out the developmental stage of being fed, or not yet developed the necessary motor skills?
- Remember, what you perceive as defiance may actually be hurt or fear. Reframe your perspective to the child's feelings and respond to those fear-based feelings.
- Be clear about what you can and cannot control. Write yourself a list if necessary. It is frustrating when a child refuses to move and we may feel instinctively that we must physically move them ourselves in order to win. Unless there is imminent danger to

the child or another, or risk of very serious damage, this is an absolute no no!

- Where you have a reoccurring theme, for example the child stopping and refusing to move when you are out, plan for a run-through of this with supportive others. You may decide to go out with a friend following discreetly. This allows you to continue walking without fear, knowing that your friend has the child in sight. This is a good strategy to establish what action the child takes when they believe they are being left behind.

Strategies during

- When your child is showing defiance, absorb the action and practise a neutral response. For example, if you need to brush the child's hair and she rolls around on the floor saying, 'No!' say, 'Okay, well let me know when you are ready, I am just off to...'
- If the child is pretending not to hear you, just carry on as if they have heard. You can also add in little tasks or natural consequences that may occur as a result of 'not hearing', such as the use of playfulness in measuring their ears, checking they are working, talking about going to the ear shop.
- Whisper about something very quietly, knowing they will want to engage.
- Use empathic commentary to give a narrative to what the child is experiencing. Look at the emotion that is being expressed and meet that head on. For example, 'I can see that you look really sad. You don't want to go and see Granny. Things seem hard for you at the moment. I wonder if it is because we were just talking about...and now you are feeling a bit stuck?'
- Do not repeat yourself. It is extremely likely that the child knows what to do. Instead, say things like, 'I know you can work this one out' or, 'That's fine you can rest for a while before...'
- Think about what immediately preceded the incident. If the child is overwhelmed with shame, they will not be able to move forwards until they are regulated and the shame reduces. Look at shame-reduction techniques. For example, 'I know you didn't

mean...to happen because you have a good heart. I saw that earlier when...'
- Remove the audience. Any reaction you are experiencing is likely to diminish proportionately to the size of the audience.
- Give the child space! Sometimes they really need us to back off so they can think straight. If they are frozen, this seems like defiance. If you spell out that you will be nearby and then leave them to 'unfreeze', the situation is often easily resolved. When the child rejoins you, avoid starting to speak about the trigger for the incident immediately.
- When you absolutely must move things on and have tried letting them 'rest' or walking off to do other things, switch on a timer and say, 'Okay, I can see you are pretty stuck right now so I am going to do... But the time will have to be paid back to me later.' This gives you back control and you can use the 'paid back time' however it fits in best with your family.
- Use 'the phone strategy' (see Part 1, Chapter 5). This allows you to disengage, comment on what is happening and remove any 'rewards' from your reactions.

Strategies after
- Defiance may be a general theme that appears to be ever present. In this case, you will find yourself taking a lot of preventative steps. Remember to adjust these occasionally as sometimes we keep preventative strategies in place for too long.
- Give appropriate praise for the child managing to regulate and move forwards but ensure it is at the right level, 'I am glad you managed to catch up as now you can do...with us.'
- Re-evaluate the incident. Think about whether you need to put a plan in place for the likelihood of this happening again.
- Discuss with a partner, friend or other adult the triggers you are experiencing. Decide on a strategy between you to allow the other person to step in where necessary (see Part 1, Chapter 5, Identifying your triggers).

- Use *Rosie Rudey and the Very Annoying Parent* (Naish and Jefferies 2016) to help the child identify with feelings around defiant behaviours.

DESTRUCTION *(see Damaging)*

DIRTY CLOTHING *(see also Chewing, Damaging, Messy Bedrooms, Sabotaging)*

What it looks like
- The child often appears messy or dirty, with a dishevelled appearance.
- The child does not put clothes in the laundry and may conceal dirty clothes.
- The child wants to wear the same clothing all the time.

Why it might happen
- Comfortable to be in a dishevelled or dirty state – the child's internal working model is such that they see themselves as someone undeserving, bad and messy.
- Recreating a familiar environment – the child is familiar with wearing dirty or dishevelled clothing and/or has witnessed a disregard for property and personal appearance.
- Lack of cause-and-effect thinking – not able to link the fact that drawing on a shirt means the shirt is ruined. The child is also unable to think through that if something is not put out for the laundry it won't get washed.
- Dysregulation – acting in the heat of the moment, particularly where there is anger resulting in damaged clothing.
- Shame – relating to feelings of unworthiness. This may also be apparent through a large amount of soiled clothing.
- A need to try to predict the environment – the child tries to keep clothing the same, and often wears the same clothes even if they are dirty or too small.

- Fear of change/transitions – regarding changes of clothing. Child does not want to 'let the clothes go' so that that they can be washed.
- Fear of drawing attention to self, especially relating to positive appearance. The child is worried that others might notice and comment.
- Dissociation – may be unaware of damaging or dirtying clothing.
- Sensory issues unaware of 'heavy-handedness' – the child may damage clothes due to clumsiness.
- Emotional age – the child may be behaving as a much younger child, especially in relation to remembering to put things out for the wash.
- Loyalty to birth parents/former carers – resisting attachment to new carers/parents by rejecting new clothes, new smells from washing powder and so on.

Reality check

Where the child self-sabotages through hygiene issues, with messy or dirty clothing being a constant theme, it's often a reflection of how the child is feeling about themselves. It's difficult for parents and carers to see the child leaving in a pristine school uniform, only to return from school after one day with holes, stains and a look of general neglect. This can be triggering as it feels like a reflection on the parent as well as an unwelcome reminder of some children's early lives.

Try to bear in mind that this is almost never a deliberate act on the part of the child. It is much more to do with disorganisation, clumsiness, dissociation and low self-worth. It's better if we respond accordingly, but not always easy to do so!

Preventative strategies

- Be aware of the child's developmental (emotional age). Does this behaviour look like that of a younger child? Would we expect a three-year-old to be able to sort out their laundry and remember to put it in the laundry basket, for example? Would a two-year-old be able to keep themselves clean?

- Use visible charts with rotas showing laundry days. It's useful to allocate one day per week per child as their own laundry day. This also prevents the child from immediately placing clean clothing straight back in the washing basket, if they are unable to put it away. It creates a natural consequence of favourite clothing items being unavailable for one week should this occur. It is also much easier to manage a household in this way and prevents arguments over lost clothing.
- Make laundry day an absolute part of the routine, with allocated time for each child to contribute to the task.
- Buy three sets of school uniform: one new, two secondhand. Start with a plan that uniform is washed every evening, so you can at least feel happy that the child starts each school day clean and tidy!
- Incorporate washing uniforms into the daily routine. I used to create snack time just after school. The children had their snack once their school uniform was with me (or in the washing machine, depending on age).
- Tell the school, in writing, why there are difficulties around clothing, and why the child may sometimes look neglected. This will help to reduce your anxiety.
- Stop worrying about matching socks! We ended up having only one plain colour for each child. A different colour for each. If they went out in un-matching socks, no one died.

Strategies during

- Although it is very frustrating when our children walk through the door with a filthy set of clothing, avoid asking why or expressing exasperation about the ruined clothes. Instead, say something like, 'Wow, looks like you had an interesting day!' This is very difficult to do and we may need to walk away first and take some deep breaths before we are able to respond in that way.
- Where you notice that, yet again, the child has been unable to put their washing in the laundry basket, try saying something like, 'I noticed that you have not put your laundry in the laundry basket yet. Do you need some help with that?'

- If the child is refusing to put their laundry out, tell them you expect them to have a good check round their room to make sure there is no laundry missing from this week's wash. Time this so that it occurs every week at the same time. Allow plenty of time for this to happen. It won't work if the child knows you are waiting to go to an urgent appointment. Settle down comfortably and say, 'That's okay if you need to rest for a while before you do it. If you need help just let me know.' Make it clear that the next event isn't happening until this task is complete.

Strategies after

- When strange stains appear, look at them with the child and speculate what might have caused them. This helps the child to link cause and effect.
- Use 'naming the need' to help the child develop awareness about why they are comfortable with a messy or dirty appearance. This needs to be handled very sensitively. Try saying, 'Sometimes if children haven't been used to having clean clothes they don't notice when things get dirty or smelly later on, because their nose forgets to tell their brain. I can be your nose until it's sorted out.'
- As the child gets older, teach them to use the washing machine. In this way, the child learns to build awareness. (Note that you will need to support the child for longer than you may think in order to achieve this.)
- If you feel the damage to clothing or the non-appearance of laundry is deliberate, help the child to 'show sorry' through the natural consequence of helping to sort the washing out, or wash the item. It does not matter if the washing is very poor. It is the action of helping to put things right that helps the child to link cause and effect. It is extremely important that if you decide to take this course of action it is done in a nurturing way, perhaps using time-in and doing it together. It's not okay to induce toxic shame and force the child to do all their washing by hand as 'punishment'. This will not link cause and effect and is likely to

make the child more determined to avoid shame in the future. The problem gets bigger!

- When a child has allowed a situation to occur where there is a large amount of washing, hidden away, and has literally run out of clothes, you have to intervene, otherwise we may be recreating an alternative version of a neglectful environment. You can use natural consequences so the child pays you back the time it took you to hunt through their room and remove all the washing (see Part 1, Chapter 5).
- A useful natural consequence to use is the sudden mysterious, but temporary, loss of a favourite item of clothing. If you have asked a child several times to put their washing out, and offered help, and the child has still been unable to comply or assist in any way, then do the washing but remove the favourite item, once washed. I used to say that it 'must still be in the wash'. Or I might speculate how 'I had so much washing to do I lost track of your orange top. I expect it will turn up next week.' I might also 'forget' to check the pockets of clothes if I was in a rush.

DISORGANISATION *(see Dirty Clothing, Memory Issues and Disorganisation, Messy Bedrooms)*

DISRESPECTING *(see Damaging, Rejection, Rudeness, Ungratefulness)*

DISSOCIATING *(see Absences (trauma based))*

DRUGS AND ALCOHOL *(see also Food Issues, Smoking)*

As this A–Z is designed to cover briefly the behavioural challenges that I am frequently asked about, I cannot include a concise overview of strategies to deal with drug and alcohol addictions and related problems, due to the complexity of the issues. Instead,

I have detailed here more specialised drug and alcohol-specific resources which I have found useful in the past.

Books to help a child understand drug and addiction issues

Children's book – *When a Family is in Trouble* by Marge Heegaard (Woodland Press, 1993).

Children's book – *I Can Be Me: A Helping Book for Children of Alcoholic Parents* by Dianne O'Connor (Author House, 2009).

Books to help parents manage and understand children and young people with drugs and addiction

Addiction as an Attachment Disorder by Phillip J. Flores (Jason Aronson Inc., 2011).

Addiction and Recovery for Dummies by Brian F. Shawe (John Wiley and Sons, 2005).

Brainstorm: The Power and Purpose of the Teenage Brain by Daniel J. Seigal (Tarcher, 2014).

Heroin Addiction: The Addiction Guide for the Amateur by Christopher J. Spinney (CreateSpace, 2016).

Other resources

Family Lives – drugs and alcohol with adolescents, includes talking to teens about drugs: www.familylives.org.uk.

Frank – for young people to access information and support: www.talktofrank.com.

Recovery.org.uk – drugs and alcohol rehabilitation and other related help: www.recovery.org.uk.

DUMMIES *(see Immaturity)*

E

EMOTIONAL AGE *(see Immaturity)*

EMPATHY *(lack of) (see Part 1, Chapter 1)*

ENCOPRESIS *(see Poo Issues)*

ENURESIS *(see Bedwetting, Urinating)*

EXAGGERATING *(see Boasting, Overreacting)*

FAKE ILLNESSES *(see Hypochondria)*

FAKE PERSONALITY *(see Charming)*

FAKE SMILE *(see Charming)*

FALSE ALLEGATIONS *(see also Lying, Overreacting, Triangulation)*

What it looks like

- The child tells school, social worker or another person that they have been physically, emotionally or sexually abused or are being neglected by their current carer/parent, when this has not happened.
- The child misinterprets a small or insignificant incident and claims that a much more serious event has taken place.
- The child tells the carer they will make an allegation against them.
- The child genuinely believes that an abusive incident has taken place, when it has not.

Why it might happen

- The child believes it has happened.
- The event *did* happen but the child has not placed the event in the correct time and space. For example, a child was kicked by a previous carer but claims the current parent/carer has done this. This sometimes occurs when the child has a real fear that it *might* happen due to a triggering event and is then unable to distinguish between thought and actuality.
- The need to feel in control and powerful.
- Lack of cause-and-effect thinking.
- Dysregulation – acting in the heat of the moment.
- Shame – something has happened so the child deflects attention by claiming a more serious incident has occurred.
- A subconscious compulsion to break a forming attachment (with the parent) – forcing a placement move.
- Fear or fearful anticipation of a negative response from the parent – the child may make an allegation to avoid returning home.
- Fear response.
- Feelings of hostility or momentary hatred towards the parent.
- Fear of invisibility/being forgotten – seeking attention/attachment.
- Recreating a familiar environment.
- Lack of empathy.
- Lack of remorse.
- A need to try to draw another adult close (see 'The sympathetic face' explanation in Part 1, Chapter 6).
- Fear of change/transitions.
- Separation anxiety – the child may make an allegation to try to return to an attachment figure.
- Dissociation – during the incident, leading to a lack of clarity about what happened.
- Boredom.
- Sensory issues – a touch can feel like a hit.

- Overwhelming need to feel loved/important – an allegation investigation places the child at the centre of the attention of many concerned adults.
- Self-sabotage – being in control of placement ending/moving.

Reality check

From my background in social work, I understand that we are trained to believe the child and to take seriously allegations that children make. I am not exploring here the disclosures made by children rooted in fact and abuse, which those of us caring for children from a background of trauma are all too familiar with. Here, I am looking at those allegations where the trauma is often the *cause* of a false allegation. It takes a very skilled practitioner to recognise the difference but often, of course, the people most closely involved with the child are very clear about what *is* real and what *seems* real.

Preventative strategies

- Communication is key – make sure that you have a very good and open dialogue with other adults who have contact with your child.
- If there is an incident at home and the child is dysregulated, ensure that you draw their attention to what is happening in real time. For example, if you are close to the child and you see that they look afraid, take a deliberate step back and say, 'I'm stepping away from you so you can feel safer.'
- Practise safe caring! This sounds easier than it actually is but it quickly becomes a way of life. Leaving doors open to ensure that other adults or children can see what is occurring can save you from allegations. Some parents use closed-circuit TV cameras in the house if there has been a spate of false allegations to protect themselves and to preserve the continuity of the placement for the whole family.
- If there is an incident, record it straightaway and send it as an email to anyone who is sympathetic to your situation, or even

send it to yourself. This gives you a time and date stamp of what actually happened, which then cannot be altered later on. It is useful if you are fostering or adopting to send it to a supporting professional who understands therapeutic parenting.

- Try to keep a daily log of events and everyday happenings. It's best to do this electronically, and it can even be in the form of messages and texts. This will help you to work out retrospectively any events that a child may claim have happened. For example, if a child alleges that he was thrown down the stairs on Tuesday, you may see from your notes that you all went out to a cafe for lunch that day and this will help you to place incidents that occurred that day.

- It is possible that the child will have threatened to make an allegation. In this case, it is essential that this information has already been recorded and passed on to supporting professionals or knowledgeable others, to help to protect you and preserve the child's security should the allegation then be made.

- Where a child is threatening to make an allegation, ideally try to respond in a matter-of-fact, low-key way. If you overreact, or reveal a trigger, it is likely to escalate the situation. When my daughter said she would phone Childline and get me arrested, I helpfully handed her the phone while wondering aloud what I might then do with all my free time. (She did not ring, but informed me that I was 'very annoying'.)

Strategies during

- Be aware that if a child is making a false allegation against you, it's unlikely that you will know about it until someone comes knocking at your door.

- If the child is making an allegation *to* you and you know that it cannot be true then it's important to ground the child in reality. For example, the child tells you that their sibling just pushed them out of the window. You know that not only is the window securely locked but the sibling is not in the house, so you can be pretty confident that this is a false allegation.

Use open-ended questions such as, 'Tell me more,' or, 'I wonder how that happened?' This helps the child to explore the reality of the situation without you prejudicing a potential genuine, linked disclosure.

- You can also use 'naming the need' to tie what the child is expressing to an earlier situation. For example, 'I wonder if you said your sister pushed you out the window because when you were very little something similar actually happened in real life? Sometimes when we are scared of something happening and remember it, we think it is going to happen again.'

Strategies after

- Where a child has made a false allegation it's imperative to let them know that *you know* the reality of the situation in a non-blaming way. It is not useful to ask the child why they did it and to place them in shame. If you take this course of action it will polarise you both and may cause long-term damage to your relationship.
- It is extremely difficult to deal with our own feelings of injustice when there is a false allegation made, and the fallout that it produces. There may be lengthy investigations and procedures. Ensure that you build in recovery time for yourself.
- Try to separate out the relationship with the child from the reason behind why they made the allegation and how you are managing on a day-to-day basis. It's too easy to get into a punitive mindset when these situations occur. Long-term improvements can be made to the child's reasoning and thinking, linking cause and effect, if the situation is handled sensitively and therapeutically.
- Access support for yourself so you have someone 'in your corner' and advocating for you. The National Association of Therapeutic Parents can help to support you. If you are a foster carer, then there are professional support organisations, such as the Fostering Network in the UK, that also give support to foster carers during allegations.

Footnote: When my son William was at school at age 15, he had several supporting professionals involved with him due to his level of need and vulnerability. One day he stole some batteries from a shop. He was caught and taken to see his (inexperienced) youth worker. William noted the concern on the support worker's face when he said he 'had to steal the batteries'. William needed to keep this sympathetic face firmly in place as that would mean that she was no longer thinking about his 'naughty' behaviour, and therefore he could avoid shame and the consequences. So, as he spoke to her, his story became embellished, and her sympathetic face grew more concerned and more protective.

He told her that he had to get batteries for his torch. He needed a torch because his room was dark. His room was dark because there was no electricity in his room. While William was saying this, he was not thinking, 'This will get Mum in trouble.' His base brain, overwhelmed from past trauma, was responding to the sympathetic face, 'That is a good face. That will keep me safe.'

Naturally, we ended up at a multi-agency meeting where professionals assumed William lived in a dark cave (probably with no food). They were astonished to visit his very comfortable room and discover his wind-up torch (which did not require batteries).

FATHER'S DAY (see Birthdays, Christmas and Other Celebrations, Sabotaging)

FEARFULNESS/FEAR RESPONSE (see Part 1, Chapter 1)

FOLLOWING (see Nonsense Chatter, Separation Anxiety)

FOOD ISSUES (see also Defiance, Controlling Behaviours, Mealtime Issues, School Issues, and Part 1, Chapter 1)

What it looks like

- The child does not know when they are full.

- The child may make themselves sick through overeating.
- The child complains of feeling hungry, even after a large meal.
- The child steals high quantities of food, often high in sugar.
- The child takes food and hoards it, often leaving it to go rotten.
- The child spoils food, deliberately preventing others from having it.
- The child cannot share food (see Mealtime Issues).

Why it might happen

- Sensory issues (see Part 1, Chapter 1, Interoception) – the child may not be able to sense when they are hungry and when they are full.
- High cortisol levels leading to a need for a high sugar intake to regulate.
- Early lost nurture, leading the child to feel 'empty inside'.
- The need to feel in control, especially where there are historical issues of neglect and the child needs to be able to control their access to food. This also relates to spoiling food meant for others or sharing food.
- Lack of cause-and-effect thinking – unable to think through the consequences of stealing food or how they might feel if they overeat.
- Dysregulation – acting in the heat of the moment, seeking food for comfort/regulation.
- Recreating a familiar environment – familiar eating patterns.
- Lack of empathy for future self – for example, how they may feel through overeating.
- Lack of remorse – the child is usually unconcerned about the effects of their actions, for example when spoiling the food of others.
- A need to try to predict the environment, especially in relation to hoarding.
- Dissociation – the child may be disconnected from bodily sensations and unaware of eating.
- Emotional age – the child may be seeking nurture, especially in relation to baby food, milk and so on (see Immaturity).

Preventative strategies

- Be aware that many of our children have high cortisol levels, so we need to be mindful of this. Use rhythmic exercise and regular snacks to help manage cortisol levels.

- Consider using a snack box or treat box which the child can help themselves to. Usually our children will eat everything in the first five minutes, but gradually they learn to ration themselves a little. This is good practice for them. Having snacks allocated just for them, which are under their control, also helps to reduce anxiety around access to food. Once it's gone it's gone! Do not be tempted to replenish the snack box during the day, and always ensure you have the same number of items going in each morning.

- Routine is absolutely critical in relation to food. Mealtimes must be very regular, with snack times also at set times. In this way, we can help our children to start anticipating hunger and also allay anxieties about the provision of food, and prevent escalation in behaviours when the child is hungry without realising it.

- If you have a child who spoils the food of others (for example, taking a bite out of each apple in the bowl), then you cannot leave food out. This is frustrating. Using individual snack boxes allocated to each child can help with this but you may need to give very careful thought as to where these are stored in case one of the children likes to help themselves to the other snack boxes.

- Where you have a child who is stealing food, a preventative strategy is to greatly reduce the amount of food kept in the house. Snack boxes can help to reduce stealing food as the child then has 'permission' to take food when they want.

- Have a safe place where you can keep food and know the child does not have access to it. When I had five teenagers in the house I did have to lock the fridge, but the children had access to other food.

- Think about how aware your child is of taking food. I remember once seeing one of my children take something, take a bite and put it back! When I challenged them, they were unaware they had done this.

Strategies during

- If you have a child who is constantly complaining that they are hungry it's useful to respond empathically, 'I can see you are feeling hungry. That can make you a bit worried or grumpy. I will be making your snack in ten minutes, I feel a bit hungry too.' Avoid saying, 'You can't be hungry!' as the child probably does not know if they are or not!
- 'I'm hungry' sometimes means 'I feel empty.' You can respond with, 'I wonder if that empty feeling is about needing a hug?'
- If you discover a child has stolen food you need to respond empathically, not emotionally. This is not easy! State that you know the child took X and explain that there won't be any for later on. For example, 'Oh, I see you have eaten some of the biscuits! You like those ones, do you? I will remember to put a couple in your snack box. It's a shame though as there's not any left for treat time later so we will have to have something a bit less interesting.'
- Where a child takes food to hoard it, 'naming the need' can be very useful. For example, 'I wonder if you took all this food because when you were little you didn't have the chance to make sure you always had food? Well, here you have a snack box you can always use. I can see that you are not eating this food, but hiding it just in case. I know it's difficult for you to feel that you don't need to hide food anymore. I think your tiny baby brain part is being in charge, so I will help you with this.'
- With hoarding, you can identify where the child hides food and remove it. Ensure that you leave one item behind. If you remove all of it, this is likely to increase the hoarding compulsion.
- Where a child has eaten a big meal and still wants to eat, place your hand and theirs on their stomach. Ask them to describe how their tummy feels from their hand. Use words like full

and hard. In this way, we can help the child to start experiencing sensations of fullness by using a different sensory pathway.

Strategies after

- Look at what your child actually *does* with food they take. If they are hoarding it then it may be related to early neglect issues. The child does not want it, but they are taking it automatically 'just in case'. This may be a hardwired survival strategy which will fade in time. In these cases, it is easier to simply keep an eye on the 'hoarding place' and retrieve the food where possible.

- Make sure you let the child know that you know what is going on. Sometimes it's tempting not to say anything in order to 'keep the peace'. This only delays an inevitable confrontation and is likely to invoke toxic levels of shame. Be matter of fact about what you know. Do not expect or require the child to 'admit' what has happened.

- Use natural consequences to deal with stealing. If an item is stolen, do not replace it. If a child has taken and eaten five chocolate cakes, sadly there are no chocolate cakes available for that particular child. You may offer an alternative that is much less attractive. This needs to be done in a 'sad, empathic' manner, not a sarcastic, punishing way! For example, 'I am sorry you don't have a chocolate cake for pudding today as unfortunately you already ate them all. I have got a spare banana though.'

- Avoid trying to have a rational discussion about taking or hoarding food. As this is an instinctive action linked to early survival strategies, it is difficult for the child to get control through rational discussions and explanations about stealing.

- Don't be tempted to use food as a punishment. If a child has just eaten a whole packet of biscuits do not say they cannot have dinner. Using food as a control mechanism or punishment will greatly increase any problems you have around food. The more controlling you become in response to your child's issues, the more likely it is that they will go on to develop more severe eating disorders.

- Be aware and clear about the link between food and nurture. Although this is one of the most exasperating challenges we face, it is also the one most likely to be a sign of evolving attachments.
- Use books such as *Love Me, Feed Me* (Rowell 2012) to further understanding, and *Rosie Rudey and the Enormous Chocolate Mountain* (Naish and Jefferies 2017) for direct help with naming the need behind the behaviour.

FORGETFULNESS *(see Memory Issues)*

FRIENDSHIPS *(see also Obsessions)*

What it looks like

- The child develops quick and intense friendships.
- The child has no friends.
- The child obsesses over a friend and becomes fixated on them.
- Friendships end within a short time period.
- The child is very controlling and/or manipulative within the relationship.
- The child is extremely obliging and ingratiating.
- The child's friendships appear mismatched or inappropriate.
- Other children avoid or reject the child.

Why it might happen

- Recreating a familiar environment – may recreate familiar relationship patterns within the relationship.
- Lack of empathy – unable to take the friend's perspective or consider their feelings.
- Lack of remorse – unable to repair a relationship or a fracture.
- Overwhelming need to feel important and loved – this need overwhelms the other child.
- Emotional age – may make friendships with younger children, closer to their emotional or developmental age.
- The need to feel in control and powerful within the friendship.
- Lack of cause-and-effect thinking.

- Attraction to peer-group activities.
- Seeking nurture.
- Fear of invisibility/being forgotten.
- Due to all of the above, other children may avoid the traumatised child.

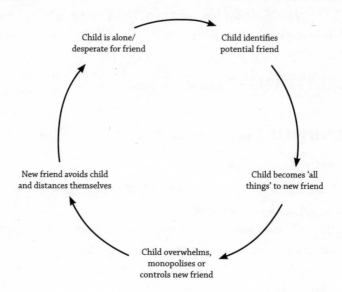

Reality check

In order to start making reciprocal, meaningful friendships, our children first need to have an idea of what that means and what it looks like. Before you start stressing about your child 'not having friends', having stressful/rejecting relationships or 'being obsessed with one friend' which then inevitably implodes, ask yourself these questions:

- Does my child feel empathy?
- Can my child share yet?
- What emotional age is my child functioning at?
- Is my child able to re-attune following a conflict?
- Does my child have at least one secure attachment/effective reciprocal relationship?

If after considering these questions, you feel your child can share, has one secure attachment, can re-attune and has some empathy, then they have a chance of forming a positive relationship with a child functioning at the same emotional age as them.

Preventative/preparatory strategies

- If your child is not yet developed enough to form and keep a friendship, then please stop trying! Chill out, and wait until they are ready. In the meantime, work on the most important relationship, which will be the one that sustains them into adulthood – the one with *you*. This is the relationship they can then start to use as a blueprint about how real relationships work and which they can later transfer to friendships.
- For parties and social events, have like-minded friends on standby who can provide children as pseudo friends. This avoids the stressful occasions such as no one arriving for birthday parties.
- Do not try to force your child's friendship onto other children. This is likely to alienate your child further.
- Concentrate on creating situations where there is not an intensity of relationship. For example, going to a soft play area where your child can make some instant five-minute 'friendships', which naturally end when you leave, can build self-esteem.
- Where there are not animal cruelty issues, friendships and attachments made through pets can help the child to feel less lonely. In particular, dogs are known to produce oxytocin and stimulate the production of this in people. Some traumatised children make their first real, reciprocal relationship with a dog.

Strategies during

- When your child has identified a new friend, make certain that you keep a realistic view. Don't get carried away imagining new-found rewarding friendships, fun days out and so on. You may be lucky, but only if your child has grown emotionally. Instead, keep a balance where your child continues to see other people and has a lot of family time. This will lessen the blow when/if the relationship ends.

- You may sense a reluctance from the other child's parent to encourage the relationship. This can be very hurtful. Sometimes we might help by speaking with the parent and seeing how open or knowledgeable they are about childhood trauma. A word of warning though: it is *very rare* for the parent to understand what the therapeutic parent is saying and to immediately become welcoming and supportive of the relationship. Be careful how much you say, as you may end up on the wrong end of some unsolicited parenting advice!

- If you are able to encourage and support the blossoming friendship, be mindful about the new friend becoming overwhelmed. The best way to do this is to supervise closely and limit the time the children spend together. Parental presence is a must. Where your child uses social media, you need to control their access to this, through monitoring wif-fi access and internet use.

- Use touch to regulate your child if you can see they are becoming overexcited and are overwhelming the new friend.

- Where you sense that a new friendship may be going awry, try using wondering aloud and empathic commentary to help your child to see what might be happening. For example, 'I wonder if Ben doesn't want to play this afternoon because he is feeling scared you might push him again?' Be aware though, it may take many friendships and a degree of emotional maturity before your child can learn from this.

Strategies after

- Our children's friendships often end abruptly and unkindly. If your child has been hurt and upset by the ending, it is not useful to immediately revisit their actions and point out the mistakes they made in the relationship. Instead, draw close to them and stay neutral. Use empathic commentary to get alongside and to help them feel less alone, 'You must really be missing X. It's so sad when friendships don't work out. I wonder what happened.'

- You can also 'name the need' at the appropriate time to help your child to make sense of their overwhelming need for a close friendship. For example, 'Sometimes when children have missed out on special friends early on, they have lots of love all stored up and it just splurges out onto new friends. This can make new friends feel a bit scared. Let's think of a way we can let the love come out a little bit slower.'

G

GRATITUDE *(see Ungratefulness)*

GRIEF *(of carer) (see Part 1, Chapter 7)*

GRIEF *(of child) (see Life Story, and Part 1, Chapter 1)*

GOADING *(see Joking and Teasing)*

H

HEADBANGING *(see also Banging, and Part 1, Chapter 1)*

What it looks like

- The child bangs their head repeatedly.

Why it might happen

- Dysregulation – the child self-soothes through headbanging or other harmful behaviours.
- Sensory issues – the child may have pain or be very sensitive to noises and lights which overwhelm. Headbanging is often a sign of sensory-seeking behaviour.
- Recreating a familiar environment – the child may have been in the habit of doing this if left for long periods of time or left in distress.
- Feeling rewarded by a distressed response from the parent.
- Fear of invisibility/being forgotten – seeking a response.
- Fear of parent/carer and other adults.
- Fear of change/transitions.
- Separation anxiety.
- Dissociation – the child may be unaware of their actions or may subconsciously use the strategy to 'bring themselves back'.
- Overwhelming need to keep the parent close.
- Boredom.

Preventative strategies

- Speak to your health visitor or GP (doctor) to explore underlying issues.
- Make sure you have lots of soft cushions and blankets everywhere so if your child starts to headbang you can make a soft space.
- Be aware of noises and general noise levels. Where children are oversensitive to sound, this can increase the likelihood of headbanging.
- Ask for an evaluation from an occupational therapist. They will check all of your child's abilities and do an assessment. Headbanging is often a sign of sensory-seeking behaviour.
- If your child is small enough, pick them up and rock them as soon as you see the beginnings of headbanging starting.
- Think about putting a protective helmet on your child if you find that you often cannot catch them in time. Be careful with this though, as where there are sensory issues the child may struggle with the sensation of the helmet.
- Use time-in and/or parental presence where you think the child is likely to start headbanging.
- Look at the structure of your home and see if it is possible to soften sharp edges and hard surfaces. This also reduces noise levels.
- Invest in a rocking chair or a swing. This can soothe the child and help to prevent, reduce or divert instances of headbanging.
- Where you can see there is going to be a loud noise or overstimulation of some description warn or prepare the child where possible.
- It's a good idea to play soft music in the background. Classical music is particularly soothing for children and can help them to stay regulated.
- Where headbanging is due to aural sensory overload, use noise-reducing headphones. These can have an immediate positive impact.

- Have a quiet space where the child can go if necessary. This is particularly important in busy environments such as schools, or if you have a lot of visitors.
- Using vibrating toys or vibrating pillows can be very effective, specifically where the child headbangs when put down for sleep.

Strategies during

- No matter what age your child is, distraction can work well. Sometimes just looking past the child and saying, 'Oh, what's that?' can distract them enough to prevent headbanging.
- Monitor your own response. You can be pretty certain that gasps of horror and rushing about will increase the behaviour.
- If you feel that an interruption will increase the banging, get close to the child with a cushion. You can then either place the cushion between the child and what they are banging on or place this against your chest, hold the child on your lap with their back to you and allow them to bang.
- Use reassuring quiet words to try to reconnect the child, especially where you feel they are 'zoned out' or dissociated. You can 'name the need' by using phrases such as, 'I will keep you safe and help you to manage these big feelings. I am here.'
- Distract to another sensory experience. Blowing bubbles, sucking, blowing, water or sand play can all help to reduce instances of headbanging. The trick is to have these items prepared and close at hand.
- Stroking the child on their face or arms can greatly reduce the intensity of headbanging. This gives them another sensory outlet.
- Where the headbanging is particularly violent and you fear for the child's safety and feel unable to stop them, using a duvet to wrap them up in can be comforting and reduce the violence of the movement. However, ensure that the child's face and airways are clear and that this is not used as a restraint method.

Strategies after

- Obviously, one of the most important things to do is check for any signs of injury, such as concussion.
- Using a weighted blanket or massage through touch can help to calm a child, reconnect and reduce further incidents of headbanging.
- Be aware that the headbanging is usually a compulsion and something the child has little control over. There is not a great deal of mileage in having a protracted conversation about this or asking them why they do it.
- Do not tell the child that the headbanging has upset you. You need to remain the unassailable safe base. It is fine to express a sadness that the child may hurt themselves and to resolve this through a nurturing response.

HIDING *(see Transitions)*

HITTING OTHERS *(see Aggression)*

HITTING SELF *(see Damaging, Sabotaging, Self-harm)*

HOARDING *(see Food Issues, Mealtime Issues, Stealing Food)*

HOLIDAYS *(see also School Issues, Transitions)*

What it looks like

- The child's behaviour is more challenging or deteriorates during school holidays.
- The child's behaviour becomes more challenging when going away on family holidays.
- The child is more anxious and fearful about forthcoming holidays.
- Holidays are very difficult times, with escalations in anxiety-driven behaviours.

Why it might happen

- Fear of change/transitions and what the holiday means.
- A resistance to emotional closeness during a holiday.
- Fear of parent/carer and other adults – there will be close proximity on holiday.
- The need to feel in control during change.
- Dysregulation – acting in the heat of the moment.
- A need to try to predict the environment.
- Separation anxiety –what is the child leaving behind?
- Sensory issues, especially where there is a lot of stimulation.
- Comfortable to be in the wrong/self-sabotage feeling unworthy of having a nice time.
- Triggers relating to past holidays.

Reality check

It's really important that we completely change our idea about what 'holiday' actually means. In the past, 'holiday' may have meant rest, relaxation and a break from routine. When we are caring for children who have suffered trauma there can be no real break in routine, and often the behaviours and challenges we face at home are magnified when on holiday. I do not say this to worry you, as you may be lucky and have some really excellent holidays, but it is important to stay realistic and think practically about what your child can cope with, rather than what *you* would like to do. Step away from any notion that your child will be grateful to you for providing such a lovely holiday. In reality, they may only appreciate the holiday in retrospect and on video!

Preventative strategies

- Minimise your child's exposure to end-of-term stress such as leavers' ceremonies, concerts and so on (see School Issues).
- Planning is key! If you are approaching long school holidays, invest in a wipe-off planner. This can be monthly or weekly. Place the planner in a visible area. Use different colours for each child. The planner does not have to be full of complex,

expensive arrangements. The important thing here is to ensure that each child has something written down for every day, morning and afternoon.

SCHOOL HOLIDAY PLANNER

WEEK 1

	MONDAY	TUESDAY	WEDNESDAY	THURSDAY	FRIDAY	SATURDAY	SUNDAY
	K-IPAD R- CAR	K TO NAN R- IPAD	SHOPS	K-IPAD R- SWIM	K TO NAN R- FRIEND HERE	K-CAR R- IPAD	K-IPAD R- CAR
	K - FRIEND HERE R- TO NAN	MAKE PIZZAS	MUM MEETING NAN HERE	* PICNIC IN GARDEN	K- AT NAN'S R- FRIEND HERE	LUNCH WITH DAD	SUNDAY LUNCH NAN
	K - FRIEND HERE R- AT NAN'S	PARK	K- JUDO R- IPAD	K-CAR R- TO NAN	SHOPS	PARK	FAMILY FILM TIME

NOTES:
* IF WET THEN PICNIC WILL BE AT SOFT PLAY

- Whether you are staying at home or going away, establish a 'holiday routine'. Naturally there will be less time pressure than school days, but your children will be able to relax much more if they can continue to predict their environment, and boundaries remain in place.
- If you are planning on going away, do not share information about this too early. The longer your child has to think about the holiday, the longer they have to feel anxious, or to escalate their behaviour to remind you that they are 'not worthy' of such rewards.
- Down play the whole 'going on holiday' anticipation. I used to appear a bit disappointed that I had to go on holiday!
- If you are flying, if possible visit the airport for a day out prior to leaving. This does not need to be connected to the holiday verbally at the time.

- Self-catering may be the best option, where you can keep to a familiar routine and children can have their own space (and you can have yours)!
- You may find you have an easier time if you return to the same holiday destination for the first few years. This builds resilience in your children as they learn to relax in a different environment.
- When travelling, ensure that one adult is the person 'in charge'. This person will have the tickets and be the one looking confident about all the arrangements. If you show doubt or hesitancy it's likely that your child will jump into the void and feel compelled to be the one in charge. Your child will be watching you closely when you are in any kind of transitional state.
- Remember that a holiday may not feel like a holiday to you. Plan a brain break (respite) and recovery time for yourself both during the school holidays and afterwards. When you are going away, if you have another adult with you, plan in advance time alone for each person.
- If you plan to use nighttime driving in the hope that the child will sleep, be aware that your child may be hypervigilant or overexcited and be unable to sleep. This can contribute to a very tense start to a holiday.
- If travelling by car, remember to ensure that each child has their own specific place which is not changed. Pack a bag with one 'present' per hour that can be given to the children. These do not have to be expensive, but can be small novelty items.
- Use electronic equipment sparingly in the days before a long journey. This way the child may have games and apps they want to catch up with.

Strategies during

- During school holidays, bear in mind that our children often suffer from sensory overload, so avoid having too many exciting activities close together.
- Explore 'day camps' and see if you can enrol your child, even if it is only for a few half days during the holiday. If they can manage

this it may help them stay in contact with people they know from school.

- Low-key activities such as picnics in a tent in the garden and paddling pools can be reassuring and easier for everyone to manage.
- If you have planned a day out, do not be tempted to share this ahead of time with the children. Something may occur that makes it impossible to go, and this leads to a lack of trust. Plan in your head that you will be going on the trip on a certain day, then share that information with the children on the morning of that day. Although this might appear spontaneous, in fact you have planned it, and of course would not be referring to the event as a 'surprise'.
- Ensure that you have made reciprocal arrangements with other therapeutic parents. This means that your children will be able to have periods away from the home in an environment where their behaviour is understood and you are not feeling blamed or judged.
- When going away, make good use of transitional objects. One of the most effective is to take the pillow from your child's bed. If this is not feasible, then take the pillow case. Do not use a freshly laundered one. Take the one that has familiar home smells!
- Keep a strong structure and routine, which includes regular snacks. This helps to punctuate the day and keep the child regulated and orientated.
- Use empathic commentary to express what you feel your child is feeling. Where there is an escalation in angry or otherwise challenging behaviour, don't be afraid to relate the behaviour back to being on holiday. For example, 'It must be really hard to feel so cross about not seeing your friends at school. I know in the past you said goodbye to people and didn't see them again. It could be that you are worried you won't see your teacher again either.'

- When planning recovery time for yourself during the school holidays, do not share the real purpose of your time with the children. The more boring and uninteresting you can make it sound, the less likely it is that the children will insist on accompanying you, or trying to prevent you leaving.

Strategies after

- As the school holidays come to an end there is likely to be an escalation of anxiety around returning to school. It is a good idea to refrain from mentioning how long it is until the return to school, unless it is very near.
- Do a review of the holidays. Write down what worked well and what you need to avoid. It's amazing how quickly we forget. Use this as the basis for your planning and preparation for the next holiday.
- Depending on the age and emotional age of your children, explore youth groups such as Cubs, Guides and Army Cadets. If your child can manage structured time away, then by joining one of these groups they are likely to be included in a weekend camp. Army Cadets go away for a two-week camp, and I have often found that children with a trauma background do very well in this structured environment.

HOMEWORK *(see also Memory Issues and Disorganisation, School Issues)*

What it looks like

- The child refuses to do homework.
- The child loses homework or engages in other stalling and avoidance techniques.
- The child can complete a task one day but appears unable to the next.
- The child uses homework to control the parent and environment.
- The child becomes extremely angry and/or frustrated about homework tasks.

Why it might happen

- Unable to manage transitions – school to home, and parent becoming the teacher.
- Emotional age – the child may be functioning at a much lower age.
- Shame – fear of failure.
- The need to feel in control and powerful – refusing homework may be creating a trigger for the parent, which the child controls.
- Lack of cause-and-effect thinking – the child cannot think about what might happen tomorrow if homework is not completed today.
- Dysregulation – acting in the heat of the moment.
- Comfortable to be in the wrong/self-sabotage/unwilling to be seen to succeed.
- Recreating a familiar environment – homework may not have been done historically.
- Fear or fearful anticipation of a negative response from the parent or teacher.
- Attraction to peer-group activities.
- Dissociation.
- Memory issues.
- Unable to concentrate.
- Overwhelming need to keep the parent close.
- Boredom.
- Sensory issues – unable to sit still for long periods.

Reality check

Many therapeutic parents do not insist on their children doing homework. The main strategy you need to know is how to deal with the expectations of the school and others, around the non-completion of homework.

If you are lucky and have a school that understands the impact of trauma on your child's learning, you are likely to be able to work flexibly together. When schools insist we spend a long time each evening doing homework there are some points we need to consider first:

- What is most important: making sure your child can make relationships (attachments) or that they get good grades? Is the priority a well-rounded person who can parent, with empathy, or a high achiever with no relationships, empathy or compassion?
- What is your child's emotional age? If it is three, would we ask a three-year-old to sit down after school and do homework?
- What memory/organisation issues are there? It is perfectly possible for your child to remember something one day and then have no recollection of it the next day. We don't need to worry, it is in there and will surface sooner or later, but sitting down to have a two-hour battle is not going to help anyone.
- Can your child cope with the transition of you changing from 'Mum' or 'Dad' to 'Teacher'? Usually they cannot, and we see an escalation in shame-avoiding behaviours.
- Is your child capable of sitting still and concentrating?
- They nearly always catch up later on, once the secure attachments are there.
- Where your child appears willing to do homework, this of course should be encouraged. Make sure they have the time and space in which to do it.

Useful strategies

- School stays at school. We do not ask the teacher to pop round to make sure our children tidy their bedrooms. If school adopts a blaming, accusatory stance, it can be useful to remind them of this.
- Where you feel a child is deliberately using homework time to get extended one-to-one attention and you really do need to move on with other tasks, set a time limit for when you will be available. There are better ways to nurture attachments than through homework.
- Be creative about learning. You can reassure the school that although you were unable to complete the homework you did an activity that promoted learning. I used to use nature walks as a good way to learn and lower cortisol levels!

- Allow 'natural' consequences to occur. If the school gives detentions for non-completion of homework, you need to allow this to happen. It is very unlikely it will make any impact on your child's motivation to complete further homework (in fact quite the opposite). It is important to 'be in the child's corner'. Use phrases such as, 'It's a shame you need to do a detention because the homework didn't get done. Never mind, I will do your favourite tea to help you feel better.' This maintains the important nurture link and stops you getting into a homework battle.
- Educate others about the effects of trauma on the brain and how your child is functioning. Don't be afraid to challenge misconceptions about your child's abilities with some fact-based research. The Bruce Perry website is a good place to start, or you can access resources through the National Association of Therapeutic Parents (see References, Further Reading and Websites at the end of this book).

HONEYMOON PERIOD *(see also*
Charming, and Part 1, Chapter 1)

What it looks like

- The child moves in with a new family and appears to be extremely compliant.
- The child's presented behaviours appear very different to historical behaviours.
- The child appears to have many interests in common with the carers/parents.
- The child presents as charming and is often described as 'a joy'.

Why it might happen

- Fear of parent/carer and other adults.
- Fear or fearful anticipation of a negative response from the parent.
- The need to feel safe – gauging the personalities and actions of others before relaxing into 'normal' behaviour patterns.

- The need to feel in control and powerful – working out the best way to retain control or elicit nurture to stay alive.
- Shame – instinctively creating a new persona in order to avoid revealing the 'shameful self'.
- Fear of invisibility/being forgotten – seeking a response.
- Recreating a familiar environment – our children stimulate the environment to replicate the one they have lost.
- A need to try to predict the environment.
- Fear of change/transitions.
- Separation anxiety – fear of abandonment.
- Overwhelming need to keep the parent close – needing to observe what the adult is doing at all times in order to feel safe.
- Overwhelming need to feel loved/important.
- Emotional age – may be functioning at a much younger age and needing to have those early nurture needs met.

Reality check

You may hear others refer to the early days of a child's placement with you as 'The Honeymoon Period'. This is when everyone is on their best behaviour and making a big effort. With a traumatised child, this period usually lasts between two weeks and six months, although you may not have a honeymoon period at all. That's good. That means you have 'the real child' from the start.

I've always felt the term 'honeymoon' for this phase is misleading. In real life, I've always thought of it as the 'pre-showtime phase'.

In the 'pre-showtime phase', the child comes to you and feels unsafe, fearing for the worst and fearing you. Their only aim is to ensure that you do not hurt them, and that you meet their basic needs. In order to achieve this, first of all they are driven to make you invest in them and keep them safe. Entirely instinctively, they may well be acquiescent, charming and delightful. They make sure that you see they pose no threat to you, by taking up hobbies and interests that may mirror your own, or doing something you have indicated you would like them to do.

Once you have bought your tickets, invested in the child and are sitting in the front row, the show can begin. Only then, when the child senses that you have invested a lot of time and effort 'buying the ticket', can they safely show their true inner behaviours and fears. Most of us do not ask for our money back, but spend a great deal of time trying to find the child who moved in originally. That child does not exist. That child wore a mask. That mask has kept them alive. You are privileged that they now feel safe enough to take it off.

It took my daughter six years to stop smiling, behaving in an acquiescent manner and generally move from pre-showtime. When she was 13, Katie carefully switched off the fake smile and sycophantic charm and called me a 'f*****g bitch'. I smiled at her and said, 'Thank you for showing me the *real* you.' Then the real work could begin.

Useful strategies

- Make it clear to the child that you accept them for who they are.
- Where you suspect that the child is feigning interest in an activity or hobby in order to keep themselves safe, in the early days it may be beneficial to allow them to do this while carefully letting them know that it is okay to have different interests.
- Use wondering aloud to help the child see that you see through the behaviours and appreciate them anyway. For example, 'I wonder if you wanted to help me with the washing because you were worried I might not like you? It's lovely having your help, and I will like you just as much if you decide you want to do something more interesting.'
- Give the child space. They may want to keep you close to make sure they know where you are, but if they want to be alone then let them have time to adjust. It's exhausting to be 'putting on a show' all the time.
- Where you see flashes of the 'real' child, welcome it. If this is portrayed as anger then simply state that. For example,

'Thank you for showing me that you are angry (sad) about that. I am here to help you manage those big feelings.'

HOSTILITY *(parent feeling towards child) (see Part 1, Chapter 7)*

HOSTILITY *(from child) (see Defiance, Rejection, Rudeness)*

HUNGER *(see Food Issues, Mealtime Issues, and Part 1, Chapter 1)*

HYGIENE *(see Bath Time Issues, Brushing Teeth, Dirty Clothing, Messy Bedrooms, Sabotaging)*

HYPOCONDRIA *(see also Self-Harming, Overreacting, and Part 1, Chapter 1, Interoception)*

What it looks like

- The child claims to feel or be ill when they are not.
- The child gets obsessed with very minor injuries.
- The child fakes illness or injury.
- The child appears to believe they are seriously injured or hurt when there is only a minor injury, or no injury.

Why it might happen

- Sensory issues – interoception: the child's brain does not receive the correct messages relating to pain sensations.
- Fear response/high cortisol levels – the child may genuinely believe they are seriously hurt.
- Recreating a familiar environment – they may have been in an environment previously where claims of illness or injury were commonplace.
- Fear or fearful anticipation of a negative response from the parent – an illness or injury may be a distraction.
- Fear of invisibility/being forgotten – seeking a response.

- Fear of change/transitions – a claimed injury may slow down or even stop a transition.
- Separation anxiety, especially where an illness or injury is intended to change the environment, for example, the child may be sent home from school.
- Dissociation – the child is unsure if they are badly hurt or not.
- Overwhelming need to keep the parent close and also elicit nurture.
- Overwhelming need to feel loved/important, especially if there is a high level of medical intervention.
- Fear of the sight of blood. This can be very triggering and we may not always know the reason behind that.
- Emotional age – for example, the child may be responding as a much younger child would to a minor scratch.

Reality check

Recognising the cause of hypochondria can help us to moderate the exasperation we feel, but it is very difficult to always be caring and nurturing when we know our child is fine and 'faking it'. This is one of those occasions when therapeutic parents need to be quite up front about what they believe is happening. Our children begin to rely on our interpretation of events to start to internalise their own response, just like babies and toddlers do. The difficulty is, you may come across as harsh or uncaring. The important thing to remember here, however, is the consistency of the message to the child. Let them know when *you* know they are either faking it or misinterpreting their body's signals, but then also give a little nurture to help them meet that potential early unmet need.

Remember, it is very common for traumatised children to complain about imaginary illnesses, yet when they are genuinely injured they may say or show nothing.

Preventative strategies

- Good communication with school is essential. If you have a child who regularly goes along to the office to have a little time-out, or even better be sent home, then let the school know what is, and is not, real. Although the school has a duty of care, frequent visitors to the sick room are usually spotted early on in the school term.

- Do not always be instantly available to deal with issues arising if you know your child is safe and are certain that the 'illness' is not genuine. Respond in a low-key manner – for example, you may not be able to go straight to the school to collect them. (Staff were always amazed how my children all miraculously 'got better' as lunchtime approached.)
- Make available some 'magic cream' or 'magic tablets' which the children can access. Naturally these might be simple vitamins and moisturising cream. If they use these to 'self-medicate' it can avoid a full-scale incident. There is the extra advantage that these can be taken to school and used there too.
- Alert others to an appropriate response. Sometimes a small complaint can escalate further, if met with a brusque no-nonsense approach, completely lacking in nurture. At other times, this approach can be effective. This is about knowing your child, and your child understanding that you know them!

Strategies during

- A tiny bit of nurture can go a long way. If a child is moaning and complaining it's useful to ask, 'What do you need to happen?' One of my children would always say, 'Kiss it better.'
- Try 'kissing it better'. It's amazing how often this is genuinely all our children actually need.
- Try to gauge how much of this is around the child seeking an opportunity for nurture. It may also be about keeping you close. This is not an unreasonable need so simply state that back to the child, 'I wonder if your tummy is hurting because you needed me to stay with you?'
- Playfulness can be really useful. When your child complains, quickly check, then say something like, 'Bet it will get better before you grow another leg' or, 'I think we need to go to the shop and buy some more ears!'

- Use the 'magic cream' to engage in some nurture. This can be a real bonding experience. It's important to get the balance right though. We want our children to grow in resilience so while rubbing the cream on I might say something like, 'I don't think this is very serious but I think you needed a little love.'

Strategies after

- Name the need – sometimes children who have had a traumatic start find it really difficult knowing when they are really hurt, or when it's 'just a little thing'. If a child has claimed to be ill or has faked it and you feel duped and angry, just chalk it down to experience. They are unlikely to fool you again. Let the child know that you know it wasn't real, but that it may have felt real to them.
- If the faking has been very well thought out and involved a great deal of inconvenience, you can use natural consequences to 'pay back time owed'. This is only likely to have any effect if the consequence is meaningful to the child, not to you. Before you embark on this course of action though, ask yourself if you truly feel the child has had their nurture need met.
- Alert others who may have been involved about the true extent of the injury or illness. They cannot learn if they are unaware of the situation.

Footnote: When my daughter Rosie Rudey was (proudly) brought out of school in a wheelchair after 'stumbling in the corridor', I simply told her to 'jump up,' which she did. At home, I invited her to play a game of hopscotch with me, which was undertaken with great enthusiasm. The school were stunned to hear about her miraculous recovery.

HYPERVIGILANCE *(see Memory Issues and Disorganisation, and Part 1, Chapter 1)*

I

IGNORING *(see Controlling Behaviours, Defiance, Lateness)*

IMMATURITY *(see also Part 1, Chapter 1)*

What it looks like

- The child functions at a younger age than their chronological age some or all of the time.
- The child's emotional needs and demands are not consistent with their age and assumed understanding. For example, the child may:
  - be unable to feed themselves
  - be overly attached to dummies and bottles
  - be much later potty training (see Poo Issues and Urinating)
  - have a sleep pattern similar to that of a baby or toddler
  - have delayed speech or use a 'baby voice'
  - choose friends who are younger (see Friendships).

Why it might happen

- Brain development impaired from early life trauma, abuse or similar.
- Developmental delay.
- Foetal alcohol spectrum disorder (see Part 1, Chapter 2).
- Grief and loss – the child is grieving and unable to move forwards on an emotional level.

- Fear of abandonment or starvation.
- Emotional age is significantly lower than the chronological age.
- Overwhelming need for nurture/unmet early need.
- Underlying mental health and physical issues.
- Sensory issues.
- Fear response – the child is in fight/flight for a great deal of time, leaving less 'space' for growth.
- Fear of invisibility/being forgotten – seeking a response.
- Fear of parent/carer and other adults.
- A need to try to predict the environment, especially where routine and boundaries have been unclear.
- Separation anxiety.

Reality check

If you are parenting a child who has developmental trauma it is almost certain that the child will be functioning at an earlier stage, at least on an emotional level. Often our children appear developmentally delayed too, but as they grow in resilience and form secure attachments, they usually catch up, although may remain physically small if there are underlying medical issues. With my own children, with all their different levels of trauma, resilience and differing attachment styles, we observed the changes recorded in the table below. You can see how the emotional age, while often at a lower age than the chronological age, still followed a general upward trend.

	On placement		Year 8		Year 15		Year 18	
Rosie	A 8	E 5	A 16	E 13	A 23	E 23	A 26	E 26
Katie	A 6	E 2	A 14	E 10	A 21	E 16	A 24	E 20
William	A 3.5	E 6 months	A 11	E 6*	A 18	E 13	A 22	E 17
Sophie	A 2.5	E 1	A 10	E 7	A 17	E 14	A 21	E 18
Charley	A 7 months	E 3 months	A 8	E 5	A 15	E 11	A 19	E 15

Key: A = Actual, E = Emotional

*William did not grow at all for four years and still wore age 6–7 clothing when aged 11. I have often witnessed that children with a very young emotional functioning age are much smaller physically, grow more slowly, and sometimes appear to be chronologically at the same emotional age.

Useful strategies

- The main strategy to use with a traumatised child exhibiting a younger emotional need is to go with it! The likelihood is that your child has been unable to get through the developmental stage that they are exhibiting in their emotional behaviours. For example, if the child wants a bottle and is very attached to it for a long time, this is an indicator of early missed nurture. The child may not have had enough time using a bottle or breast.

- Look at the younger emotional stage as an opportunity to engage with the child at a younger level. Theraplay® (a type of therapy) can be extremely useful in engaging with children at their emotional age (see Rodwell and Norris 2017).

- Spend some time observing your child and then look at developmental milestones. See where you think the child fits. You may find that in some areas your child is functioning at their developmental age but in others they are functioning at a much younger age. This does not mean that your child is capable and is merely pretending.

- Where the child is shouting and making a noise at night, relate this to a young baby crying at night and how you might respond to them. This is a really useful way to break negative patterns of behaviour. For example, you would not go into a room with a baby or toddler crying and try to reason with them that it's late and they need to go to sleep. You might instead offer reassurance, a cuddle and some milk.

- State out loud which emotional need you are meeting, 'Oh, I see I have baby Emma today! Let's wrap the baby up.' You can then use playfulness to make it into a game.

- If the child often uses a baby voice and you find it difficult to respond empathically due to feelings of irritation, try exploring that with the child. When Katie, aged 11, was still using a baby voice I found it really hard not to snap at her sometimes, so one day I just said, 'You know, when you use your baby voice I find it really hard to understand you. I think sometimes you use your baby voice because that's the voice you used when you were a tiny girl and needed to try to make the scary grown-ups be kind to you. I will be able to answer you better, and understand you better, if you use your big girl voice. The one you use when you are bossing the dogs around!' After this conversation, I was able to use trigger words when I heard the baby voice again. It disappeared within two weeks.

- Where a child appears unable to play alone and amuse themselves, it's unlikely that they have developed the skills to play with age-appropriate toys. Try introducing younger activities and build in time to revisit games you might play with a toddler, such as peek-a-boo, blowing bubbles, and singing nursery rhymes.

- Where there are issues around eating, you may need to return to feeding the child. Again, this is an important opportunity to invest in time missed if the child did not live with you during their first months or years.

- Develop a thick skin! You may well find that as you lower your expectations and increase parental support, there might be a queue of people waiting to tell you how the child 'needs to learn'. This is a good opportunity to share resources around therapeutic parenting and the effects of trauma. The National Association of Therapeutic Parents can help you with resources for this.

J

JOKING AND TEASING *(see also Anxiety, Immaturity, and Part 1, Chapter 1)*

What it looks like

- The child does not 'get' jokes.
- The child teases or taunts others to a greater extent than is acceptable.
- The child claims they are 'joking' after saying unkind things.

Why it might happen

- The need to feel in control and powerful by controlling the environment and actions of others through joking and teasing.
- Fear – concealing their true identity beneath a 'clown' persona.
- Fear of invisibility/being forgotten – seeking a response from a parent or another child in order to keep themselves centre stage.
- Fear of drawing attention to self – the 'jokes' or teasing focus attention on others.
- Recreating a familiar environment – teasing may have been a prevalent part of past family life.
- Lack of empathy – the child is unable to think about the effect on others.
- Lack of remorse – the child is unable to care about the impact of their actions.

- Fear of parent/carer and other adults – making fun of adults in order to try to 'reduce' them to a manageable level.
- Fear of change/transitions – may increase teasing or taunting behaviours.
- Boredom.
- Self-sabotage/internal working model.
- Emotional age – the child is younger developmentally than chronologically and has not yet reached the correct stage of development to use and understand humour.

Useful strategies

- Be aware of the child's literal thinking. What may seem like a joke may actually be the child taking things literally, and asking literal questions, such as, 'Is the sauna warm?' It may be difficult not to laugh when you have a very literal child, inadvertently making jokes, so to avoid invoking shame or the ridicule of others, teach them that they are clever, have made people laugh and encourage them to smile. This is much easier than looking puzzled and asking, 'What?' My children became quite skilled at this. Even as young adults, people think they are quite talented comedians. Driving past a church with solar panels Charley Chatty said, 'Why does that church have a sunroof? It doesn't even look nice.' She remembered in the nick of time to join in the laughter, and wallowed in the glory of being 'very funny'.
- If the child is targeting you as the parent with 'jokes' or teasing, try taking them literally to engage a different part of the child's brain. You can use the same strategies from 'Rudeness' to deal with this.
- Think about the emotional age of your child. What would your response be if a much younger child made this joke? Is it *actually* teasing? Respond in the same vein.
- If you are tempted to respond with, 'Just be quiet!' or similar, change your reaction to, 'That's wonderful news!' with a happy smile, or something equally out of context.

- If the child is teasing other children and gaining a reaction from them, first of all work with the responders. Take them to one side and explain that they are giving the 'teaser' a little gift each time they respond. We would make it a game and have small prizes to see who could last the longest without being drawn in to the teasing. This effectively changes the temperature in a similar way that the 'parental reward chart' does for rudeness.
- Where a child constantly says unkind things then claims to be 'just joking', this is often learned behaviour. 'Naming the need' can be quite effective: 'I think maybe you say unkind things as jokes because that happened to you. You must still be feeling sad about that.'

K

KICKING *(see Aggression)*

LATENESS *(moving slowly, lagging behind, staying in bed) (see also Controlling Behaviours, Defiance)*

What it looks like

- The child refuses to get out of bed.
- The child dawdles behind, gradually increasing the distance (see strategies for Running Off).
- The child moves deliberately slowly (see Mealtime Issues for eating slowly).
- The child is often late for school, buses and so on, despite leaving in plenty of time.
- The child frequently returns home late with no awareness of time.

Why it might happen

- Unable to manage transitions – the child may be unwilling to go to the next place.
- Memory issues and disorganisation generally, which contribute to difficulties in timekeeping.
- Lack of awareness of time.
- Rewards the child with a reaction – if this is a trigger for the parent.

- Lack of cause-and-effect thinking, especially in relation to being unable to visualise outcomes – the child is unconcerned about the consequences of 'being late'.
- Blocked trust – delaying leaving in order to prolong current status quo. The child is uncertain of where they are being taken to.
- The need to feel in control and powerful.
- Fear or fearful anticipation of a negative response from the parent regarding arriving home late.
- Attraction to peer-group activities, especially when arriving home late.
- Fear response – fear of the 'next thing'.
- Feelings of hostility or momentary hatred towards the parent.
- Fear of invisibility/being forgotten – seeking a response.
- Overwhelming need to feel loved/important.
- Comfortable to be in the wrong/self-sabotage.
- Emotional age – the child is functioning at a younger age, particularly in relation to time keeping and the meaning and importance of punctuality.

Preventative strategies

- Be prepared! If you know you have a child who moves slowly and likes to find lots of last-minute distractions to delay exiting, start moving earlier. You might decide that you need to be at school for 8.30am. State this is the time you need to be there. It can take a huge amount of pressure off you if you know you have a spare 15 minutes in hand.
- If lateness in the mornings is a particular issue, get everything packed and sorted the night before. Put all packed lunches, PE kits and so on in school bags and place them in the locked car or other inaccessible area. This prevents sabotage and last-minute 'losses'.
- Think about where your child is developmentally. Sometimes we expect our children to be able to function at their chronological age rather than their emotional/developmental age. Is your child late because they are not physically able to dress themselves or

organise themselves at their chronological age (see Memory Issues and Disorganisation)?

- Remember, what you perceive as the child deliberately being slow in order to make you all late may actually be fear of the change (see Transitions). Re-evaluate your perspective if appropriate, and respond to those hidden feelings.

- Avoid saying things like, 'You are going to make us all late!' This may be experienced as, 'You now have complete control of our day.'

- Where you have a reoccurring theme, for example every morning the child brings in obstacles to prevent leaving on time, engage the help of a supportive friend or partner. This way, you can continue moving forwards and leave the house on time without worrying about making others late, or leaving the 'late' child home alone. The supportive friend or partner just happens to suddenly be around, just at the usual leaving time, making you free to leave on time and giving you good insight into how the child might respond. This can also effectively remove a trigger by changing the dynamics of this particular interaction.

- Think about triggers for the child. When we are rushing to get somewhere on time we are often distracted and preoccupied. This means that our facial expressions change and we might appear stressed. This alone can trigger the child. Think about where you are trying to get to and what immediately preceded the delaying tactics.

- Where a child is late coming home, don't expect them to keep an eye on the time and remember to leave in good time. When you are out of sight you may cease to exist for a few hours! Well-timed text messages can help a child stay on track.

- For morning lateness/staying in bed turn on all the lights in the house and a lamp on in the child's room 45 minutes before actually having to get up.

- Plan the routine so that the child gets moving straightaway (in case there are high cortisol levels) and the best thing happens once all the dull stuff is done. I found that December was a very good month as the children got their advent calendar chocolate just before we left. A square of chocolate can work wonders and can also help to regulate the child.

- Happy music that comes on at a set time, before it is actually time to get up, is less triggering than an adult saying, 'Time to get up now!'

Strategies during

- Keep moving forwards. A lot of these behaviours are around seeing if the child can be the one who is in charge and can get a response. If you appear unconcerned and just keep going, this can resolve a lot of these issues. For example, if they are still in their pyjamas, or have still not got their shoes on, just say, 'That's fine, you can always get changed at school. I will put your clothes/shoes in a bag for you.' Most children will not want to arrive at school looking different so they either rush about or change quickly in the car.
- To keep children on track, ask, 'What should you be doing right now?'
- Remove the audience. Say, 'Okay, well let me know when you are ready, I am just off to...'
- Use empathic commentary to give a narrative to what the child is experiencing, 'I can see that you are a bit wobbly so you are pretending to have lost your shoes to make it longer before we leave for school.'
- Using happy, loud alarm music can also promote playfulness. Sometimes I used to dance into the children's bedroom in a silly way so they would start off by laughing. This can help to set the right tone.
- Use wondering aloud to explore the emotions behind the behaviours, 'I wonder if you are trying to be late because you get upset when you aren't with Mummy?'
- Allow the situation to play out. Some parents have found this the most effective strategy of all. It is quite disconcerting for a child who is using lateness as a controlling behaviour to find the

parent unconcerned and appearing relaxed, perhaps even taking advantage of unexpected 'relaxation time!'

- Use 'the phone strategy' (see Part 1, Chapter 5).
- Where TVs and gadgets are contributing to lateness, remove access through wi-fi controls and so on. I used to find that my children would move around very quickly in the morning if it then created ten minutes' TV time prior to leaving.

Strategies after

- Where you have a child coming home late you can use natural consequences to 'pay back' time. If a child is ten minutes late home one night then you can take ten minutes back next time. This is only ever effective if the child will actually acknowledge and stick to this. It's not appropriate to use if it is catapulting you into a downward spiral of control. In this case, you take back the time in a different way, 'As you were one hour late home last night, I stayed up one hour later and am too tired today to...'
- If you have a child who stays in bed and refuses to get up, you are normally left with natural consequences. As far as possible, keep moving forwards and do not show annoyance. If it happens a second or third time (or 1000 times), plan a surprise that you know the bed blocker would really like. As long as you have enlisted the help of another adult, you can keep going and announce at the last minute that it's a shame they are not ready as you are leaving now for (favourite place). Do *not* be tempted to stop and wait otherwise the next time there is no linked cause and effect. This is a natural consequence of staying in bed. You miss things.
- Think about how the routine of the house can be altered. This is particularly relevant in relation to the body clocks of teenagers and electronic gadgets causing tiredness.

LAUNDRY ISSUES *(see Defiance, Dirty Clothing, Messy Bedrooms, Sabotaging)*

LIFE STORY *(see Part 1, Chapter 3, Be honest!)*

LITERALNESS *(see Joking and Teasing, and Part 1, Chapter 1)*

LOSING THINGS *(see Memory Issues and Disorganisation)*

LYING *(see also Boasting, Charming, False Allegations, Overreacting, Triangulation)*

What it looks like

- The child tells a blatant lie when the truth is very obvious.
- The child lies habitually about unimportant matters.
- The child refuses to tell the truth under any circumstances and sticks rigidly to an untrue story, even when presented with contradicting fact or evidence.

Why it might happen

- The avoidance of overwhelming and toxic shame.
- Overwhelming fear or fearful anticipation of a negative response from the parent.
- Lack of cause-and-effect thinking – the child is unable to think through logically the course of events or to see the situation from the viewpoint of others.
- Comfortable to be in the wrong – there may appear to be no benefit to 'doing the right thing' or 'being a better person'.
- Emotional age – the child may simply be at a much earlier emotional developmental stage.
- Blocked trust – the child cannot trust that the adult will do what they say they will.

- Dysregulation – acting in the heat of the moment.
- The need to feel in control and powerful by controlling information.
- Feelings of hostility or momentary hatred towards the parent.
- Fear of invisibility/being forgotten – seeking a response.
- Recreating a familiar environment – lying may be very familiar and the child may have trouble distinguishing between fact and fiction.
- Lack of empathy, especially for future self and understanding the consequences of the action.
- Lack of remorse – the child is unable to access feelings of remorse for their behaviour.
- Dissociation – the child may believe what they are saying.
- Overwhelming need to keep the parent close – having a long dialogue about whether or not a child did something engages the parent in lengthy discussion.
- Overwhelming need to feel loved/important.

Reality check

Traumatised children lie as if their lives depend on it, because the overwhelming feeling of toxic shame is too difficult to bear. I refer to this as 'mad lying'. It's when the child has clearly eaten the chocolate bar, you can see the chocolate round their mouth, they are still holding the chocolate bar, yet they look you straight in the eye and claim never to have seen it! Remember, they are not doing it to annoy you. This is an early survival-based mechanism, so it's instinctive.

Sometimes parents and carers really struggle with the idea of the child 'getting away with it' or 'winning'. If you often find yourself in that mindset, try to momentarily pause and think, 'I wonder what the child is thinking right now.' The important outcome is to make sure the child knows that you know they are lying, or are at least struggling to maintain a grasp on reality. That is how we 'win', by showing the child that we are not taken in and that we won't be joining in with this charade. Met with this response, lying definitely decreases over time but our response needs to be:

- sure
- clear
- unthreatening
- a statement of fact, not emotion.

Useful strategies

- There is *definitely no mileage* in insisting the child tells you the truth as they are often unclear what the truth is or means. If you place yourself opposite the child demanding an explanation the child is likely to have high levels of cortisol and be in flight or fight mode. We need to take a step back if we want to resolve lying (see Part 1, Chapter 6).
- Our children are often scared of our reaction – properly scared, as in terrified – so once you have said you know the truth and have decided the consequence is X, they are able to be less fearful and sometimes even admit the lie!
- I tend to meet lying head on, not by correcting or arguing, but by simply stating what the truth is and saying I will apologise later if that proves to be wrong. This method has the added advantage of allowing us to disengage and get on with other issues. It also keeps stress levels lower.
- Where the child is frozen and unable to admit what has happened, we need to reduce their fear of what might happen, as it is too overwhelming. For example, your child comes home from school. You know they have had a very bad day and are in a lot of trouble. You ask how their day was and they reply that all is wonderful. I would just let the child know that I know things have gone badly at school today. Then when they deny it I would just say, 'That's interesting. Well, I am sure you can sort it out. You know where I am if you need me', disengage and move on. The child's brain then unfreezes as the fear of the consequences diminishes, and later they can access higher thinking. You may even get an explanation or conversation about it!

- Empathic commentary leading into a statement of natural consequence can be very effective with lying, 'I can see you are really struggling to tell me that you took the chocolate. It must feel very scary thinking that I might be really angry if you tell me the truth. Well, I am going to help you with those scary feelings. I have decided that you *did* take the chocolate and because of that, there will not be any more chocolate today.'
- It is better to follow your instinct and appear certain than to hesitate and show doubt. If you believe your child in a lie, it can make them feel unsafe. If you call time on the lie, stating clearly that you will apologise later if you discover the child is telling the truth, this enables you all to move on.

Footnote: When they were very little, I told my children that they got a little blue spot on their tongue when they lied. Only adults could see it. Even when they no longer believed this, there would be an involuntary movement as they closed their mouth when telling fibs! Over 17 years with five children, I followed my instincts with lying. I always used, 'I will apologise later if we find out you did not...' I had to apologise and put it right once. Had I believed all the protestations and claims of innocence there would have been many thousands of unsafe moments!

M

MAKING DECISIONS *(see Choosing Difficulties)*

MANIC LAUGHTER *(see Overreacting)*

MEALTIME ISSUES *(see also Controlling Behaviours, Defiance, Food Issues, School Issues, and Part 1, Chapter 1)*

What it looks like

- The child is very fussy about meals/food offered.
- The child eats very slowly.
- The child eats very fast.
- There is arguing and tension at mealtimes about sharing.
- The child refuses to eat or often rejects meals offered.
- The child cannot sit still at the table/gets down and so on.
- The child is very particular about food touching on the plate, the colours of different foods and so on.
- The child makes a lot of mess at mealtimes.

Why it might happen

- Child may not have been weaned appropriately and may have missed out key stages. This is particularly relevant where the child favours only one or two types of food.

- A subconscious compulsion to break a forming attachment (with the parent), especially in relation to rejecting food offered (nurture).
- Sensory issues, especially relating to hot/cold, spiciness, colour and texture.
- High cortisol levels – making it difficult for the child to sit still and do one thing.
- Emotional or developmental age, especially in relation to being able to feed oneself, avoid messiness and so on.
- The need to feel in control and powerful, especially in relation to having choice, where previously there may not have been. This also relates to 'fussy' children who are very particular, for example about the arrangement of food on their plate.
- Loyalty to birth parents or former carers – rejecting food is a powerful rejection of care and nurture.
- Recreating a familiar environment – food may be unfamiliar and the child may not have experience of structured mealtimes.
- Feelings of hostility or momentary hatred towards the parent.
- Fear of invisibility/being forgotten – seeking a response, especially where slow eating ensures that the focus remains on the child.
- Overwhelming need to keep the parent close.
- Overwhelming need to feel loved, important and centre stage.

Preventative strategies

- Consider starting the whole weaning process from scratch if you feel this may be a cause of the child rejecting the majority of different foods. You may need to supplement milk only with vitamin supplements, etc., so ask a health professional about this. Ensure that the nurture element is strongly present when using this strategy, i.e. feed the child with bottles or spoons wherever possible, rather than leaving the child to feed themselves. Relate this to the child's emotional age.
- Keep mealtimes the same. Incorporate them into the routine of the house, making sure that mealtimes are predictable in timing and content.

- Allocate each child their own set of crockery and cutlery. When this is on the table it assures the child of their place at the table. The message is, 'you will get food'.
- Use reverse psychology. If you have a child who refuses to drink, put a drink out anyway and say, 'Try not to drink that, so I can save it for later.'
- Be aware of the relationship between food and nurture. It feels hard when children reject our food because they are rejecting our nurture and therefore it feels as if they are rejecting us. It's important to be aware of this as a potential trigger.
- Cover the table in a heatproof vinyl tablecloth to reduce your anxieties around mess and damage.
- With a child who eats very quickly, put their meal out in small portions, adding second and third portions after a suitable pause.
- Do not put out sharing platters, for example in 'party teas'. This is too triggering for our children, who will be frantically counting all the cakes on the plate and eyeing up the opposition at the same time. Instead, where there is a celebration, put the same savoury food on each child's plate, then afterwards refill with the dessert or sweet treats. Ensure that everyone has the same number!
- Where a child is a very messy eater, try taking a subconscious step backwards and observe what the child is doing. Try to establish how much is developmental. How much practice have they had with a knife and fork? Do you need to go back a stage and reintroduce aprons or help the child learn to improve coordination?
- Also with messy eating there are often sensory issues to consider. Some therapeutic parents have had their children assessed and discovered that they cannot tell whereabouts the food is in their mouth. A game you can play to help with this is to take a very small sweet, like a sherbet pip, and see who can keep it in their mouth the longest. Then you can progress to moving the pip about to specific places in the mouth. This will take some weeks to see an improvement.

- Manage portion sizes carefully. In Food Issues, I describe how difficult it is when our children don't seem to have sensations of hunger and fullness. Because of this we need to be their 'sensor'.
- You can try to involve the child in menu planning. Some parents have had limited success with this. In our house it was a disaster, leading the children to indulge in some intense arguing about meal choices!
- Be 'King or Queen' of the house! You do not need to cook five different meals for five different children! While we can try to accommodate individual choices over the week, it's important that our children see us as a parent who is confident and in control. If we constantly bow to this week's latest food fad, we are undermining that security.
- If you have a child who is very fussy and particular about food touching, colours and mess, this is an indicator of a need to introduce some messy play! You can do this quite spontaneously, maybe making up a game involving food, doing baking, and ensuring the flour and other ingredients make a bit of a mess. As the child learns and experiences some mess around food and associates it with fun and joy, the anxiety they experience will lessen.

Strategies during

- Where a child is eating very slowly, simply keep moving forwards, making it clear that they can take as long as they like but that you will continue in the usual timeframe. If this happens due to a child wishing to exert control over the rest of the family, this therefore removes that as a reward.
- Use a big roll of paper to cover the table so they can draw on it where there are issues around sitting still or attention.
- If the child triggers you then position yourself so you cannot see what the child is doing, whether or not they are eating or drinking. Remember, the child may well be watching you for a response, and that response could be reinforcing the negative behaviours. You need to be good at acting to ensure you show a 'not bothered' face.

- Empathic commentary can be used in most situations around mealtimes. For example, 'It looks as if you don't want my dinner. I know you are hungry. It must be really hard to say no to food when you are hungry. I wonder if you think (previous carer) will be upset if you eat our food?'
- With a fussy eater, don't be tempted to skip straight to the sweet stuff because they 'need to eat something'. If you are worried about the child's development make sure you get them weighed regularly. I found it much easier to say 'no pudding' (when almost the entire contents of the main dinner were still on the plate) when I was secure in the knowledge that they were gaining weight. I later discovered how adept my children were at borrowing from other children's lunch boxes...
- With a child who does not like different food touching, I nip this one in the bud. It is reasonably straightforward to downplay this and tell the child they can move things around on their plate if they wish. I know some parents buy plates with separate sections to use with children who have very entrenched behaviours and simply will not eat. I would tend to use tray bakes in these situations, such as cottage pie and lasagne, where the meal is all 'touching'. I did once put all the food in a blender and made 'soup'!
- Use wondering aloud, 'I wonder if you are thinking that if you eat one cornflake at a time it will mean it's longer before we leave for school?'

Strategies after

- Where you have decided to 'keep moving forwards', it's important to see this through. Say to the child, 'I can see you need a bit more time to finish your meal so let me know when you are done.' Then leave the table and involve yourself in a task elsewhere. This helps to resolve challenges where children are deliberately eating slowly, and 'popping back to check' also reassures the genuine slow eater.

MEMORY ISSUES AND DISORGANISATION

(see also Absences, Lateness, Messy Bedrooms)

What it looks like

- The child forgets equipment, books and so on.
- The child is disorganised, runs late and has incorrect equipment.
- The child often loses things.
- The child appears generally forgetful, unkempt and unconcerned about the consequences of this.
- The child forgets major events such as holidays.
- The child forgets a whole section of work learned.

Why it might happen

- Brain development impaired from early life trauma or similar – for example, dyspraxia, especially in relation to clumsiness and disorganisation.
- Compartmentalised thinking – the child's brain stores things in such a way that they are not easily accessible.
- Sensory issues, especially in relation to feeling overwhelmed and losing concentration.
- Lack of cause-and-effect thinking – the child is unable to recognise or think about the effect that the loss will have.
- Comfortable to be in the wrong/self-sabotage – the child expects to be blamed or 'in trouble'.
- Emotional age – the child may be functioning at a much younger age.
- Recreating a familiar environment – material items may hold little interest or value.
- Fear of invisibility/being forgotten – seeking a response or help to find a lost item.
- Lack of empathy – for future self. The child has no concept of the impact of the disorganisation or loss.
- Dissociation.
- Overwhelming need to keep the parent close.

Reality check

There is a plethora of information and research about how trauma affects memory. Two of the most useful resources are Bruce Perry's website http://childtrauma.org and the book *The Body Keeps the Score* by Bessel Van der Kolk (2015). Memory issues are *very* common in our children. When they are traumatised and have high levels of cortisol, the brain simply prioritises survival over housekeeping. However, as the adrenalin and cortisol levels lower over the years, and routine and predictability make them feel safer, we begin to see marked improvements. It does help parents and carers if they know that the child genuinely can't help it. Try not to worry too much as I have found this definitely improves as they get older. Lack of memory directly impacts on organisation and losing items as well, making this a medium to high priority to tackle.

I found that the children's memories appeared to be 'compartmentalised', so they only had to deal with what their brains allowed them to manage at one time. For example, I took my children to Paris. Three months later Rosie had to do a project on Paris at school but had no recollection of going. I showed her a video and she vaguely remembered it. Three months after that she recalled going.

Hypervigilance was a contributory factor to why my children didn't remember learning at school. Think of it like this – if you had a man walking into a room holding a knife, you wouldn't recall what the lady standing behind him was called. It's just the way the brain prioritises for survival.

Useful strategies

- Routine and structure are an excellent way to help your child improve their memory. If life is predictable and organised, it's less difficult for the child to forget where they are supposed to be and what happens next.
- Use lots of memory aids. You can get charts and organisers, which can be put up with tick charts and picture guidance. If you search 'autism aids' or 'now, next, later boards' these are easily found.
- Bear in mind that your child may be as frustrated as you are about always losing things and being disorganised. If you empathise with the child about this, you may also find that you feel better about it too.
- Using an Omega 3 supplement can really help our children improve their memory function. Sometimes children are resistant to taking it in tablet form, especially the fish-based supplement, so you can include it in their diet if possible, or use a vegetarian supplement, which can be disguised in food quite easily.
- Patience is key. The difficulty is that therapeutic parents have to have so much patience and tolerance so much of the time! If this is triggering you, then try to re-allocate one of the tasks you

know may be difficult. For example, we used to have 'bag sort out time' at the end of each school day. This usually involved lost items and property belonging to others mysteriously appearing. This might be a task you decide to allocate to another person, or do it all at once around the table. The temptation is to 'not look' in order to avoid exasperation and possible conflict, but be warned, this will probably only store up trouble for you. Having a Friday night off is fine though!

- Let school know about your child's memory issues and agree on strategies between you that do not rely on the child remembering. We used to give the school spare PE kits and do a physical handover to avoid items going astray.

MESSY BEDROOMS *(see also Dirty Clothing, Damaging, Memory Issues and Disorganisation, Sabotaging, Urinating)*

What it looks like

- The child's bedroom is extremely messy, untidy and/or dirty.
- The child may be very disorganised with clothing and posessions frequently hidden and in the wrong place.
- The level and scale of the issue is far beyond the range of acceptable untidiness and may even be hazardous, including items such as used sanitary towels.
- There may be urine and faeces in the room (see Poo Issues and Urinating).
- The child may hoard food which is rotten (see Food Issues).
- The child may wet the bed and leave it wet (see Bedwetting).

Why it might happen

- The room is often a reflection of how the child is feeling about themselves, and sometimes a direct view of their internal working model.
- Emotional age/developmental delay – the child may be functioning at a much younger age than their chronological age. We may be expecting too much from them.

- Controlling behaviours/fear of change – the child may have control over very little in their life and controlling their personal space may be very important to them.
- Recreating a familiar environment – the child is familiar with the smells of neglect and dirt. It is not offensive to them. They may have witnessed a disregard for property and hygiene.
- Lack of cause-and-effect thinking – the child is not able to do forward thinking about the fact that leaving rotten food to fester will create a smell.
- Rewarded by a trigger from the parent – the child may know that making their room very messy and dirty guarantees them some lengthy interaction with the parent. It does not matter if this is mainly negative.
- Sensory issues – the child may be heavy-handed or clumsy, so things get broken easily.
- Dysregulation – acting in the heat of the moment, particularly where there is a loss of control leading to 'trashing' the room.
- Shame – relating to feelings of unworthiness or bodily functions. This is especially noticeable when girls start their periods and hide used sanitary towels in the room.
- Dissociation – the child may be unaware of the true state of the room.
- Loyalty to birth parents/former carers – resisting attachment to new carers/parents by deliberately sabotaging the room and not accepting unfamiliar, new items.

Reality check

A messy or dirty bedroom is often a reflection of how the child is feeling about themselves. This is one of the issues that parents find the most trying, especially if they have put in a lot of time and effort making the room nice. It can be soul destroying to find the bedroom yet again stinking of wee or poo, with rotting food secreted in corners, drawers upended, and clothing all over the floor. It's difficult to think that the child is not doing this on purpose and it can be really hard to remember that this is often an instinctive, entrenched pattern of behaviour that no amount of logical discussion will alter. It is triggering for the parent or carer where they feel the child is recreating an environment they wish them to disconnect from.

To be clear, we are not talking about normal levels of untidy rooms here. It is completely normal for most children to have messy bedrooms at one stage or another, particularly during the teenage years. The bedrooms of traumatised children are on a different level. This can be difficult to understand for supporting professionals as, obviously, we work hard to keep the rooms respectable. The relentlessness and depths of the dirt, mess, smells and hygiene issues are truly on a different scale and that is what grinds down the parent, making it difficult to respond therapeutically. After all, the room is in our home.

Preventative strategies

- Planning of the room is essential. We need to work hard to limit the potential hiding spaces. Use open shelving with labels, fixed to walls and floor. No drawers whatsoever. Many of our children cannot remember or visualise what is in a drawer, and this is why they are often all pulled out. Get a bed that goes right down to the floor so nothing can go underneath. Ikea was my second home when the children were young, as I found the furniture exceptionally hardwearing. I know it may seem like a big task to plan a room this way, but it will save you literally hours of torment.

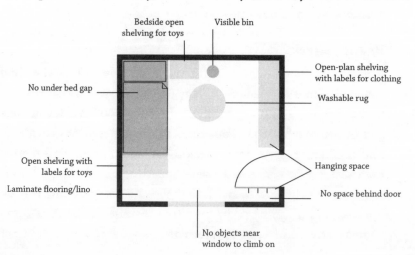

- Think hard about your child's emotional stage of development. Are they doing things a toddler might do? In this case, plan the room accordingly.
- If your child has dyspraxic tendencies, memory issues and is disorganised, we need to organise the room for them and stay on top of it. Boring I know, but essential for everyone's mental health.
- Incorporate room tidying into a weekly routine. Make sure that there is a regular 'tidy-up time'. Ours was just before pocket money on a Saturday morning as that was what the children cared about.
- If you have a regular 'tidy-up time' it may mean that you can live with the interim mess, knowing that it will all be okay in a few days' time. An effective strategy is just to close the bedroom door.
- Limit the number of items the child has in their room. If the child is clearly struggling to manage the number of toys they have, remove two-thirds and then circulate them. This also reduces breakages. You can do the same with clothing.
- Ensure that the room reflects the child. They are more likely to feel comfortable and contribute to keeping it at an acceptable level of tidiness if it feels as if it is truly their space.
- Where a child is urinating in their room provide a 'wee pot' (see Urinating).
- When you feel that the room is completely unacceptable, ask a friend who also has children to take a look and let you know if they also think the levels are unacceptable. You need your energy for the important battles and you may find that this may not be one of them, although it feels like it at the time.

Useful strategies

- Remember, they cannot dig their way out without your spade.
- Avoid long, blaming rants. They may feel cathartic but you are likely to end up feeling more frustrated.

- For a complete sort out, instigate a five-point plan:
  1. First, don't take everything away in a punitive way, as you may be replicating early abuse and also reinforcing feelings of unworthiness. Instead, do a joint major sort out. Be warned, you must feel strong enough to do this, so plan ahead. Have a good look first on your own so you have a rough idea about what needs to go.
  2. Tackle the joint sort out together on the basis of, 'I can see you are struggling with this' and a bit of 'naming the need', 'When you were little you may have been surrounded by a lot of mess and chaos. Sometimes children copy that later on, but they can't help it.' Have four piles:
     i. Save for later (attic/storage)
     ii. Give away (charity shop, not friends they can get stuff back from)
     iii. Throw away (straight to the tip, not in a bin where it can be rescued from)
     iv. Keep – at this point, you may discover stuff in the room that is causing the child anxiety. In one of my children's cases it was a photo in their life story book that was traumatising them.
  3. Replace the 'keep' stuff in the room, after redecorating with lining paper so the child can draw all over the walls if they wish. This also saves you stress.
  4. Stand back and watch.
  5. When the room deteriorates, decide what you can tolerate and what you can't. Basic hygiene levels need to be kept. Sometimes, I made a large pile of objects that needed sorting out again and allocated a time for the child to do it. It can be a good idea to do this early on, as soon as you notice more serious issues developing.

MOANING *(see Whining)*

MOTHER'S DAY *(see Birthdays, Christmas and Other Celebrations, Sabotaging)*

MOUTHING *(see Chewing)*

MOVING SLOWLY *(see Defiance, Lateness)*

N

NIGHT TERRORS/NIGHTMARES *(see Sleep Issues)*

NONSENSE CHATTER *(nonsense questions)*
(see also Anxiety, Separation Anxiety)

What it looks like

- The child asks a constant stream of nonsense questions but does not appear to listen to the answer.
- The child gives a running commentary on everything.
- The child makes nonsense statements repeatedly.
- The child says 'I love you' or similar repeatedly.

Why it might happen

- Separation anxiety.
- Anxiety.
- A need to try to predict the environment, especially where the questions and chatter centre around immediate events.
- Fear of invisibility/being forgotten – seeking a response.
- Dissociation – the child is often unaware of what they are saying.
- Overwhelming need to keep the parent close and engaged.
- The need to feel in control.

- Lack of cause-and-effect thinking, especially in relation to being unaware about what they are actually saying and the impact of that.
- Emotional age – the content of the questions and chatter may be related more to a child of two or three years of age.
- Avoidance of shame.
- Fear of change/transitions – nonsense chatter may be more marked at these times.
- Sensory issues – lack of awareness.

Reality check

Nonsense chatter can be really draining! There are not too many strategies you can use that are preventative, as the main aim is to get the child to be conscious of what they are saying, thereby lessening the frequency and intensity by changing awareness and pathways in the brain. It's useful to remember that nonsense chatter and questioning is very often to do with a younger emotional age and is often seen later, and for significantly longer, in children who have suffered trauma. My youngest child, Charley Chatty, definitely had 'nonsense chatter' from about four to ten years of age. Even now as a young adult she is talkative, although the 'nonsense' element is no longer apparent!

Useful strategies

- If the child is saying 'I love you' all the time or a similar phrase, simply pre-empt it and say it more often and at random times.
- Try saying, 'My ears are full up of all the nonsense words at the moment. They need a bit of a rest. They can still hear sensible words though.'
- Ask the child to go and write down what they are saying. Explain that you do not want to miss anything so you can read it later. This is very effective as it engages the higher brain. Children (usually) cannot access or remember the 'nonsense' words to complete this task.

- Use an empathic response such as, 'I can see you have a lot of words to get through today. My ears are a bit full up at the moment, but at 4 o'clock I am going to sit down with you and help you get all those words out.' Make sure you then follow through with this at the set time. Again, as the child now has to engage their higher brain to have a direct conversation, you normally get either meaningful conversation or gazing at the ceiling, 'trying to remember'.

- If you have electronic media that answer questions, such as Alexa (Amazon) or Siri (Apple), direct the child's questions to those.

- Use playfulness with 'silly words'. So, for example, if a child is repeating and repeating, but not actually asking a question, I might also point out to the child what they are doing through a trigger word (such as 'elephant'). This surprises the child out of the playback loop, and over time can help them to regulate themselves. So, for example, in a calm moment I would explain to the child that I think sometimes her brain isn't in charge of her tongue, so in order to help her I am going to say 'elephant' every time I notice this. The next time my child then starts commentating on the fact that we are crossing the road, 'We are crossing the road, aren't we Mummy? Aren't we Mummy?' (48,000 times), I reply, 'No the elephant is crossing the road.' The child is then jolted from the questioning cycle by the unexpected response. Again, this engages their higher thinking brain. Normally they will say, 'What elephant?' or, 'No it's not! We are crossing the road!' You can simply reply, 'I knew you were too clever for that.'

- If you are really struggling and the problem is entrenched and pushing you into compassion fatigue, say, 'I am so glad you have some more nonsense words for me today! I get to listen to my favourite song.' You then insert headphones, stay physically present with the child, but have a nice time singing along to the tune. Most parents report that even reaching for their headphones enables their child to switch from 'nonsense chatter' to meaningful talk.

- Touching the child, without engaging in the nonsense questions, can help the child to regulate and feel more grounded.
- It's the fear of invisibility that drives this behaviour, so it can also help to 'name the need' with them and explain to them why they do this, 'Sometimes I feel you may be worried that I have forgotten about you. When that happens, your mouth says lots of emergency words but your brain isn't thinking them. I will let you know that I have not forgotten you with this secret signal.' Then give the child a signal like a thumbs-up or a touch on the arm.
- *Katie Careful and the Very Sad Smile* (Naish and Jefferies 2017) and *Charley Chatty and the Wiggly Worry Worm* (Naish and Jefferies 2016) can help to 'name the need' behind these behaviours.
- Try giving the child a dictaphone to speak into. This is useful if you have a child who cannot write things down. Then get them to listen back to the talking and try to do a summary. This can be very funny and sometimes interesting!
- Be alert for the 'kernel of truth'. Sometimes, within the nonsense chatter is a grain of a real worry or fear. Our children are very skilled at hiding these.

NOT LISTENING *(see Controlling Behaviours, Defiance)*

NOT GETTING UP *(see Lateness)*

O

OBSESSIONS *(see also Friendships, Sabotaging, Ungratefulness)*

What it looks like

- The child goes on and on about a desired object obsessively, then discards it immediately or loses interest on acquisition.
- The child becomes obsessed with an event, party or similar, happening a very long time in the future.
- The child becomes fixated on inanimate objects.
- The child develops obsessive routines which look similar to obsessive compulsive disorder.

Why it might happen

- The internal working model, feeling of emptiness/badness, compels the child to always look for distractions to 'fill the hole'.
- Obsessive, ritualistic routines give the child a sense of security and safety over their immediate surroundings. This may be especially apparent where children have experienced significant chaos, lack of routine and exposure to danger, so 'keeping safe' habits develop.
- Sensory issues, especially related to attachment to inanimate objects such as elastic bands, which reward the child with feelings when 'pinged'.

- Lack of cause-and-effect thinking, specifically relating to pets and the need to care for them.
- Seeking nurture – the child may feel that a desired item will provide a nurturing experience or that it will somehow 'prove' the parent's love.
- The need to feel in control and powerful – sometimes to see if the adult can be manipulated to give the item to the child.
- Fear of invisibility/being forgotten – this gives the child a focus to talk about the desired object at length and work on receiving it.
- Recreating a familiar environment – there may have been an early pattern of giving material objects in place of time or nurture.
- Lack of empathy, especially for future self and the impact the object of their desire may have on their life.
- Lack of remorse, especially where the object desired is a replacement for an identical, broken item (see Sabotaging and Ungratefulness).
- Overwhelming need to feel important and loved, validated by the desired item.
- Emotional age – the child may be functioning at a younger age and not really understand the true implications of receiving the object they are obsessing over.
- Immaturity – rituals and routines may be reminiscent of younger-age thinking.

Reality check

Obsessions often happen because our children struggle to be still and 'comfortable in their own skin'. When they are still, the trauma, anxiety and emptiness seem bigger and make them feel uncomfortable, driven to action and to find a distraction. An analogy I use for obsessions is as follows:

The Monster Bait

Imagine that whatever it is that frightens the child is in the shape of a Trauma Monster. As the child learns to start to feel safe, they put the Trauma Monster in a cupboard and shut the door. However, they can hear it constantly banging on the door. They know that sooner or later he is going to get out and get them again, so the child starts looking for something to distract the Trauma Monster with. They may hear banging on the door whenever they are still. They might make a lot of noise, to keep themselves busy, so they don't hear the Trauma Monster. The child gets fixated on the one thing (the monster bait), which they are sure will keep the Trauma Monster busy, once and for all.

They go on and on about this one thing. This keeps the child very busy, so they can't hear all the noise the Trauma Monster is making. The child must make sure they get the monster bait at all costs. They can think of nothing else. The prize is won. This will be a very wonderful, distracting thing. It may be the new game they had to have, a pet, or even a new friend. The child cannot even hear the Trauma Monster, and it seems the monster bait has done the trick. Sadly, the door suddenly breaks and the Trauma Monster is free. In a panic, the child throws the Monster their hard-won monster bait. It is all-consuming and it provides some very good bait to keep the Trauma Monster busy for a while. Then, once the Trauma Monster has finished with the bait, the child realises that the trauma is still very much alive and kicking. Bigger monster bait is needed...and so we begin again.

Many of the parents we work with find obsessions to be very common, particularly where a child hankers after something obsessively, devoting every waking thought to obtaining the object, yet seems to then disregard or break the object soon afterwards, or move swiftly on to the next obsession. An interesting parent–child dance develops around obsessions, which the following figure demonstrates.

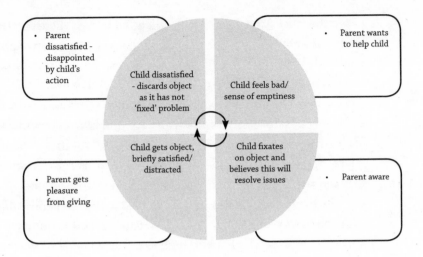

We want to make our children happy, and where there has been child trauma it can be very tempting to fall into the belief that giving the child this item will genuinely resolve an issue at least temporarily, or stop the noise of constant requests! Our children can grind us down and of course we do want to give them treats. With obsessions, we have to be very careful about what this actually means and resolve the underlying issues.

Useful strategies – obsessing about getting an item

- Think about the underlying trauma, the driving force to the obsession. It is usually a distraction so focus on the 'Trauma Monster' not the 'monster bait'.
- If the child manages to get the desired item, it is *nearly always* an anti-climax. I use 'naming the need' with this and explore the gap the child is trying to fill with the new obsession. I may even use 'The Monster Bait' story above.
- Prepare yourself for disappointment (see Sabotaging). You may be feeling really excited about getting something for the child when it genuinely appears it is the *one thing* they believe will 'fix them'. Then, when the item is quickly discarded, due to its lack of effectiveness in distracting from trauma-based feelings, this can be very hurtful.

- Meet the obsession head on, 'I know you really believe that having the new game is the only thing that will make you happy, but really I wonder if you need the game to stop your head worrying about scary things instead?'
- Say no! Don't be afraid to simply state that you have decided that the child does not need this item and you won't be entering into any further discussion about it.
- Don't be tempted to give examples of why the child won't manage the focus of their obsession. Saying things like, 'You are not having a hamster as you won't look after it properly' is another way of saying, 'Would you like an opportunity for a lengthy argument?' It's better to say, 'I have decided you are not yet ready for a hamster, but I will look at this again in three months.' Then do not discuss it (for strategies see Whining).
- Use a variation to the parental reward chart (see Rudeness) and let the child know that every time you hear the word, you will be rewarding yourself with £1. Keep a visible tally. This changes the dynamic and removes the trigger. The money doesn't come from the child. It's just your little treat to yourself.
- You may also find that 'being curious' about the need the child is trying to fill can give some surprising answers.

Useful strategies – obsessing about rituals and procedures

- Distraction is the first technique to use. Use it as soon as you see a ritual starting to develop.
- Tell the child what you think is happening, 'I wonder if you feel you need to check that the door is locked 15 times because you are worried about someone frightening getting in.'
- Share explanations relating to control. If the child is obsessed with having the radio volume control on at a set limit (Sophie Spikey still has to have it on 5 or 10 as it's 'tidier'), you might say, 'I understand that having everything set very strictly and just so makes you feel safer, because there is some order.'

- Consider if this needs even to be an issue. What level is the obsession running at? If it is damaging the child or others in some way, or starting to impact on family life, it may be time to address it. If it's not, then step away and see if you can let it run its course.

Useful strategies – obsessing about birthdays or special events a long time in the future

- State that you feel the child may be secretly worried that you will forget the event.
- Make a plan with the child about what will happen on the day and mark it on a visible calendar, so it is clear that it cannot be forgotten.
- If the child continues to obsess, just point at the calendar. You can also distract them with planning tasks.
- Use empathic commentary to explore the anxieties around this, 'I wonder if you are talking about X a lot because you are worried about what might happen? Maybe you are worried I will forget because that may have happened before.'

Footnote: William 'pinged' elastic bands on his wrist from ages 3 to 11. If he lost the elastic band he would go into a meltdown until a new one was found. They all had names and they were all his friends. An elastic band went everywhere with him. We did not intervene and just kept a spare box in case of accidents or losses. He used it to help himself to stay regulated. I realised later on that in the neglectful circumstances he lived in for his first two years, elastic bands were probably enthralling toys and his only 'friends'.

OVEREATING *(see Hunger)*

OVER INDEPENDENCE *(see Rejection)*

OVERREACTING *(see also Boasting, Lying, Triangulation)*

What it looks like

- The child jumps or overreacts to loud noises.
- The child often makes statements such as, 'I nearly died', or claims to have narrowly escaped serious injury.
- The child laughs in a manic way (see Shouting and Screaming).
- The child throws themselves to the floor or against a wall if someone brushes past.
- The child screams in pain, as if their life is at risk, when they have a very minor injury.
- The child acts as if the world has ended when told 'no' or thwarted in any way (see Controlling Behaviours).

Why it might happen

- Sensory issues – the child may experience noise and touch differently.
- Brain development impaired from early life trauma or similar, leading to a gap in the ability to experience sensory input relating to pain appropriately. The child may be oblivious when they are actually hurt, but be very fearful that they have been hurt when this is not the case. They may depend on visual clues.
- Fear of parent/carer and other adults – the child genuinely believes that they are in danger or are going to be hurt.
- Dysregulation, especially in relation to manic laughter.
- Trigger for the parent – if the child knows that manic laughter or throwing themselves to the ground is triggering for the parent, the behaviour is likely to increase.
- Lack of cause-and-effect thinking – the child may see a small injury and not be able to relate this to the actual outcome or feeling.
- Fear response – generally the child may have high cortisol levels and is wired for fight, flight, freeze or defensive rage. When a triggering event occurs, the child responds instinctively.

- Fear of invisibility/being forgotten – seeking a response, especially relating to manic laughter, or claims of having nearly died.
- Dissociation, especially in relation to pain or sudden startling noises.

Useful strategies

- Continue to react to the child as if they had reacted 'normally'; for example, you brush past the child. They hurl themselves to the floor exclaiming, 'Ow! You nearly knocked me down the stairs!' You might say, 'Oh dear, you seem to have fallen over. Would you like a hand up?'
- Avoid getting into a confrontation and saying things like, 'I didn't even touch you! Why are you doing that?' and similar. This only heightens the child's response and is unlikely to resolve anything.
- In the moment, it is sometimes useful to just state what is happening, especially if you are worried that the child genuinely believes you might have hurt them. 'Goodness me! You have flattened yourself against the wall in case I touch you, but look how far away we are. Let's count the steps.'
- Make a short response. For example, you cross the road safely then a car passes. The child exclaims, 'I nearly died!' Smile and just say, 'Phew, lucky you have me to keep you safe.'
- Where the child is overreacting to a slight injury, be aware that the fear the child is experiencing is very real. They may not be aware that a small cut does not lead to death, especially if blood has been triggering in any way in the past. Think about the way you might respond to a very small toddler. Lots of reassurance is needed without logical explanations.
- Use empathic commentary, 'I can see you are feeling really scared that you might be badly hurt. Even though you are not badly hurt, it's still very scary for you.'
- With manic laughter, it can be useful to wonder aloud, 'I wonder if you are laughing in that way because you are worried I might

forget about you?' Some parents join in the manic laughter and find themselves 'unable to speak' for a short while. This is a useful strategy if you feel the child has some control over this action.

- Many of our children overreact to loud noises and seem to have an over-developed startle reflex. This reflex only changes over a very long period of time, where frightening things no longer happen and there is routine and predictability. If you can see there is going to be a loud noise, warn the child. This at least lessens the startle response.

- With some children who have oversensitive hearing, parents and carers can use noise-reducing headphones. This has been found to really help children concentrate, especially in busy environments like school.

- Use *Charley Chatty and the Wiggly Worry Worm* (Naish and Jefferies 2016) to explore overreacting and exaggerating.

OVERSENSITIVITY *(see Anxiety, Overreacting, and Part 1, Chapter 1)*

P

PACIFIERS *(see Dummies)*

PEE *(see Bedwetting, Potty Training, Urinating)*

PRETENDING NOT TO HEAR *(see Controlling Behaviours, Defiance)*

POO ISSUES *(see also Messy Bedrooms, Urinating)*

What it looks like

- The child poos themselves and appears unaware.
- The child poos themselves and is aware but unconcerned.
- The child poos in different areas of the house or in their bed.
- The child hides their poo in different places.
- The child 'holds' their poo and gets constipated.
- The child is very late in potty training or regresses once potty trained (see also Immaturity).
- The child does not flush the toilet or wipe themselves properly.
- The child plays with their poo.
- The child wipes the poo on walls and furniture.

Why it might happen

- The need to feel in control and powerful – the child at least has ultimate control over bodily functions. 'Holding poo' may be the ultimate control for a child where there has been very little in the past.
- Shame – the child may experience shame around bodily functions, depending on how this was handled when/if they were potty trained or had nappies changed.
- Sensory issues – the child may lack feeling and be unaware of the usual impulses.
- Fear of transitions/loss, especially in relation to holding on to poo to prevent a change of activity or another child playing with their toy.
- Unable to leave an activity – the child may suppress poo in order to allow themselves to continue with what they are doing. This invariably leads to soiling.
- Immaturity/emotional age – the child is simply at a much younger developmental stage than they are at chronologically.
- Trauma-related issues, particularly around neglect and/or sexual abuse.
- Rewards the child with a reaction – trigger for the parent.
- Recreating a familiar environment – may be normal past entrenched behaviour. The child may have played with poo. It may have been their only toy.
- Comfortable to be smelly or dirty – the child has no sense that this is not socially acceptable.
- Medical issues, particularly in relation to sensation. The child may be unaware of the usual warning signals.
- Fear response – the child may poo themselves in fear or may be frightened to ask to go to the toilet, or even frightened of the toilet.
- Blocked trust – the child cannot trust others enough to poo, or let the poo go down the toilet.
- Lack of cause-and-effect thinking – the child is unlikely to link 'I will hide my poo' to the fact that the poo will be found!

- Fear of invisibility/being forgotten – seeking a response.
- Fear of parent/carer and other adults.
- Fear of change/transitions.
- Separation anxiety.
- Fear of drawing attention to self by asking to go to the toilet.
- Dissociation, especially where it appears that the child is unaware (see also Absences).
- Overwhelming need to keep the parent close, especially to involve them in personal care.

Reality check

This is easily the topic (along with wee) that we get asked about the most on our Therapeutic Parents Facebook Group! It can be exhausting, long-standing and really difficult to cope with. First of all, bear in mind that you are almost certainly dealing with an issue that presents as behavioural, but has its root in trauma, fear and control. This is one thing *you* cannot control! The child does not poo themselves to exert control over us, it happens because they need to feel they have control over *something*. Sometimes the child simply feels they cannot 'let go'. Where there are issues around neglect and feeling hungry, this can exacerbate the problem:

> As a child growing up in foster care, I held on to my poo all the time. I got so used to doing it. After all, I did not know where the next meal was coming from, so how could I let go of what I had? I did not realise I had done this until I was an adult. (Sarah Dillon, attachment therapist and former child in care)

This is not done deliberately, so as parents we need to be mindful of that. Look at ways to take the pressure off both yourself *and* the child. The child may well have had confusing cues around their bodily functions, and be surprised to find that their poo is not a toy, or that you do not delight in its existence. Similarly, they may experience high levels of shame. Perhaps they were told off for having a dirty nappy. These kinds of early life, pre-verbal experiences often lead to the child experiencing overwhelming shame. That's when we find the poo hidden in all kinds of bizarre places.

Preventative/minimising strategies

- Ask for a referral to a specialist nurse dealing with bowel issues. The National Institute for Health and Care Excellence (NICE) guidelines recommend this. Sometimes parents are provided with a sacral nerve stimulator where it is found that there is a lack of sensory function due to nerve damage. You may also need to have the child assessed for issues relating to constipation. We often find, however, that there is not a straightforward medical explanation for children whose soiling issues are trauma based.

- Put to one side any expectations around chronological age development. If the child is aged seven and doubly incontinent, then they are clearly functioning at a younger age, especially where medical issues have been ruled out.

- Be prepared to start potty training again. Right from scratch. Often this can be really effective at helping our children to start to learn their bodily signals. If you approach it exactly as you would with a two-year-old, you won't go far wrong. If the child is chronologically two and has a background of trauma, it is likely that you will need to start potty training much later. Step away from the pressure of perfect parents and 'helpful' advice!

- Where a child is 'clenching' and holding on to poo in order to avoid changing activity, make it clear to the child that you know they are doing this and tell them. The child may not be interpreting their body signals correctly. For example, 'I have noticed that when you are playing with the Lego and don't want to leave it, sometimes you do a little shiver, as if your body is trying to hold the poo in. I think that is why you are getting tummy aches. In order to help you, every time I notice this happen, I am going to keep the toys safe for you so no one else can get them while you go to the toilet. That way you won't have tummy ache and the toys will be safe.'

- Where there has been neglect and the child had used excrement as a toy, recreate the sensation and experience in a positive way. I called this 'poo play'! I used to use chocolate powder, butter, and flour. While you are helping the child to play with this and make 'poos' it essentially reduces the shame the child is experiencing. Naturally, playfulness occurs during this activity! Some people worry that this will increase the child's tendency to play with their actual poo, but I have found that it decreases and the child gradually replaces it. Obviously, it tastes nicer!

- While doing 'poo play' you can 'name the need' a little, by saying, 'This is a lot like poo, isn't it? Sometimes when children have been left on their own too long they get very bored and they play with their poo. Then later on it's really hard to stop doing that. This is much more fun though!'

- Establish a routine relating to 'toilet time'. With young babies, parents can often anticipate the times that their baby will poo, related to mealtimes and sleep. Make a note with your child and see if you can find a good time to encourage a visit to the toilet. When going to the toilet say, 'toilet time'. Don't ask the child if they need to go as they probably don't know.

- Make a game about the amount of poo the child does. A lot of children do not fully empty their bowels properly as they are rushing to get back to something, or are afraid of missing out. Although generally we do not do reward charts as such, it can be effective to provide different size treats immediately after the child has emptied their bowels, dependent on the amount of poo.

- If a child is sent to the toilet, they are effectively alone. Recreate the way that a toddler is potty trained and consider reintroducing a potty. This can be used alongside where you are, or you can go to the bathroom with the child. If the child is afraid they will be 'forgotten' while they are away in the toilet then you need to think creatively about how this can be minimised. A two-way baby monitor can be useful, so you can have a little chat.

- Some parents have found that switching their children to a gluten-free diet has dramatically reduced soiling.

- Similarly, parents have reported discovering that their child had a milk protein allergy and this was causing diarrhoea and affecting the child's ability to get to the toilet in time.

Other strategies

- Finding a child covered in poo (again) can be very triggering. If you need a moment, walk away calmly saying you need to go and find something to help you clear up. While you are away, take some deep breaths.
- If the poo has been smeared or made into a shape, try asking the child, 'If this poo had words. I wonder what they would be?' This can give good insight into where the trauma is based.
- If you find a hidden poo, tell the child you have found it but try to reduce shame. You may feel that the child does not feel shame about what they have done, but if this is the case, why is the poo hidden?
- I found it really handy to buy disposable pants. Swim pull-ups are useful as they stop the poo going through to the clothing (usually) but you can see quickly when the child has soiled.
- Access up-to-date help and resources through the Enuresis Resource and Information Centre (ERIC), a charity supporting parents dealing with bowel and bladder problems – www.eric.org.uk.

Here are some useful phrases to use when dealing with poo issues.

Instead of	Say/do
'Why have you pooed yourself again?'	'I see you have had an accident. Do you need some help with that?'
'Right, you can jolly well clean it up!'	'Let me help you sort it out, then you can jump in the shower.'
'What is this poo doing here?'	'I see there is a poo under your bed. Come and help me sort it out. Let's think where it needs to go.'
'No one will want to play with you because you smell!'	'I can smell that you have had an accident. I think sometimes it's difficult for you to smell when this happens.'
'There are streaks of poo in your pants again! You need to wash them.'	Check that there is not a medical issue relating to constipation. If poo has broken off inside the rectum the child may have no sensation of this. Never use shaming consequences to try to address any behaviours with traumatised children, particularly those relating to bodily functions. Just say, 'I see you have had an accident. Pop your pants in the laundry basket. Here are some fresh ones.'
'Who wiped all this poo on the wall?'	'I see some poo is wiped on the wall. Come and help me clear it up.'
'Do you need the toilet?'	'Time for the toilet now.'

Footnote: If you are frantically trying to get a child out of nappies or pull-ups before they start school, remember that nurseries and schools are not allowed to discriminate against or disadvantage children with medical conditions, including continence difficulties. Your child can't be prevented from starting at the school just because they are still in nappies or are soiling.

POTTY TRAINING *(see Bedwetting, Immaturity, Poo Issues, Urinating)*

Q

QUESTIONING *(see Nonsense Chatter)*

REFUSING FOOD *(see Mealtime Issues)*

REFUSING TO FOLLOW INSTRUCTIONS
(see Defiance)

REFUSING TO HURRY *(see Lateness, Moving Slowly)*

REFUSING TO SAY SORRY *(see Part 1, Chapter 5)*

REJECTION *(of parent) (see also Controlling*
Behaviours, Defiance, Rudeness)

What it looks like

- The child says hurtful, rejecting things to the parent.
- The child will not ask for help from the parent.
- The child avoids spending time with the parent.
- The child rejects the parent's morals and values.
- The child ignores the parent or pretends they can't hear (see Defiance).

Why it might happen

- A subconscious compulsion to prevent or break a forming attachment.
- Uncomfortable feelings around being disloyal to birth parents/former carers.
- Fear response – this may be overwhelming. The parent may be the *source* of fear.
- Recreating a familiar environment – the child anticipates rejection themselves.
- The need to feel in control and powerful.
- Shame.
- Fear or fearful anticipation of a negative response from the parent.
- Feelings of hostility or momentary hatred towards the parent.
- Fear of invisibility/being forgotten – seeking a response.
- Lack of empathy.
- Lack of remorse.
- Fear of change/transitions, especially if trying to control the ending of a placement.
- Overwhelming need to keep the parent close – engaging in rejecting arguments may achieve this and may keep the child central in the parent's thoughts.
- Overwhelming need to feel loved/important – the child is unable to express this so they reject rather than risk rejection.
- Comfortable to be in the wrong/self-sabotage – the child's internal working model allows them to believe that they are 'not worthy' of caring parenting.
- Emotional age – the child may be at an emotional stage where they might normally seek independence.

Reality check

There is little you can do *preventatively* to stop the child feeling the need to demonstrate rejection towards you. We need to try to reduce rejection through our responses to the behaviour. We can temper our emotional response through ensuring that we are not looking to the child to be our *reward*. By looking for emotional reward elsewhere we can mitigate some of the feelings of hurt and sadness that are provoked when a child behaves in a rejecting manner towards us.

Where the child is rejecting our morals and values they may do this through absconding or absenting themselves to realign with another family (see Absconding). It's useful to avoid patterns of thought such as, 'After all I've done...' and, 'I can't believe they choose that way of life after learning a new way!' Children who are fostered and adopted often feel compelled to 'try out' what feels familiar to them. If they spent their early life in a home where drinking, the smell of cigarettes, shouting and neglect were commonplace then don't be surprised if that is what they seem to gravitate to. This is not about you or the way you have brought them up. This is about the child exploring for themselves the two contrasting worlds. They will make a choice, and usually choose the more comfortable, safer life you have shown them. Be careful not to react to their rejection of your values with a rejection of your own. You may be storing up long-term heartache.

Here are some useful responses to statements which may be hurtful.

Child says	You respond
'I hate you.'	'It must be really hard to feel that you hate your Mum/Dad.'
'You are not my Mum/Dad.'	'I'm not?! Oh my goodness! And all this time I've been (*name tasks child needs/wants you to do*). I didn't know that! I could have been... (*name activities you enjoy*).'
'You can't tell me what to do – you're not my Mum/Dad.'	'Sorry but I am your (*state relationship or say* 'the closest you have to a Mum/Dad') right now, so I am going to keep right on loving (or being here for) you no matter what, and making sure I keep you safe.'
'I wish I never came to live here.'	'That's really sad you feel that way. I am so glad that you came to live with us but I know you feel really mixed up about it.'
'I want to go back to X'	'I can see you miss X very much. Do you want...' (*offer nurture*)
'I know you hate me and I'm glad.'	'I wonder how that feels to think that I might hate you? It must be really scary.'

Useful strategies for over-independence

- Where the child is refusing to ask for help and you can see they are struggling, use parental presence. Sit down near them and say, 'I can see you are struggling with that. If you would like me to help you at any time just let me know.' You may have to sit nearby and keep quiet for a long time.
- If your child manages to ask for help, don't make a big deal about it. Acknowledge in a low-key way that you have noticed they have been very brave in asking for help, and then complete the task for them. The bigger the deal you make, the less likely it is the child will ask for help again.
- Where things have gone wrong because the child has not been able to ask for help, wonder aloud about how things might have ended differently had they been able to ask for help.
- You can use *Sophie Spikey has a Very Big Problem* (Naish and Jefferies 2016) to help with over-independence issues and *Rosie Rudey and the Very Annoying Parent* (Naish and Jefferies 2016) to tackle rejection and rudeness.

REMORSE *(see Part 1, Chapter 1)*

RESPITE *(see Transitions, and Part 1, Chapter 7)*

REWARD CHARTS *(see Part 1, Chapter 6)*

RUDENESS *(see also Defiance, Joking and Teasing, Rejection, Swearing)*

What it looks like

- The child responds in a rude way to an adult.
- The child is often defensive and rude to other children.
- The child makes loud, rude comments to others.
- The child complains loudly, using insults.

- When reprimanded, the child responds with aggressive rudeness and insults.
- The child uses name calling.

Why it might happen

- The need to feel in control and powerful – acting in a rude way tends to make people steer clear of the child so this gives them control over their immediate environment.
- Lack of cause-and-effect thinking – the child is unable to think about the consequences of being rude.
- Dysregulation – acting in the heat of the moment.
- Shame – avoidance of shame and deflection is a powerful precursor to rude behaviours.
- A subconscious compulsion to break a forming attachment (with the parent).
- Attraction to peer group – mimicking actions and reactions of peers.
- Fear response.
- Feelings of hostility or momentary hatred towards the parent.
- Fear of invisibility/being forgotten – seeking a response.
- Recreating a familiar environment – the language, tone of voice and rudeness may be very familiar to the child and they may be unaware that it sounds rude.
- Lack of empathy.
- Lack of remorse.
- Fear of parent/carer and other adults – a need to keep them at a distance.
- A need to try to predict the environment – a need to control endings.
- Fear of change/transitions – rudeness may be a reaction to a transition.
- Overwhelming need to keep the parent close.
- Boredom.
- Overwhelming need to feel loved/important.

- Comfortable to be in the wrong – the child's internal working model dictates that they are unworthy of nice things so rudeness is the protective shell.
- Emotional age – the child may be functioning at a younger age and appear rude when they are not.
- Blocked trust – defensive rudeness.
- Loyalty to birth parents/former carers – resisting attachment to new carers/parents.

Preventative strategies

- Try looking at things differently. Sometimes our children come across as rude when they are anxious or frightened.
- Think about the emotional age of your child. What would your response be if a much younger child said or did the same things?
- Conceal your triggers! If your standard response is to say something like, 'How dare you speak to me like that!' or something similar, you may as well be saying, 'Please feel free to be as rude as possible to me and I will reward you with 100 per cent of my attention.'
- A reward chart for parents can really help to change the entrenched patterns that develop between parents and children with rudeness and arguing. You may have to make your own so you can tailor-make it to fit the rude behaviours you are dealing with. You need to be open and share with your child what you are doing. The rewards must start off low key, maybe a luxury bath and a glass of wine, building up into a night out or evening away. The effect of this strategy is that when the rudeness happens the parent can respond with, 'Brilliant I get a star!' When we used this with one of my children the rudeness diminished significantly and quickly.

REWARD CHART FOR PARENTS

YOU WILL COLLECT A STAR WHEN YOUR CHILD DOES ANY OF THE FOLLOWING;

- SLAMMING THE DOOR
- BEING RUDE
- HITTING
- SPITTING
- BITING
- STEALING
- BREAKING THINGS
- SHOUTING
- _____
- _____
- _____
- _____
- _____
- _____
- _____
- _____

PARENT	MONDAY	TUES	WEDS	THURS	FRIDAY	SAT	SUN	TOTAL STARS
MUM								
DAD								

REWARDS

★ _____   ★★★★ _____   ★★★★★★★ _____

★★ _____   ★★★★★ _____   ★★★★★★★★ _____

★★★ _____   ★★★★★★ _____   ★★★★★★★★★ _____

Strategies during

- Use an empathic response to explore feelings behind strong statements. For example, 'I hope X dies...!!' Response, 'Wow, it must feel really scary to feel so angry', showing empathy for the child, not the statement.
- Use playfulness. This can help to give the message that the rudeness is not triggering you (even if it is)! I used to do 'the rude dance'. The ruder the child was the more I would dance, normally singing 'Here is the rude dance, the rude dance, the rude dance' to the tune of 'Following the leader'.
- Say, 'Shall we have another go? Because I don't think that came out how you meant it to.' This gives the child the chance to try a different way without invoking shame.
- Use playfulness to say in a robotic voice, 'I'm sorry, there is a rudeness filter activated at this time. I cannot understand your request/statement as it contained words that were blocked by the filter. Please rephrase and try again.'

- Another playful response is doing a rewind. You can make a rewind noise and move your actions backwards to let the child 'try again'.
- Try deliberately misunderstanding. This can be done a number of ways. You can say, 'Sorry, I literally have no idea what you just said...try again' and then adopt a confused expression. Or say, 'Sorry, what did you say? Can you repeat it again as my ears didn't understand those strange words?'
- Simply adopt a confused expression, say nothing and wait. This can be very effective as long as you don't look threatening!
- Give the child a chance to 'rest and reflect' on what they need to do, 'You sound as if you need to tell me something but it feels as if you need a moment to compose yourself before telling me what that is. You know where I am when you are ready to use good words to tell me about it.'
- Responding in a similar manner removes the trigger. If a child blows raspberries at you, blow them back. Have a raspberry blowing competition.
- Use an incongruous response to engage the child's thinking brain. For example, 'Get me my lunch right *now*!' Response, 'I can't, it just went out in the car.'
- Look at what they are *doing* – if the rudeness is accompanied by the child doing as they are asked (for example, putting clothes away while muttering or blaming some higher power), just thank them for doing as asked.
- Where a child tells you to shut up, try bursting into a related song (such as 'Shut up and Dance'). Alternatively, you can find yourself unable to speak. When the child asks you something or needs a response you can mime, 'Sorry, I can't talk to you as I have to shut up.'
- Demonstrate that the rude words hold no power to shock you. Say something like, 'It must feel really cluttered inside you having all those rude words there. Let's get them all out.' This exercise is best done on the top of a hill in a loud voice. Perhaps an isolated hill!

Strategies after

- If your child has called you a 'fat pig', 'stupid cow' or similar it's a good idea to add in some natural consequences to the specific rude words. I may be 'too fat' to get up and make dinner, or possibly 'too stupid' to remember how to drive. You can say (with empathy), 'As I am stupid, I have forgotten how to drive! I don't want you to feel unsafe in the car with me.' You need to see this one through and not immediately cave in after a fake apology.
- You can express sadness for hurtful words once your child is regulated. It's important not to go overboard on this. It also gives the child a chance to repair. Saying something like, 'I can't see you want me to feel better about that; try showing it by...'
- Go back through the insults and rudeness and examine them with the child. Agree with any that have a foundation of truth, and then state your positive feelings for the child despite these words.
- 'Name the need' to look at where these words came from. For example, 'Sometimes when children have felt very scared, they use unkind words to try to keep people away from them.' *Rosie Rudey and the Very Annoying Parent* (Naish and Jefferies 2016) may help with this.

Footnote: When on holiday in Florida, unfortunately I had my work cut out trying to help my children overcome their reactions to overweight people. I would say to the children, 'Don't look, don't stare, don't point.' The children looked, stared and pointed. They stared open mouthed in horror at large people in wheelchairs. Rosie Rudey would loudly exclaim, 'God, they should make fat people walk, that way they'd lose some weight!' I realised to my cost that I had, inadvertently, handed the children my 'rudeness trigger' on a plate.

RUNNING OFF *(see also Absconding, Controlling Behaviours, Defiance)*

Why it might happen

- Fear of invisibility/being forgotten – seeking a response.
- Comfortable to be in the wrong/self-sabotage, especially if this happens during a positive experience.
- Testing the 'safety boundary', especially in relation to emotional age of the child.
- Emotional age – the child may be merely behaving as a toddler would.
- Sensory issues, especially in areas of high sensory exposure, such as supermarkets.
- The need to feel in control and powerful.
- Overwhelming need to keep the parent close – ensuring the parent notices and returns.
- Lack of cause-and-effect thinking.
- Dysregulation – acting in the heat of the moment.
- Shame.
- A subconscious compulsion to break a forming attachment (with the parent).
- Fear or fearful anticipation of a negative response from the parent.
- Fear of change/transitions, especially where this behaviour happens during transitions
- Separation anxiety – where the child is delaying moment of separation.
- Overwhelming need to feel loved/important – needing the parent to express love/concern and to 'reunite'.

Preventative strategies

- If you are going on a car journey or similar, and your child is having to sit quite still, they will be likely to have high cortisol levels on arrival and already be in fight or flight mode!

Take regular breaks and ensure that where you stop the child can move around freely for a while to reduce the risk of running off.

- Think about their emotional age, not their chronological one. If you have a four-year-old who is running free in the same way that an 18-month-old might, then consider reintroducing reins or another method of keeping the child close. We gave the children rucksacks that had long handles on for us to hold.

- Get the children to repeat 'the rules' about staying close, not running in the road and so on, so this gradually becomes hardwired. You can make it into a little song or a game. It's a good idea to get them to do this just before going out. Emphasise the need to be safe.

- If you have a little 'runner bean' then don't set everyone up to fail! Practise with small local outings in safe environments, like a park, far from the road. Keep the practices short. Let the child know you are helping them to practise so you can go on to other things. Name some ideas you know the child will like.

- Be aware of your own expectations. If you are expecting a traumatised child with ADHD tendencies and sensory issues to walk nicely in a supermarket with overhead bright lights and a myriad of distractions, you are going to be disappointed.

- It's important for your own peace of mind to establish what action your child would ultimately take if they run off. Parents often overcompensate in their reactions because they imagine the child being lost or kidnapped. In reality, our children often hide nearby and keep us in close sight, waiting for us to notice they are missing, having fun, running further and faster as we give chase. Set up an event with a friend or partner where you are confident the child will probably run off. The friend is nearby and stays close to the child observing what they are doing and where they go. Where it is observed that the child quickly runs to catch up with you again, this will give you confidence for future episodes.

Strategies during

- If you are out and the child runs away, the natural consequence for not being safe is that the activity has to stop. This gives a strong message to the child and immediately links cause and effect.
- Walk in the opposite direction! It can be very powerful to walk away, while using a friend, a phone or another child to give you a running commentary on what the child is doing.
- If you can see that the child is nearby and you are concerned that if you approach them they will run further away, simply stand your ground and use 'the phone strategy'. This enables you to assume an unconcerned air and effectively removes the audience, while allowing you to do some empathic commentary to a 'third person'.
- Tell the child they will need to hold your hand in order to stay safe. Do not allow this to be negotiable. You can just say you will be resting for a while so everything stops until the child holds your hand.
- Use playfulness to interrupt the thought processes. For example, if the child has run off and is holding onto a lamp post, hold onto the next lamp post and speculate who has the nicest lamp post.
- Avoid running after the child or shouting, 'Get back here now!' or other standard parenting responses. This increases the child's adrenaline levels and enables them to run faster!
- Use parental presence to regulate. You can run *with* the child if you are able, or run a race, do marching or make up a game that is active and can be done together.
- Try not to show worry, concern or fear. This often escalates the situation.

Strategies after

- Remember to pat yourself on the back every time you manage an outing and resolve this issue. This behaviour does decrease, generally quite rapidly when met with the right therapeutic response. Baby steps will get you there in the end.

- Revisit the episode with the child. You can explain what might have happened and how it is your job to keep the child safe. During these moments of nurture and connection it's important not to hand the child your 'trigger on a plate' by making statements such as, 'I was *so* worried! Don't *ever* do that again!'
- Use 'naming the need' to explain about cortisol levels (we called it 'busy juice') and how this makes children want to run. Give the child alternative strategies, such as running in circles around you, or jumping up and down.
- Don't be afraid to use natural consequences to limit the kinds of places you can go until you feel this can be managed safely. Explain to the child that you need to practise 'staying close'.

S

SABOTAGING *(see also Birthdays, Christmas and Other Celebrations, Damaging, Holidays, Ungratefulness)*

What it looks like

- The family have a nice day out and the child's behaviour then deteriorates and 'spoils everything'.
- The child becomes dysregulated and more challenging approaching treats, celebrations and special days such as Christmas.
- The child disrupts the celebration or event (see also Birthdays, Christmas and Other Celebrations).
- The child's behaviour worsens as a promised treat approaches – the parent feels they need to remove the treat as a sanction.
- The child destroys good work that has received praise.
- The child destroys own belongings, even treasured ones (see also Obsessions).
- The child often appears messy or dirty with a dishevelled appearance (see also Dirty Clothing).

Why it might happen

- Comfortable to be in the wrong – the child's internal working model convinces them that they do not deserve nice things. This creates conflict within the child.

- Blocked trust – the child does not trust the honesty or motivation of the person providing the positive praise or gift or event.
- Recreating a familiar environment – the child is unfamiliar with receiving nice things or being given special time and/or has witnessed a disregard for property and personal appearance.
- Disappointment – the child may believe that the gift, event or special day would make them feel differently but then they find that they still feel the same, i.e. they still have trauma.
- Lack of cause-and-effect thinking – not able to remember that if something is broken, it stays broken.
- Dysregulation – acting in the heat of the moment.
- Shame – relating to feelings of unworthiness.
- A subconscious compulsion to break a forming attachment (with the parent), especially following positive bonding times spent.
- Feelings of hostility or momentary hatred towards the parent.
- A need to try to predict the environment – the child tries to keep everything the same, avoid surprises and so on.
- Fear of change/transitions.
- Separation anxiety – if the treat takes the child away from the parent.
- Fear of drawing attention to self, especially relating to positive praise.
- Dissociation – the child may be unaware of damaging the item, especially in relation to damaging their own clothing.
- Sensory issues – unaware of 'heavy-handedness'. May be clumsy.
- Emotional age – the child may be responding as a younger child would.
- Loyalty to birth parents/former carers – resisting attachment to new carers/parents.

Reality check

Remember that when a child sabotages a day out or an exciting event or destroys a precious gift, it does *not* come from a well-thought-out plan to ruin everything. It is spontaneous and driven by an early unmet need.

When our children break gifts that we have saved hard to give them, ruin days out that we thought they were looking forward to, or generally sabotage anything positive we try to create, it's extremely difficult not to show a *rewarding* or triggering emotional reaction. We can perfectly well retain a sense of understanding about why our children behave like this. We can even appreciate the conflict created within them when presented with a positive alternative view of life, but the sense of failure as a parent can be overwhelming, and frustration and anger boil over. It feels as if whatever we do is not enough, or that they will never be able to change. When sabotage occurs, it is like a flashlight being shone on the child's inner world, often leaving us feeling helpless. That's why we must always prepare, and lower our expectations. I learned the hard way not to expect too much from my children. Once I lowered my expectations, we often had a nice surprise.

A useful mental image I kept in mind was a kind of graph (see the following graph). I learned that the level of sabotage (or rejection) seemed to have a direct inverse relationship to:

- my expectations
- the child's expectations
- the amount of conflict created by the positive event.

In other words, the nicer the time we plan and expect, the more we will pay!

It won't *always* be like this! But it will be like this until our children can believe that they are worth what we give them.

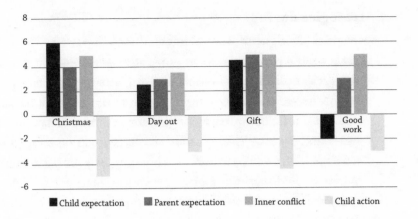

Preventative strategies

- The main preventative strategy is to keep your own expectations low. A positive result is a bonus!
- Don't be tempted to over-hype the forthcoming experience or gift. A casual off-hand stance is easier for the child to integrate into their own expectations and sense of self.
- Avoid surprises! Do not even use the word 'surprise' unless your child is very well established with you and secure.
- Be cautious about embarking on days out and events that incorporate trauma-inducing responses. Some examples of this might be people in costumes (especially where the face is concealed) and pantomimes (where there is a 'baddy' who may appear threatening).
- When planning a gift, try to separate out your thought processes and replay previous incidents. How did the child respond once they received the gift? Was it about a) actually having the item and investing in it long term, or b) achieving the ownership alone? If you conclude b, then you know what to expect.
- Avoid using threats and bribery to 'make' the child behave during the forthcoming event. This will just signal to the child that you are anxious, and increase their levels of anxiety. It's better to warn others at the event that you may need to take some time out if your child becomes dysregulated, and make a plan in case things go wrong.

Strategies during

- Wonder aloud, while reinforcing your view about why the child deserves the treat. This works especially well where you suspect the escalation in behaviour is a direct attempt to sabotage a forthcoming treat. For example, 'I wonder if you did X because you feel you are not worth having Y? Well, I think you have a good heart and deserve Y, so no matter what, Y will be happening; however, there will be other consequences for your behaviours.'
- Where a child presents a piece of work, muted praise is more likely to ensure the work survives! Don't be tempted to launch into how wonderful it is and how clever the child is. The child is usually unable to believe you so you suddenly become dishonest and unreliable. So, for example, I might say, 'That's an interesting picture. Who is that there?'
- It's okay to show your disappointment when the child ruins something, but we need to relate it to the child, not ourselves. Instead of saying, 'I can't believe you did that! I spent £100 on that for you!' say, 'What a shame you broke your new phone! You won't be able to have one for a long time now. I expect you feel a bit sad about that.'

Strategies after

- 'Naming the need' is very effective where there is sabotage. You need to understand that the child may feel as if they do not deserve nice things, so they need to remind you they are not 'good'. I therefore use phrases like, 'I know you have a good heart' and give evidence for positives I have seen. It's really important that we don't just give vague examples.
- Do not replace a damaged item. Although the child has normally acted in the heat of the moment and may be uncomfortable with the conflict created by their internal working model, replacing the item will not suddenly make the child feel better! It is more useful to continue working on their self-esteem, and help them to work towards a partial replacement at a level they can accept.

- Where a child's behaviour has escalated due to a forthcoming treat or event, it is a good idea to maintain natural consequences but put the forthcoming treat outside the consequences. Although it is tempting to say, 'Right, you are not going to the birthday party now!' remember this is an unrelated consequence which merely reinforces the child's negative view about themselves.

Footnote: When my daughter, Katie Careful, was 15 we had a forthcoming birthday treat planned. Just Katie and I were to have a special day out together. As the birthday approached, her behaviour escalated. There was increased hostility, rudeness and aggression. This culminated in her attempting to jump out of a moving car. I told her that I understood that the behaviours were trying to make me take the special day away, but that I had decided she was worth this special day and no matter what she did we *would* be going. At the same time, of course, we were unable to take her out in the car for one week due to safety concerns. This caused her much inconvenience, but the behaviours immediately began to subside, and we did have our day away. During the day, she was physically sick several times, which demonstrated to me the level of conflict this created within her.

SADNESS *(see Part 1, Chapter 1)*

SAYING SORRY *(see Remorse, and Part 1, Chapter 6)*

SCHOOL ISSUES *(see also Homework, Memory Issues and Disorganisation, Transitions, Triangulation)*

What it looks like

- The school seems to have a different view of the child to you (see also Triangulation).
- The child is resistant to going to school and appears overwhelmed.

- The school's expectations are not consistent with your child's abilities, and there is disagreement around disciplinary issues (see also Homework).
- The child's behaviour is significantly worse at school, leading to possible or actual exclusion.
- You often feel criticised and blamed by the school, especially in relation to eating, aggressive behaviours, and soiling and wetting.
- The child is fearful of school and appears frozen and unable to learn, and/or is functioning well below expectations (see also Immaturity, and Memory Issues and Disorganisation).

Why it might happen

- School's lack of knowledge around effects of trauma and attachment.
- Fear or fearful anticipation of a negative response from adults, leading to triangulation.
- Fear of, or unable to manage, change/transitions.
- The need to feel in control and powerful.
- A need to try to predict the environment – this can be difficult in a school environment at times.
- Lack of cause-and-effect thinking, especially where consequences are not linked, or are too far in the future.
- Dysregulation – overwhelmed by overload of sensory input leading to possible outbursts of aggression. Additionally, high levels of cortisol make it difficult for the child to sit still and concentrate.
- Feelings of hostility or momentary hatred towards the teacher, especially where the child is anxious about having another adult 'in control' and experiences this as a threat to the parent's authority.
- Fear of invisibility/being forgotten in a class with other children.
- Emotional age – the child is placed in a class of children by chronological age.

- Hypervigilance – the child tries to remember where everyone is and what they are doing, so has no capacity for further learning.
- Separation anxiety – may be exacerbated through unskilled use of time-out in school.
- Fear of drawing attention to self in class by asking for help.
- Dissociation – the classroom environment may be too overwhelming (see Memory Issues and Disorganisation).
- 'If we cannot all learn to sing from the same hymn sheet, we should not be surprised when our children are the ones left conducting the entire orchestra!'
- Overwhelming need to keep the parent close.
- Comfortable to be in the wrong – the child's negative internal working model means that standard school reward charts and similar systems are usually ineffective.
- Sensory issues – the child may be flooded with information that they cannot separate out and make sense of.

Reality check

One of the questions I am most frequently asked is, 'How do I deal with my child's school?' Many therapeutic parents feel frustrated, undermined and disempowered by well-meaning teaching staff, who stick firmly to tried and trusted methods which seem to work well with securely attached children. It is *our* children who linger in the 'dark cloud' on the behaviour chart, and are the ones who cannot sit still and disrupt the class. We know that standard parenting does not work for our children, so by the same token, standard teaching methods won't work either.

I do a lot of work with schools, and there are many other excellent training courses and books that help schools to adopt a more 'attachment friendly' approach. One of the most important services we can do for our children is to identify an attachment-aware school for them. It is essential, not only that the school understands the effects of trauma and what therapeutic parents are trying to do, but that the therapeutic parent is proactive in ensuring information is shared effectively.

Strategies around communication

- *Communication is absolutely fundamental and critical.* Responsibility must be shared equally between the parent and the school. This communication cannot rely on the child carrying messages in a book, or relaying them in any other way. Direct communication, preferably face to face at pick up and drop off is the best way to avoid misunderstandings. It is also better for the child to be transferred securely. Failing that, direct phone calls or emails work well.

- If it looks as if the school may have made a mistake, it's more useful to adopt a neutral stance with the child until you have the facts. Use phrases such as, 'I don't know what happened, but I have confidence in you to sort it out. If you need help, let me know.' Then contact the school to find out what happened from their perspective.

- Provide useful resources that the school can refer to which explain why your child needs a different approach. On the website of the National Association of Therapeutic Parents there is a letter for schools, which members can print out. Refer the school to current legislation and NICE guidelines, which recommend attachment-aware practice. Also see the recommended books and websites at the end of this book.

- Make absolutely sure that you attend parents' evenings. My children's school had a strange arrangement where the children were responsible for making the appointments. Clearly it was a coincidence that the teachers who had been left off the appointment list were the ones who had the most vital information for me! I always ensured that I made a particular point of seeing any teachers missing from the list. These were the teachers who 'hoped I had recovered from my recent hospitalisation' and said how sorry they were to hear about the loss of our dog. Naturally none of this had happened, but Charley Chatty had found an excellent new strategy for avoiding project deadlines.

Strategies to manage conflicting management styles and discipline

- It's really important that school stays at school! We simply do not know exactly what happened, and sometimes our children are set up to fail. If we align ourselves completely with the school, our children no longer have a safe base and can feel alone. This can spiral downwards very quickly. This does not mean we deliberately undermine the school either. The neutral stance can be helpful all round.

- I discovered, once my children were grown up, that many, many incidents had been created by the school mishandling my children's anxieties, and their lack of understanding around attachment disorder. I once said to their school, 'I don't ask you to come here and get them to tidy their bedrooms, so don't ask me to punish them for something that happened at school.' This is particularly relevant if the child has been told there will be a consequence, but the school has failed to follow through. It is not up to you, as the parent, to put that consequence in place instead. This might damage your relationship if it transpires that the child was put in an untenable position.

- Many schools use behaviour management methods that are unhelpful to our children. Reward charts are a particular issue. Make it clear to the school that these kind of incentive-driven methods have been shown to be ineffective with children who have suffered developmental trauma. You might share books with the school that specifically address trauma and attachment issues, such as the ones by Louise Bomber (2011) and David Colley (2017).

- We need to reassure our children that our view of them is not defined by the classroom reward chart. When one of my children's teachers told me with a sad face that unfortunately William had not managed to 'get off the dark cloud this week' I simply turned to him and said, 'That's fine. I know you have a good heart and you can be in our shiny sun every day.'

- For strategies around the child claiming to be ill at school, see Hypochondria.

Strategies around helping your child to resolve issues at school

- Reinforce your belief in your child's ability to resolve the situation when they get in trouble with school, 'I know things are looking very muddled at the moment, but I know you have a good heart as yesterday you were so kind with X. I am sure you can sort this out too.'

- Tell your child that you know what happened. With good communication, you should be kept in the loop. If you have been contacted and told about an incident, let the child know that you know about this, without giving an opinion about what you think happened. I might say, 'I hear you had a difficult day at school today.' Then leave it at that. The child may react angrily and protest that nothing happened, in which case just let them know you can help them if they need you to. Avoid passing judgement, as you cannot be sure about what has happened.

Strategies around structure and routine

- I moved my children 120 miles to put them in a village school where they kept the same teacher and class for three years. Although this may seem a little extreme, the benefits were enormous and we forged an excellent relationship with the school, who embraced information around attachment difficulties and developmental trauma. Look very carefully at class sizes and the school structure when choosing a school.

- Normally, schools have fairly good structures and routines, but this can deteriorate towards the end of term, or around special celebrations. Our children can really struggle with this lack of structure. Forewarned is forearmed, so write formally to the school telling them that it is essential that you are kept informed if there is to be a change of teacher or a break in the normal routine. In this way, it gives you a chance to prepare your child. Sometimes, I would attend school with my children in order to keep them regulated, at times of maximum disruption.

- If the school have leavers' ceremonies or similar, you may want to carefully consider if your child can attend, or if they only attend part of the event. Our children have often suffered so much loss that a ceremony such as this can really throw them off balance.
- Where schools run non-school uniform days, it can be really difficult for our children to manage. As they are often hypervigilant, our children struggle when it is non-uniform day. This is because everyone looks different and the child now needs to take account of all the different appearances as well. There is more information to absorb. Sometimes my children would choose to wear school uniform on a non-uniform day. If your child states a wish to do this too just say, 'I understand that when things look different and change a lot, it can make you feel wobbly inside. If you want to wear your uniform, you might be the only one in school uniform today, but that is fine.' In this way, they are prepared. You may also want to rehearse what they may say to a curious comment. When my children did this, I used to also say, 'That's amazing! You went to school in your school uniform and you knew that you would be different from everyone else. It takes real courage to do that. I am proud of you!'

Strategies around school lunches

- Make sure the school understands how our children are often unable to interpret signals around pain, hunger, body temperature and so on. If you make sure this is written down, it can help to alleviate issues when they arise if the teacher expresses concern, for example, that your child is 'always hungry'. My son used to eat his packed lunch on the way to school, or the majority of it, and then explain how hungry he was to his unsuspecting teacher. He wasn't consciously trying to be manipulative (see Food Issues). It can be very frustrating and parents may feel blamed and judged, especially when a kindly teacher sends home a guide to healthy packed lunches!
- Make sure you hand the child's lunch box directly to the point of contact (such as a teaching assistant). If your child also has a

snack in their pocket then at least the school understands that the child has arrived with a full lunch box and snack!

- The school (and others) is less likely to raise meaningful concerns around lunch boxes and hunger if your child is weighed regularly. I found this to be good practice generally.

Footnote: Don't stress too much about children 'falling behind' or 'going backwards' at school. Nearly all our children make up for lost time later on when their brains have matured and their attachments are more secure, with lower cortisol levels and fewer anxieties. Four of my children simply could not manage school in the teen years on top of everything else. I just let go of what we couldn't control and tried to support them the best I could. It's trying to control the uncontrollable that makes us feel so helpless. All the children went on to further education and did much better there in smaller class sizes studying subjects that interested them.

SCREAMING *(see Shouting and Screaming)*

SELF-CARE *(see Part 1, Chapter 7)*

SELF-HARM *(see also Headbanging, Sabotaging)*

Self-harming behaviours are complex and need careful consideration and responses. In this A–Z with brief strategies for intervention, I am only touching on the more common self-harming behaviours that therapeutic parents frequently ask about, often in younger children. If these are not responded to and interpreted correctly, it can lead to much more significant problems later on, especially during adolescence. An excellent resource is *The Parent's Guide to Self Harm* (Smith 2012).

What it looks like

- The child hits themselves in the face.
- The child picks at scabs and makes them bleed.

- The child wobbles teeth to loosen them.
- The child swallows harmful substances.
- The child burns themselves.
- The child or young person moves on to more serious self-harm, such as cutting themselves or using other implements/substances to cause harm to themselves, for example bleach.

Why it might happen

- The internal working model of the child creates feelings of 'badness', emptiness, worthlessness and overwhelming shame.
- The need to feel in control of themselves.
- Lack of cause-and-effect thinking.
- Dysregulation, especially where the self-harm is an entrenched behaviour. Young people report having a feeling of release once they have cut.
- Dissociation, particularly in relation to picking scabs, pulling out hair and wobbling teeth. The child may be unaware they are doing this due to a lack of sensory input.
- Attraction to peer-group activities, especially relating to cutting or inscribing symbols on skin.
- Fear of invisibility/being forgotten – seeking a response, especially where the child knows this behaviour triggers a fear response in the adult.
- Overwhelming need to feel loved/important.
- Emotional age, especially in relation to wobbling teeth and thinking about the tooth fairy.

Reality check

I once worked in a specialist residential unit for young women who self-harmed on an extreme scale. One young person, T, had a very long conversation with me one day where she explained that the need to cut was like 'a volcano of pressure building inside'. She said she did not want to cut herself, but the only thing that released this feeling of pressure was cutting. Over the years I found there was often a divide in self-harming behaviours between those determined and prolific self-harmers (perhaps older children and adolescents where the behaviours are secretive and often involve cutting) and lower level self-harming behaviours (sometimes seen in younger children, such as hitting themselves and picking scabs). Some children describe the feeling of 'being brought back' by inflicting pain. Some children say they do not feel any pain, but just need to 'see the blood'.

The way we react to early signs of self-harm can have an extremely significant impact on the development of longer-term issues. It is essential to seek help and reassurance from mental health professionals at an early stage if you are concerned about a child or young person in your care showing signs of developing entrenched self-harming behaviours.

Preventative strategies

- Feelings of blame/shame are most likely to catapult the child into self-harming behaviours. Ensure that if there is an accident or incident the response is non-blaming and does not induce shame.
- Practise being present and available. Parental presence and time-in minimise the opportunity to self-harm.
- Focus on activities that promote oxytocin, such as stroking a dog, stroking the face, shoulders, and some Theraplay® techniques. This makes the child less fearful and therefore less likely to engage in behaviours meant to help them to self-regulate. The book *Parenting with Theraplay®* (Rodwell and Norris 2017) is useful for this.
- Avoid having long discussions about the long-term implications of their actions. As our children often lack cause-and-effect thinking and may be unaware of what they are doing, this only serves to alert the child to your high levels of concern.
- Agree on a system for the child to communicate to you non-verbally if they are feeling as if they want to self-harm.
- Moderate your response if the child comes home from school having taken part in a 'game' where self-harming actions have

taken place. An over-the-top reaction is likely to increase the child's drive to continue. Instead, give a muted response, but then follow up your concerns very proactively with school or through covert monitoring. When I discovered one of my teenage daughters had started this type of low-level self-harming behaviour, I simply asked if she was okay and let her know where the first-aid box was. I then ensured that I took her shopping to try on new clothes so I could check that the self-harming was no more serious than I thought. With this particular child, the lack of reaction was key in ending the behaviours.

- If the child is wobbling teeth because they want to get money from the 'tooth fairy' you need to make sure that you plant the right seeds early on! When William started to do this, I explained that the tooth fairy can tell if they are 'old teeth' or 'young teeth' and she doesn't take 'young teeth'. This seemed to stop early dental issues!

- Distract the child with alternative sensory experiences. Elastic bands on the wrist are frequently used by children with difficulties in self-regulating. They can ping it on their skin, causing only very low-level pain. Blowing bubbles, sucking, blowing, water or sand play can all help to reduce instances of self-harm. Keep activities prepared and close at hand so you can divert attention to them as necessary.

- If a child or young person 'needs to see the sight of blood' in order to feel calm, make some ice cubes using red juice. The child or young person can then squeeze the ice cubes which produces a cold, slightly painful sensation and also mimics the sight of blood. They can also draw red lines on their skin. This helps them to gain control of the self-harming behaviours.

- Be vigilant about everyday objects that can be used to self-harm. Use plastic tumblers rather than glasses and keep sharp knives locked away. Someone who is very determined to self-harm will find a way, but minimising opportunities helps us to be more available should an incident occur.

Immediate strategies

- Where a child appears distracted and is picking scabs, pulling hair or wobbling teeth, distraction techniques work well. Suggest something where they need to use their hands.
- Mute your own response. It can be very difficult not to feel panic stricken if we see blood or what looks like a serious injury, but try to maintain a matter-of-fact approach.
- If you feel the child is dissociating and unaware of their actions, remind them that you are nearby. You can use empathic commentary to help the child make sense of their feelings, 'Oh dear, you picked that scab again and made it bleed. Maybe you were feeling wobbly today?'
- Where a child is hitting themselves in the face, gently take their hands and say, 'It looks as if your hands are hurting your face. That's sad. Let me help you to feel better.' If you then calmly sit and stroke the palms of the child's hands this can give them a calming, sensory experience.
- Give the child a hug. This can interrupt most self-harming behaviours.
- Use balanced, appropriate nurture to deal with any injuries.

Strategies after

- Check for any signs of serious injury and take appropriate action, but try to do this without making a great deal of fuss. Keep things low key.
- Be aware that the self-harming is usually a compulsion and something the child has little control over.
- Explore the relationship between emotional pain and physical pain, as some children are unaware of this. Let the child know that you understand that the self-harm is an outward expression of inner pain. Empathise about how this might feel.
- Wonder aloud if there may be a better way to express the pain that the child is showing to you.

- Seek medical advice and support from mental health professionals if you are concerned.
- Always use up-to-date advice from websites such as Mind (www.mind.org.uk). This has excellent free booklets and information to help with self-harming behaviour.

SENSORY ISSUES *(see Headbanging, Overreacting, and Part 1, Chapter 1)*

SEPARATION ANXIETY *(see also Anxiety)*

What it looks like
- The child sits physically very close.
- The child follows the parent around.
- The child climbs onto the parent or holds on to their clothing or person.
- The child becomes dysregulated and distressed when the carer or parent is absent.

Why it might happen
- Fear of abandonment.
- Early lost nurture – the child may feel they almost need to 'crawl inside the parent's skin' to feel secure.
- Fear of invisibility – the child fears they might 'disappear' when the parent is absent.
- Blocked trust – the child cannot trust that the parent will return.
- Fear of adults – a need to know where they are at all times.
- Needing to control the movements of the parent.
- Needing to get between the parent and other children.
- Overwhelming need for physical contact and reassurance.

Reality check
Ask yourself, 'Why does this need to be changed?' It may not be about your child's behaviour so much as your need to have some space. This is completely understandable. Our children's stress

and anxiety around separation and their overwhelming need for nurture and safety can be suffocating and difficult for us to manage, especially as we know this is due to real distress or fear.

Preventative strategies

- Think about what levels of separation there were for your child in their babyhood. Have they ever had that special bonding time? If not, this is a stage that needs to be gone through.
- This is hard I know, but if your child is clinging to you due to overwhelming fear, a large part of resolving this is to allow it to happen, only reducing the times very gradually over a long period of time in a manageable way. We reduce through a gentle persistent cycle, which helps the child to separate by tiny increments.
- Give the child something special of yours to look after. This can be as simple as a piece of material sprayed with your perfume/aftershave.
- Look at the child's emotional age. If the behaviour is telling you that there are big developmental gaps where the child cannot meet the milestones (for example, of being unsupervised, playing alone) then lower your expectations accordingly. If you gauge the child at six months of age, go back to that stage.
- Put in a dedicated 'nurture time'. This will be when your child knows you will be having a hug, sitting closely together or doing a joint activity with physical closeness.
- Give the child a countdown for when you need to move off to do other things.
- Give the child something of yours to hold or look after, when you need to move freely.

Strategies during

- Recreating early nurture experience when the child is clingy, and giving them the experience of being a baby, can really help to progress a child who is 'stuck' (see also Immaturity).
- Wondering aloud about the child's need to feel you close by and the reasons behind that can be effective.

- Playfulness can help to relieve the tension around clinginess, 'Oooh, I wondered what that was holding on to my leg! I wonder if I am strong enough to walk along with you still holding on?'
- Use reverse psychology and give the child as much time-in as you can manage. Theraplay® (Rodwell and Norris 2017) games are useful for building attachment and security. Our children often really enjoy 'baby games', particularly if they have missed out on this stage.
- If the clinging behaviours are around stopping you from interaction with others, be clear that your interactions will continue, and comment on this, 'I think you might be holding me tight to stop me picking up X. Well I am going to pick up X and you can sit next to me.'

Ongoing strategies

- 'Name the need' around clingy and anxious behaviours, 'Maybe because you have lost some people from your life, you are worried that I am going to disappear too.'
- Name the feelings for the child, for example, 'I know you are worried about leaving Mummy.'
- Take a piece of string and cut it in half. Give one end to the child and you take the other. Tell the child the piece in between is magic and if the child pulls the string during the day when he is anxious you will feel it on the other end. (You can make general comments about feeling the tugs throughout the day.) This also helps to reassure the child that you have not forgotten them when they are away.
- Where a child is following very closely, reverse psychology works well. You will have to do some mental preparation *and* build in an escape plan for mid-way through the day. Basically, from the moment the child wakes up, stick to them like glue. Whatever they do, follow them! Don't go anywhere unless they go too. This will create all kinds of dialogue about what might happen next. When you are the follower, the child may well start to move away.
- Use the *Katie Careful and the Very Sad Smile* (Naish and Jefferies 2017) book to name the need around separation anxiety.

SEXUALISED BEHAVIOUR *(see also Social Media)*

Sexualised behaviour is such a huge topic, I cannot do it justice in a short A–Z listing on basic strategies. Instead, I have covered a few of the questions that are frequently asked, and signposted parents and carers to fuller, more specific resources relating to this subject.

What it looks like

- The child acts in a way that appears sexually provocative at an inappropriate age.
- The child appears to have clear and inappropriate knowledge of sexual acts, which are demonstrated in play, through drawings, speech or in re-enacting sexual acts.
- The child exposes genitals publicly.
- The child masturbates publicly.
- The child attempts to, or actually does, touch others inappropriately.
- The child uses sexual violence or threats involving sexual language.

Why it might happen

- Emotional age – the child is experimenting and exhibiting the developmental stage more in line with that of a younger child.
- Dysregulation – masturbation may have been used as a self-soothing mechanism at times of stress.
- Indistinct boundaries – the child may have witnessed or been a victim of sexual abuse and be unaware that the behaviour is inappropriate.
- The need to feel in control and powerful, especially where the sexualised behaviour is used to intimidate or threaten.
- Dissociation – the child may 'zone out' and be unaware of their actions.
- Fear of invisibility/being forgotten – seeking a reaction.
- Overwhelming need to feel loved/important, especially where the child has been groomed and believes that sex is a tool to elicit love.

- Sensory-seeking behaviour.
- Shame.
- Attraction to peer group activities, particularly in relation to social media.
- Recreating a familiar environment, especially where there were paedophiles and sexual abuse within the child's immediate environment during the formative years.
- Lack of empathy – unable to access empathy for the victim.
- Lack of remorse – may not feel any remorse for threatening sexual behaviours.
- Comfortable to be 'in the wrong' – the child's persona may be that of sexualised behaviour being normal and rewarded.

Reality check

Over the years, I have come across many children who are inappropriately labelled as sexual predators. This is the experience of many supporting professionals, foster carers and adopters working with traumatised children. I often think that if as much attention was given to the effects of neglect as it is to sexual abuse, there would be many more children living in better circumstances.

I have seen five-year-old boys labelled as sexual deviants or abusers because they pulled their trousers down at school. I have witnessed a 14-year-old experimenting with masturbation alone in his room described as demonstrating 'predatory sexualised behaviour'.

It can be very frightening, even horrifying, to come across a very young child who is, or, appears to be, sexually knowledgeable and active; but if we can put to one side our own horror and revulsion and see what the behaviour is really telling us, we can at least start off with the right mindset.

Where children have been subjected to sexual abuse, they have missed out key stages of development. The abuse might include being forced to participate in full or partial sexual acts with adults, peers or siblings. The child may have been photographed, filmed or abused on multiple occasions within a paedophile ring. The child has therefore learned that sexual activity gained attention, something that looked like love and approval from powerful adults. This has then hardwired within the child as a way to survive. An abused child may have an extremely confused concept of love and sex. Teenagers may have been sexually aroused while being abused and have a very complex guilt/arousal response.

'Always remember, the revulsion we feel when our children act out sexually, belongs to the original perpetrator, not the child.'

Preventative strategies

- Practise safe caring. This quickly becomes a way of life and is a helpful strategy to use alongside all therapeutic parenting methods. Safe caring helps to keep you *and* the child safe. Leaving doors open and ensuring there are not blind corners in the house can help other adults or children to see what is occurring and enables everyone to feel and be safer, minimising the opportunity for sexual intimidation. You will need to specifically state that 'this house does not have any secrets' and make sure you avoid using the word 'secret'.
- Think about the layout of your house. Where are the bedrooms? Can a child who may be a risk easily enter the bedroom of another child? These are issues that need careful thought and action, as supervision *must* be your number one priority.
- Talk to the child about behaviours that are not acceptable, and *why* they are not acceptable. This needs to be done with empathy for the child and in a matter-of-fact manner. It is extremely unlikely that following this explanation there will be a sudden change or dawning of realisation, but all too often we start off assuming that the child should 'just know'. But they do not.
- Give clear explanations about what touch is, and is not, acceptable, both to and from the child. The National Society for the Prevention of Cruelty to Children (NSPCC) website has good resources, which you can print off and use with your child to facilitate this. An excellent book, which I have used in the past, is *Let's Talk About Sex* (Harris 2010). This covers all aspects of puberty, bodily development, sexuality and relationships.

- Talk to an empathic listener to make sure that *you* can access calm feelings and empathy when you need to deal with this situation. It is so emotive that it will take all your therapeutic parenting skills not to recoil in horror, overreact and catapult the child into toxic shame.
- Where you have more than one child living with you, keep an open dialogue about what is and is not appropriate sexual behaviour. This can be introduced when watching a TV programme or on a family holiday. Sometimes, my husband and I would plan a conversation we would have when sitting at the dinner table, ensuring we had a captive audience (they would not leave their food)! I might say, 'I was talking to X today and she said that her 13-year-old son had got his willy out in front of his sister! The sister ran away laughing but I don't think it was a very kind thing to do. They must both be feeling very mixed up.' This is a useful strategy on many levels:
    ◦ It demonstrates matter-of-fact, non-hysterical thinking.
    ◦ It gives the children permission to disclose.
    ◦ It does not induce shame.
- If you are concerned that one or more of your children may be at risk from the sexual overtures of another sibling, equip them to deal with it. Practise what they would say or do if approached. You might rehearse a key phrase or a secret code so they can communicate to you that they are feeling threatened. Let them have locking door handles on their bedrooms if they wish, so they can feel secure in their rooms when dressing and undressing.

Strategies during

- If the child starts to masturbate openly in front of you, treat it exactly the same way as you would for any other socially unacceptable behaviour, such as picking their nose. You might say, 'If you want to do that, it's fine, but we do not want to see it, so you need to go and do that in private.' Our children do not like to miss anything, and always want to know what is going on, so this often becomes a natural deterrent.

- If the child tries to touch you or another person/child inappropriately, gently move their hands or turn slightly so this stops. Address what is happening immediately. Embarrassment may make us freeze and try to convince ourselves it was an accident. Sometimes a child may get on the parent or carer's lap and start wriggling about to try to elicit a sexual response. If this is understood as behaviour that brought reward and safety in the past it's easier to deal with. Tell the child they can sit next to you but they cannot sit on your lap. You might say, 'I always want to make sure you feel safe with me and to understand I will never do anything to hurt you. Some children have been very confused by grown-ups, so to help you to stop being confused we will just sit next to each other at the moment, and only touch each other in the places where we have agreed.'
- Be careful not to react at either end of extremes. A rejecting, revolted response or a kind, sympathetic one are equally likely to give the child confused messages about their sexuality.

Strategies after

- Reinforce the 'goodness' in the child, 'I know you are confused about what is and is not acceptable touching. This touching is not acceptable and I am here to help you to learn. Luckily, I know you have a really good heart because (give example of positive behaviour), so we will get this sorted out together.'
- As sexualised behaviour can be so overwhelming to deal with, it's essential that if you are feeling out of your depth you access sexual therapy for the child. See the websites below for current advice.
- Finally, do not panic! Just because a child is acting out sexually, this does not mean they are automatically going to grow up and become a paedophile. Very often we are seeing our child's inner distress and confusion manifested. If we can deal with this, we can normally manage the sexualised behaviours to an appropriate level.

Footnote: As I had one boy and four girls, teenage years were challenging. I made sure that I equipped my daughters with a strong sense of what was and was not acceptable behaviour. Their favourite form of protection was to pretend to laugh hysterically at their brother if he started acting out sexually. I have to say, it worked wonders and stopped any sexualised behaviour in its tracks! We also built a new bedroom to ensure we had excellent supervision of William. Extreme behaviours require extreme proactive responses.

Further resources

Stop it Now! – to talk through your concerns about a child's sexualised behaviour: www.stopitnow.org.uk/concerned_about_a_childs_behaviour.htm.

NSPCC – this site gives an overview of sexual behaviour, what to look for, and what to do about it: www.nspcc.org.uk/preventing-abuse.

SHAME *(see Part 1, Chapter 1)*

SHARING *(see Competitiveness, Controlling Behaviours, Sibling Rivalry)*

SHOPPING DIFFICULTIES *(see Controlling Behaviours, Running Off, Shouting and Screaming)*

SHOUTING AND SCREAMING *(see also Arguing, Banging, Rudeness)*

What it looks like

- The child shouts loudly and frequently.
- The child shouts demands at parent or others.
- The child screams apparently for no reason and at random times.
- The child screams when thwarted.

Why it might happen

- Dysregulation – defensive rage, or frustration.
- Fear of invisibility/being forgotten – seeking a response, reminding others of their presence.
- The need to feel in control and powerful – shouting and screaming makes others react.
- Sensory issues – the child may be unaware that they are shouting.
- Overwhelming need to keep the parent close and engaged.
- Emotional age – the child may be functioning at a younger age, possibly around the age of two years old on many levels.
- Dysregulation – acting in the heat of the moment.
- Brain development impaired from early life trauma or similar – high cortisol levels giving the child a need to act.
- Fear or fearful anticipation of negative response from parent – shouting and screaming may block out a response.
- Fear response of a new situation.
- Feelings of hostility or momentary hatred towards the parent.
- Fear of change/transitions.
- Separation anxiety.
- Overwhelming need to feel loved/important.
- Fear of abandonment or starvation.

Preventative strategies

- Think about when the child shouts or screams. Is it around a transition or a time when you are normally distracted?
- A simple change of routine or implementing some of the strategies around anxiety and separation anxiety can help to reduce any underlying contributory factors.
- Keep the mood and volume of the house generally at a low level. This may seem like an impossible task! If we lower our voices and speak quietly, our children often follow suit, or at least they may not feel they need to shout over the noise.
- Playing background classical music can help to promote an atmosphere of calmness and to regulate our children.

- Reframe your thinking. How might you respond to a two-year-old having a screaming session? How much is to do with frustration?

Strategies during

- If the child is shouting at you and demanding attention from some distance away, you simply don't hear it. It will not take long for the child to connect this. If you decide to go to the child because you feel that the situation may escalate, do it in such a way that you are not being summoned. For example, you are in the kitchen and the child starts shouting from the bedroom, 'Get me my school bag! I can't find my school bag!' After a short while you might happen to pass the child's bedroom door on another unrelated errand. Say something like, 'Are you okay? I thought I heard a noise a minute ago.'

- Try stating, 'I see you would like my attention. When you stop screaming and shouting I will talk to you, but my ears shake when there is a loud noise and I can't understand what you are saying.'

- You can also comment on the noise level, 'Wow you can make a very big noise!'

- Use playfulness and identify a trigger word to remind the child. If the child starts talking in a screaming voice, avoid using the word 'screaming.' Instead, say 'squeaky', 'That's a funny squeaky voice you have there! I thought there was a mouse in the kitchen!' Then later you can refer to the mouse noise again if needed.

- Wonder aloud about the child's fear of invisibility. For example, 'I wonder if you are shouting so loudly because you are worried I might forget about you.' Then give the child a signal you will use in the future to reassure them that they are not forgotten.

- Parental presence may be sufficient to help your child to regulate and stop shouting or screaming. When using parental presence in this way, I would just sit quietly with the child. Don't respond to what they are saying with the shouting or screaming, just respond to their dysregulation, 'I am just going to sit here quietly and wait for you to be able to speak to me quietly.'

- Offer nurture to reduce the screaming, but be aware of the child's body language and state. If they are throwing themselves on the floor in a screaming tantrum, they are unlikely to be receptive to a hug. This could escalate the situation.

- You can use distraction techniques quite effectively. If the child is screaming and starting a full-blown tantrum, simply suddenly look past the child in a distracted way, as if you have suddenly just noticed something fascinating. The child will often stop mid flow and turn to see what you are looking at. Depending on the unfolding situation you can then either turn this into a playful moment or prolong the distraction, buying you valuable thinking time.

- Make a completely random statement, unrelated to what the child is shouting or screaming about. This helps the child to see that you are not angry. You have connected to them, but it appears to be unrelated to the shouting. If this is done using humour it can also help shift the child's thinking as they cannot feel fear and joy simultaneously.

- Try joining in. This can go one way or the other! I used to do loud, screamy operatic 'singing' in an over the top, extravagant, playful way. Usually the children would fall about laughing or walk off in a huff. In an enclosed space though, this did not work and they all shouted or screamed louder!

- If the screaming is very loud and constant, and you have tried all the usual empathic nurturing responses, you can simply put headphones on and appear to be really pleased that you get the time to listen to your favourite tunes instead. Headphones can help you to take yourself out of the moment if the noise is causing you to feel stressed.

- If possible, go out into the garden and take some deep breaths to change the soundtrack of your life for a couple of minutes.

Strategies after

- State, 'It seems like you wanted my attention earlier when you were shouting. Shall we think of a better way?' You can then agree on the 'better way'.
- You may also 'name the need' behind the shouting, 'Did you feel lonely? I think you may have felt lonely earlier because...'

SIBLING RIVALRY *(see also Arguing, Competitiveness, Controlling Behaviours, Sneaky Behaviours)*

What it looks like

- Children argue with each other almost constantly.
- Siblings hurt each other, sometimes seriously.
- Children compete to 'be the best' or win.
- Children compete at a violent level for adult attention.
- Children compete and fight for space such as car places, seats at the table.
- Children take each other's possessions.
- Children 'block' or trap others (see Controlling Behaviours).
- Children perceive that they get less than other siblings and that the parent is 'unfair'.

Why it might happen

- A fight for survival, recreating early childhood patterns, especially where there was abuse/neglect.
- Fear of invisibility, in particular the need for others to notice the child above the other children, especially when the other children might be getting attention for positive *or* negative behaviours.
- One or more children need to feel powerful and in control.
- Rewards the child with a reaction – the parent responds to the rivalry, for example by refereeing.
- Recreating a familiar environment, for example older children behaving as the parent.

- One child feels the need to 'protect' the parent from the needs of the other children.
- Disruption in sibling order and placement, for example a child who was the oldest is placed in a family with an older child.

Reality check

Sibling rivalry between children who have developmental trauma is *nothing* like 'normal' sibling rivalry. Few statements are more irritating to a therapeutic parent, struggling with sibling rivalry, than 'all children do that', or similar. The rivalry we see between our children is literally a fight for survival. It is often early, learned behaviour with strong foundations in real visceral fear and jealousy. It differs from standard sibling rivalry with securely attached children in its intensity, relentlessness and longevity. For this reason, siblings are very often separated because it is felt that most parents cannot manage the diverse behaviours, competitiveness and rivalry. Having raised five adopted full siblings myself, I hold the view that it is almost always best to keep the children together, *but* the correct level of experience, brain breaks (respite) and individual attention must be part of the support package.

Preventative strategies

- Put in place cast iron boundaries that lower the children's anxiety and reassure them of an equal status, for example each child has a 'turn' at favourite activities and this is not changed.
- Ensure that places are protected. Make sure each child has a designated place at the table, in the car and even in the lounge.
- Make mealtimes structured if necessary, with everyone being given a turn to speak (see Competitiveness).
- Put in place 'special time' for each child. This can be ten minutes alone with the parent each day at a set time, or one evening or afternoon out with a parent once a month. This can be difficult with large sibling groups of four or more but if you enlist the help of another person the task is easily shared.

- Make sure each child is easily able to protect their own property from others or can escape if needed. We used locking door handles on bedrooms so the children could go in and turn the handle, preventing others from entering (naturally, we always kept a spare key).
- Avoid comparing the children to each other, even in a positive way!
- Remind the children of any previous written statements you have made around fairness (see 'Strategies after').
- Minimise or remove physical barriers that prevent supervision. Our children's arguing and fighting escalated when the parent left the room to make dinner. This is not a coincidence. We knocked down the wall between the kitchen and lounge.

Strategies during

- Sibling rivalry can be a constant theme, rather than a specific incident. If this is the case in your house then pick the main issue you want to deal with first and stick with that one!
- Check yourself when tempted to referee. Think about what would happen if you did not intervene. Often the behaviour is about getting us to mediate. The more we do, the worse it gets. Making statements such as, 'I am sure you are able to work this out for yourselves', can be empowering for the children and remind them that you have them in mind.
- Do not be tempted to have long, logical conversations with the children. Keep in mind that the rivalry may literally feel like a fight for survival for the child, and they are probably not regulated enough to be able to think things through rationally during an incident.
- Use wondering aloud to let the child know you have seen what is happening and to help to explore alternative outcomes, 'I wonder if you are pushing each other because you want my attention?'
- State what you know in a matter-of-fact way, to let them know what is going on. This is also effective where you have a 'hand grenade child' (see Sneaky Behaviours) who is causing trouble,

for example, 'I can see you just took your sister's book and hid it and that's why she punched you.'

- You can also use empathic commentary where hurtful things are said or done to try to move anger to sadness. Anger is usually unexpressed sadness, and the sad feelings are much easier for us to help the children to resolve, 'It must be really sad to feel as if you hate your brother, when you have already both had such a tough time.'
- Use empathic commentary to draw attention to the child's actions and effect on their sibling. For example, where there has been violence, 'Look at your sister's face. Can you see the tears in her eyes? She is crying because she is hurt and scared.'
- Tell the children that if they continue doing x then the consequence will be y. If you cannot think of the natural or life consequence in the moment, then state that there will be a consequence which you will let them know later. You can use *William Wobbly and the Mysterious Holey Jumper* (Naish and Jefferies 2017) to help with this.
- If safe to do so, simply walk away. Removing the audience can be very powerful. You can explain that your ears are full up with all the noise and you will return when they have recovered. If possible, go out into the garden and focus on a different sound and sight to free your mind. It's amazing how simple this strategy can be to help us to re-frame our response.

Strategies after

- Revisit any particularly negative incidents once the children are calm. Now is the time to talk through how everyone felt. Occasionally you will get a breakthrough. Usually you may see an escalation and more accusing, so be careful to pick the right moment and incident!
- When you feel upset and exhausted by constant fighting and arguing, instead of spending your energy always diffusing and refereeing, plan to leave the house so you can have a

brain break. You may not be able to stop the arguing and fighting for a very long time, so it's important to build in recovery time.
- Use 'showing sorry' to help the children put things right.
- Think about what led to any particularly bad incidents and consider changing visibility, structure or routine to prevent a reoccurrence.
- Where there has been an incident with a child saying, 'It's not fair! X always gets more than me', do a list to compare what each sibling has had. Make sure the complainer's list is the longest. Then later on, show this to the complainer and say, 'I was thinking about what you said, so I decided to write down what I remembered.' You can then use this as a preventative strategy next time by reminding the child of the list.

Footnote: I used to do a structured time-out for everyone, including myself. Now before you all gasp in horror and say, 'therapeutic parenting doesn't use time-out', it wasn't possible in those moments to have five arguing children doing time-in! So, we *all* went to our rooms or safe place to help feel calm then met in a neutral place to 'reflect'. I enjoyed these moments of time-out for me, I must admit, and even if the arguing immediately started again, I had had a little brain-break recharge.

SLEEP ISSUES *(see also Banging, Bedtime Issues, Bedwetting, Defiance, Shouting and Screaming)*

What it looks like
- The child is unable/unwilling to settle.
- The child cannot sleep.
- The child disrupts others at night.
- The child wakes up very early.
- The child leaves the room at night.
- The child has nightmares/night terrors.
- The child sleep walks or moves around in other ways that may be disconcerting.

Why it might happen

- Emotional age may be much younger and expectations of ability to settle and sleep too high.
- The child is fearful of being alone.
- The child finds that traumatic memories surface when quiet and without distraction.
- Fear response – often very pronounced, increasing levels of cortisol and adrenaline make it very difficult to settle, driving the child to movement.
- Flashbacks.
- Fear of invisibility or being forgotten when in bed or quiet.
- Recreating a familiar environment.
- Fear of parent/carer and other adults and scared of what they may be doing.
- Fear of abandonment.
- Fear of dying/disappearing during sleep.
- Unable to manage change/transitions.
- Separation anxiety.
- Overwhelming need to keep the parent close.
- Boredom.
- Sensory issues.

Strategies for going to sleep/staying asleep (see Bedtime Issues for 'going to bed')

- Think about parental presence. If your child has missed out on early nurture they may well be stuck at an earlier emotional stage. Think about what your child's behaviour is saying. Is it the same as you might expect for a six-month-old? A one-year-old? It may be that the only way your child can feel completely secure all night through is to be close to their primary caregiver in the same way that a baby is with a similar routine, and then to move through the developmental stages.
- Weighted blankets are frequently found to be very helpful by therapeutic parents. They can really help to promote the child's feeling of security and enhance deeper levels of sleep.

- Melatonin helps to induce sleep. This can be found in natural sources such as bananas and milk, so these two items used together as the last snack can be really helpful. Some parents have found that two squares of milk chocolate, melted into warm milk and then drunk just before bedtime has a very dramatic sleep-inducing effect with children.
- Stroking the child's face, especially the cheeks, helps to dramatically increase delta waves in the brain, which induce sleep.
- A pop-up tent that fits over the bed often gives the child increased feelings of security, enabling them to go to sleep more easily.
- Using empathic commentary in a soft soothing voice, can be helpful, 'You look so tired, I can see you really want to go to sleep. I wonder what I can do to help you?'
- Some parents have invested in a 'Dreampad'. This is a pad that goes under the pillow and vibrates and/or plays soothing sleep-inducing sounds. Naturally, care needs to be taken when considering your child's curiosity and ability to dismantle items!
- Set up the child with coping strategies so they can feel better while awake. This is helpful if you have a child who wakes up and does not leave the room but might make noise. I used to put a few items such as a mini DVD player or favourite game in my daughter's room at night when I went to bed.
- Make a recording of you reading stories or singing. The child can then play this to help them go to sleep or to soothe them if they wake.
- Experiment with night lights. Some parents find that switching them off as soon as the child goes to sleep promotes deeper and longer sleep; other parents find that having night lights and music or a heartbeat noise, which automatically turn off after half an hour, is helpful, then if the child wakes in the night they can turn them on independently again.
- Play audible stories/mindfulness relaxation either in the bedroom or just outside for them to fall asleep listening to.

- Try leaving quiet classical music playing all night. This can help to regulate the child.
- If you have been using parental presence for a long time and the child is still not settling, it may be time for a change. Stage a gradual withdrawal, first of all sitting next to the bed for a couple of evenings, then move the chair further away until eventually you just leave your slippers peeping round the door. My daughter slept well for over two years before she realised I wasn't in my slippers!
- Leave a little torch so the child can switch it on for comfort and to find their way to the toilet with some security.

Strategies for waking others/ leaving room/returning to bed

- Fit some door alarms so you can hear straightaway when the child leaves their room at night. This will at least discourage the child from wandering. You can also use alarms that just send a signal to a light so you are alerted without the rest of the house being woken up.
- Using a baby monitor can help to reassure you and the child, especially two-way ones, if you're feeling strong enough. It can help the child to remain in bed without physically needing to come and find you.
- Where a child has left their room and appears downstairs, simply say, 'Oh dear, it looks like you are lost!' then guide them back to bed. Use strategies from Bedtime Issues to help with this.
- If you have a child who wakes up other children the only sure-fire way is using parental presence to prevent this. I know this can be an exhausting prospect but once you have completed the nurturing bedtime routine (and the mindfulness meditation is playing in the background), install yourself comfortably in a separate chair. Use the time to have a cup of tea, read or use an iPad or tablet with headphones to watch a downloaded favourite programme. The very fact that you are physically present may enable the children to feel calm enough to go to sleep.

Strategies for nightmares/night terrors/sleep walking

- General advice is not to touch the child unless you are certain they are awake. It can work well to put on soft music when you first hear the child crying or shouting. Without touching them, sit where they could see you if they were to wake. Let the child act out what they need to and make sure they are safe. It may be terrifying to watch but just remain calm and present. Remember that the child will almost certainly not remember the event.

- It sounds obvious, but make absolutely sure that accessible windows and doors are locked. I once found my five-year-old son fast asleep and trying to climb out of the window! Also as a safety feature, consider reintroducing stair gates.

- Where the child shares a room and frequently screams for long periods, some parents have found that wrapping them securely in a blanket and taking the child to the parents' room or into a different part of the house can be helpful. Some parents have found going outside and looking at the moon or stars very grounding if the child has awoken with a nightmare.

- Where a child is acting out dangerous movements, such as climbing on the window sill or attempting to get out of the window, a firm command can be effective. I used to say in a strong voice, 'Get back into bed, I'm here, you're safe.' This seemed to get through.

- Getting the child to touch something in the room can also help. We may need to help the child with this if we are unsure how asleep or unaware they are. We had 'stars' on the ceiling and would start counting them out loud. Counting backwards can also be soothing.

- If you feel the child is waking and coming out of the terror then stroking their face or shoulders will increase feelings of calmness and help them to go back to sleep.

- Monitor what time the night terror happens each night, then for three or four consecutive nights, rouse the child about 30 minutes before the night terror is 'due'. You only need to say, 'You are safe, I am here, go back to sleep now.' This can interrupt the depth of sleep and stop the pattern of nightmares or night terrors.

- Avoid asking questions. If the child is walking out of the back door, you may need to turn them around. This is preferable to shouting, 'Where are you going?'
- Restrict exit routes. If you ensure that the only path out is past you, this can dramatically reduce risk and help you to feel more secure.

Strategies for waking early/angry

- If your child is behaving and thinking as a much younger child, think laterally. What would you do with a toddler, say two years old, who woke too early? How would you 'teach' them that it's not 'waking up time' yet? I used to put certain cherished special toys in the child's room after they had gone to sleep. Sometimes I would add a banana or cup of milk (nurture and melatonin).
- Think oxytocin! If our children are waking angry due to high levels of cortisol this can be addressed in several ways. After long periods of inactivity, the child's cortisol level may have risen to a point where they are fearful, anxious, angry and generally full of energy! A snack can help to reduce the cortisol levels, which is why I used to leave a banana or biscuit for the morning. A friend of mine lets her (resilient and much loved) dog go into her daughter's room when she wakes early and angry. She then hears her daughter calming, speaking to the dog and stroking it. This activity produces oxytocin. Do note, however, that you need to be confident about the child's treatment of animals for this!
- Another strategy for waking angry (if it is not too early) is to get the child moving. Forget a slow, long, drawn-out morning routine. I would get my children marching up or down the stairs and doing quite a lot of activity first thing. This lowers their cortisol levels.
- Use empathic commentary to explain to the child what you think they are feeling and also to 'name the need', 'I can see you are

feeling really wobbly today. I wonder if being asleep and lying still all that time built up all the wobbliness or busy juice. Maybe some breakfast will take some of the wobbliness away.'

- Where you are unsure what behaviour and attitudes you might be facing in the morning, prepare everything possible the night before! I cannot tell you how many hours of stress I avoided by preparing PE kits, lunches and school bags and putting them in the car the night before. I also used to lay the breakfast table and get nearly everything out ready for the morning.

- Some easy-view toddler clocks which show when it is 'waking-up time' can be really useful, but don't expect immediate and dramatic results, although alarms generally, especially novelty ones with happy music, can be more effective and less triggering than a parent's voice.

- Sometimes you just need to allow the child to get into bed with you and go back to sleep. There is quite a lot of negativity around co-sleeping, especially where there has been abuse, particularly sexual abuse, so it's important to take sensible precautions. It is a question of weighing up the early missed nurture and bonding time, the importance of that close, attachment time with the parent, and risk. Our children have often missed so much, and waking early is often about needing to be close. Again, think how you might respond if this was a two- or three-year-old waking early.

- If the child needs to return to their room, simply use the same withdrawal process as putting them to bed. After a couple of weeks of returning the child and slowly withdrawing, the child may start to settle and amuse themselves with the interesting things you have left for them until their clock shows 'waking-up time'.

- Some parents have a blow-up bed which can either be placed next to the parent's bed, or next to the child's. Try not to get too stuck in control issues here. Nurture triumphs over control every time. It's also really important that you get your sleep as you cannot therapeutically parent from a point of exhaustion.

SLEEP WALKING (see Sleep Issues)

SMOKING (see also Drugs and Alcohol)

What it looks like

- The child or young person smokes openly.
- The carer or parent suspects the child or young person is smoking.
- The child or young person smokes secretly in their bedroom or elsewhere in the house.

Why it might happen

- Addiction to nicotine.
- Replacing early lost nurture.
- Sensory-seeking behaviour.
- The need to feel in control – in particular, this is an activity that is very difficult for well-meaning adults to control.
- Dysregulation – smoking can help to self-regulate.
- Lack of cause-and-effect thinking and impulsivity – the child or young person is unable to relate to or accept longer-term health risks, or even more immediate health or physical issues, and is driven by immediate needs and impulses.
- A subconscious compulsion to break a forming attachment (with the parent).
- Fear or fearful anticipation of a negative response from the parent.
- Attraction to peer-group activities.
- Fear response – smoking can help the child or young person to feel calmer.
- Feelings of hostility or momentary hatred towards the parent.
- Fear of invisibility/being forgotten, especially if this triggers a response from the parent/carer.
- Recreating a familiar environment – the smell of tobacco might be a familiar or even reassuring smell.
- Fear of change/transitions – there may be an increase in smoking or increased attraction at times of transition.

- Fear of drawing attention to self in relation to peer-group activities and not wishing to be the 'odd one out' if others are smoking. Also, the child may gain favour and temporary popularity by procuring cigarettes for others.

Reality check

This is one of the issues where therapeutic parents can sometimes lose their way and go over the top with control issues (I know, as I did!). Putting in unrelated consequences and punishments will not resolve this issue. Rather, we need to keep communication open and work in partnership with the young person.

Useful strategies

- Avoid vilifying the child; instead, speak about how you are confident they will be able to sort this out. You can reference their strength of personality and the fact that they have overcome difficulties in their life as proof.
- The best strategy to cut down or end smoking is to closely monitor money available to the child or young person. Cigarettes are expensive, and limiting funds automatically limits access to cigarettes through legitimate channels. This does not mean they won't take them from others. If you or anyone else in the house smokes then you need to make sure that tobacco and cigarettes are securely locked away.
- Put boundaries around smoking in the home. Providing a tin and placing it by the back door, making it clear that smoking is only allowed outside, makes this a less attractive habit. Our children do not like to be excluded and usually want to know what is going on.
- It is reasonable to insist that the child or young person does not smoke in the house, and this includes their bedroom. Tamper-proof smoke detectors should be fitted in the bedrooms and bathroom to keep everyone safe. Some therapeutic parents have a designated smoking area some distance from the house, in an unattractive part of the garden. This often cuts short smoking!

- Use 'naming the need' and empathic commentary to link the child's need to smoke to possible stress factors and any early lost nurture. For example, 'some children and young people smoke because they need something to do with their mouth. This happens especially if they missed out on some baby things.'
- Provide lollipops as an alternative.
- Our children are often unable to link long-term health risks to the immediate act of smoking, so although we can give our children literature and advice, don't be surprised if they do not take this on board. This can be especially difficult if there has been a long discussion that felt positive, which is then followed by a return to smoking. Remember that our children study us closely and often say what they think we want them to say!
- Letting the child or young person know about some of the more immediate risks that impact on them more directly can be effective. These include skin getting dry and breaking out in spots, and teeth becoming stained and potentially decaying if they're not looked after (pictures of rotting teeth can help)!
- Give the child fiddle toys to play with, especially if they are anxious and needing a cigarette.
- If the child enjoys a certain sport or singing, let them know that smoking will have an impact on this. You can also tie in a reward for when they cut down. One of my children wanted singing lessons, but obviously we were not going to provide these until the smoking stopped. This created the desire to stop smoking, which was much easier to work with.
- Imposing a straightforward ban could lead to high levels of anxiety as the child suffers nicotine withdrawal symptoms. If the child or young person has expressed a desire to give up smoking, or has asked for help not to start, we need to use small, achievable steps when aiming to help them. In order for this strategy to stand any chance of success, they must help to negotiate and agree the targets set, such as limiting the number of cigarettes in a day or agreeing times when a cigarette can be smoked.

- Give the child positive encouragement and praise for what they are achieving but make sure this is not too over the top, for example, 'I can see it's really hard for you not having any cigarettes, but you managed your angry feelings really well today.'
- Replacement patches, nicotine gum, vapers or any other form of nicotine replacement products are useful where a child or young person is addicted and wishes to give up smoking, but medical advice needs to be sought in relation to the use of these. Some therapeutic parents have had some success replacing the cigarettes with more 'tasty' nicotine-free vapers.

SNEAKY BEHAVIOURS *(see also Joking and Teasing, Lying, Sibling Rivalry, Stealing, Triangulation)*

What it looks like
- The child tells tales on others.
- The child sets up a situation to get another child into trouble.

Why it might happen
- Fear of parent/carer and other adults – as an early survival strategy, the child works hard to keep negative attention off of themselves.
- Recreating a familiar environment – the child pointing out faults or creating negative attention on others may have kept themselves safe in an earlier environment.
- Overwhelming need to feel loved/important – the child attempts to present themselves in a more favourable light.
- The need to feel in control and powerful – by controlling the affections and attentions of the parent/carer.
- Lack of cause-and-effect thinking – the child often does not realise that the parent is fully aware of their actions.
- Dysregulation – diverting attention to avoid blame or further conflict.
- Attraction to peer-group activities, particularly in relation to stealing money or valuable items and using these to win friendships.

- Fear of invisibility/being forgotten – seeking positive reaffirmation/comparison from the parent.
- Lack of empathy – unable to think about the effects of their behaviour on others.
- Lack of remorse – unable to feel sorry about what they have done (avoidance of shame).
- Emotional age – the child may be functioning at an earlier stage.

The 'hand grenade child'

These kinds of behaviours are often typical of children whose prevalent attachment style is ambivalent or avoidant. My little Sophie Spikey fitted in well here! I called her my 'hand grenade child'. Sophie could walk into a room of peaceful, cooperating children and two minutes later might appear to be the only well-behaved child in the room. Meanwhile, the hand grenades she had carefully set went off at regular intervals. The hand grenades consisted of 'helpfully' telling her siblings exactly who had been saying what about whom, who appeared to have misappropriated possessions of others, and speculating about who might be getting an extra treat.

Useful strategies

- If you have several children and one appears to be 'too good to be true', take a step back and *really watch* the behaviours and interactions. Sometimes the child we always notice behaving badly is the one who responds emotionally and quickly to the hand grenade thrown by the 'good' child.

- You must tell the children that you see what is happening. There is less reaction when the victims of the hand grenade child know that the adults see what is really happening, 'Oh William, poor you! I can see that when Sophie just took your plate away, pretending to tidy up, it really upset you. Sophie, give it back now.'

- When you confront the hand grenade child be gentle! You may provoke a panic response where the child is very fearful that you will no longer love them and keep them safe. I might say, 'Sophie, I saw what you did just then. I see you, remember? I am always watching because I want to keep you all safe and happy. Let me help you put that right.'

- Treat protestations such as, 'It wasn't me, I wasn't even there' in the same way as 'lying' but using some additional empathy.

- 'Naming the need' with empathy is helpful, but be careful not to overuse this, 'I wonder if you are telling me that Katie has been naughty so I love you more? Sometimes, if children worry about not being loved, or if they are scared they might be in trouble, they tell tales about other children. Well, I love you all the same no matter what.'

- Where you have a child telling tales on other children, the absolute best way of responding is by *not* responding to the information contained within the tale! I used to take all the information on board (some of it was very useful and often used at a later date), but I did not give the reaction that was sought by the hand grenade child. For example:

  Sophie: Mummy, William has wet the bed again!

  Me: Lovely! Thank you so much for offering to help him to sort it out. You are so kind!

Sophie: Mummy, Charley has a whole packet of biscuits in her room.

Me: Goodness she must be hungry! Lucky Charley.

SOCIAL MEDIA ISSUES *(including phones) (see also Friendships, Obsessions, Sexualised Behaviour)*

What it looks like

- The child is addicted to social media sites.
- The child shares inappropriate information online.
- The child visits inappropriate websites.
- The child seeks contact with people they must not be in contact with through social media.
- The child becomes very tired, using phone and computer at night.

Why it might happen

- Immediate gratification – as our children often lack impulse control, the rewards and attraction of social media are very powerful.
- The need to feel in control and powerful, especially in relation to creating an alternative online version of themselves, and also making sure that they know everything that is going on at all times.
- Lack of cause-and-effect thinking – the child is unable to process the effects of their online actions.
- Addiction to social media.
- A subconscious compulsion to break a forming attachment (with the parent) – the child can be emotionally absent when online.
- Attraction to peer-group activities.
- Boredom, especially if the child struggles with face-to-face real-life friendships. Online 'friendships' may be easier to sustain.
- Overwhelming need to feel loved/important – instant gratification and recognition are available through social media.
- Emotional age – the child is unaware of or oblivious to the risks.

- Loyalty to birth parents/former carers – trying to contact them through social media.
- Brain development is impaired from early life trauma or similar.

Reality check

Social networking is now a fact of modern life. It is very difficult to prevent children and young people from using Facebook, Snapchat and other similar platforms. Even where parents and carers are very vigilant and restrict usage, our children are gifted at obtaining access from the phones and gadgets of others. Our challenge is complex as our children often function at a much younger emotional age and they are simply not capable of managing the intricacies and dangers of social media.

Completely preventing children from taking part in social networking could lead to social exclusion among their peers. Our task is extremely complex in trying to help our children explore the positives of social networking while keeping them safe, particularly when considering their additional needs. Children who have experienced past trauma and have low self-esteem can be more vulnerable to the dangers associated with the internet.

Strategies for minimising risk

- Establish firm boundaries! Tablets, phones and so on were under *my* control and only issued at times when I wanted the children to be able to use them. Naturally, this was at a time within our set routine.
- Understand what children and young people are doing when they are online. The best way of doing this is to become conversant yourself. If you are not sure about how social media works, either ask a member of your family to show you, or undertake a course. Ignorance cannot be used as an excuse.
- Make it clear that no phones, tablets or computers are allowed in bedrooms. You have no visibility of this and there is significant heightened risk. The child also becomes more isolated and spends less time in a family environment.

- Establish a regular and open dialogue with the child about how you intend to keep them safe online, house rules about internet usage, and your expectations.
- Think about the type of phone or tablet your child needs. Many social media platforms are not suitable for children under the age of 14. Some of our children are much younger than this chronologically and emotionally. My children all had basic phones without internet access to start off with and then we saw how it went from there, gradually increasing their access as I felt they were able to manage it.
- Ensure that the child understands how to use the privacy settings in order to 'hide' their profile in searches and block unwanted contacts. Be aware that some social media apps give real-time reports about where the person is located and what they are doing.
- If you have a computer screen, make sure it is facing outwards and located in the living room or an area that can be viewed by others easily.
- Try to understand what a child is doing online through becoming involved in their sessions, and ask them to guide you in understanding social networking sites and the internet. Don't be afraid to ask a child for help in understanding new applications and the language used, as they may well know more than you!
- Be aware that it is very likely that people who have acted inappropriately towards the child in the past will target and access them through social networking sites such as Facebook. If it is agreed by all parties that a child may have a social media account (and is chronologically and developmentally mature enough), then set the account up yourself, or ask a trusted friend. In this way, you can ensure you have the passwords and can access information should the need arise.
- Place blocking and filtering controls on computers that can easily be accessed online and provide the parent with information about sites that are visited and so on. Parental controls can also be set up on tablets and phones, but you will need to be involved at the set-up stage for this.

- Make sure your own equipment is securely password protected and that you do not leave it in an accessible area. Our children can be extremely quick at noting passwords and codes. They can then log on as you and make purchases. It is very useful to change your settings so that an extra layer of security is required, such as touch ID.

Strategies for managing children's obsessions with social media

- Remember that you are in charge of the wi-fi! This is very powerful. It is now possible to buy a wi-fi blocker which restricts the amount of time a child or young person can stay online, and also limits the type of sites they can visit through your wi-fi. However, this will not affect where they can go through a phone data plan.
- Make a rule that all phones, tablets and computers are not allowed in bedrooms. When the child goes to bed, the 'charging station' needs to be centrally located, and this is the only place where charging happens. If you notice that the child has taken the phone to bed, you can either go to the room and remove it, or wait until the child has fallen asleep and remove it. The natural consequence for this happening is that you will not want them to get tired so the phone will not be returned until the following day. I used to say, 'Let me help you to stop feeling so tired. I think you forgot the rules yesterday about no phones in bedrooms, so you must be very tired indeed. I will look after the phone and give it back later/tomorrow.' I also used, 'I am sorry I did not realise that you could not manage your time on your tablet yourself. I will be helping you with that in the future.' The natural consequence is right there.
- Make sure the child is responsible for their own phone/tablet. If it gets broken, it stays broken. You might help the child to save up or work towards getting a new one, but resist the temptation to immediately replace it. This does not help our children to learn cause and effect.

- Do not, under any circumstances, be tempted to take out a contract under your name for the child's phone. This invariably ends in disaster, and has many far-reaching implications. If the child has taken their phone to bed and you decide to switch off the wi-fi, the child is unlikely to care if they have unlimited data! If the child is responsible for paying for their own data on a pay-as-you-go plan, this means they have less money available for less healthy options such as cigarettes and alcohol.
- Keep a check on your child's behaviour after they have been online. If they suddenly become secretive and do not want to say where they are going, don't be shy about following them if at all possible. As a matter of course, you should be able to check any messages so you can be reassured they are not at risk from a sexual predator or another dangerous person from their past. The NSPCC website has up-to-date information about the risks of grooming online and how to keep your child safe and recognise risks.
- Make good use of online resources (below) and appropriate books such as *Your Brain on Porn* (Wilson 2015) and *Bubble Wrapped Children* (Oakwater 2012).

Further resources

Parents Protect – for up-to-date information and top tips on keeping your children safe online: www.parentsprotect.org.

XXXAware – this site gives step-by-step instructions on how to set up parental controls on a range of broadband providers and tech products and is very user friendly. It's a one-stop shop for parental controls: www.xxxaware.co.uk.

NSPCC – this site gives an overview of normal and abnormal sexual behaviour, what to look for and what to do about it, with links giving information about such subjects as grooming and online porn: www.nspcc.org.uk/preventing-abuse.

SOILING *(see Poo Issues)*

SPITTING *(see also Aggression)*

What it looks like

- The child spits at people in an aggressive way.
- The child spits on other objects, the floor and so on.

Why it might happen

- Sensory issues – an oral sensory issue may be an underlying cause.
- Dysregulation – acting in the heat of the moment. Spitting creates a sensation that may help the child to regulate.
- Feelings of hostility, rejection or momentary hatred towards the other person.
- The need to feel in control and powerful, particularly where the spitting provokes an extreme negative reaction. Spitting may be being used in order to trigger the other person into responding.
- Boredom and lack of stimulation – this is especially apparent where there has been neglect and the child has been left alone for long periods. Saliva may have been their toy.
- A subconscious compulsion to break a forming attachment (with the parent).
- Fear response – the child may spit either through aggression or fear.
- Attraction to peer-group activities – copying the actions of peers.
- Recreating a familiar environment – it may be a normal habit which the child has witnessed or had themselves due to a lack of stimulation over a number of years.
- Comfortable to be in the wrong/self-sabotage.
- Emotional age – the child may be actually replicating a younger stage of development. This is apparent if spitting is also accompanied by body curiosity, dribbling and so on.

Reality check

Spitting is really emotive. If this is a deliberate act of aggression it can be extremely difficult to respond in a measured way. I am always surprised when therapeutic parents say they have reacted strongly and add, 'I wasn't very therapeutic.' I disagree – having strong boundaries is definitely a foundation of therapeutic parenting and there is nothing wrong with saying, 'This is unacceptable.' The trick is to respond without reinforcing the behaviour. If the child is targeting you with spitting to provoke a reaction, and you reward them with a strong emotional response, you are unwittingly reinforcing the behaviour, making a reoccurrence more likely.

Avoid the temptation to have long dialogues about spitting and continuously telling the child it is wrong or bad. Of course, we do let them know it is unacceptable, but telling them off and reinforcing the idea that *they* are 'bad' will not make the child stop.

Preventative strategies

- Set some time aside to monitor the child closely. Where spitting is a habit this needs to be intercepted immediately at the time it happens. You will probably need to plan ahead to have time to address this.

- All behaviours are a form of communication and some are indicative of an unmet need. Anything that is oral needs to be thought about first in terms of lost nurture and sensory issues.
- It's a very good idea to plan in advance what you have decided the natural or logical consequence to being spat at might be. It's really hard to think of this at the time it happens.
- Where the spitting is due to oral sensory issues you need to give the child frequent oral stimulation five to ten times a day. This doesn't have to be very time consuming. You can:
  - blow bubbles
  - give the child food that is very chewy
  - engage in sensory water play
  - use massage around the jaw and face area
  - play blowing games using straws.

Strategies during

- Tell the child that spitting is unacceptable. Don't be afraid to say it how it is. If you miss this bit out, you can't then put in the natural consequences another time, as the child has breached an invisible boundary!
- When a child spits at you, the first thing to do is remove the emotional response to that act. You may need to actually practise and rehearse this as it's not easy to do. Removing an emotional response does not mean we remove any type of reaction or natural consequence. Say calmly (while moving away to wipe the spit off), 'That's a shame that you chose to do that, as you know that spitting is not allowed. Unfortunately, now:
  - 'I will need to go and wash my face and redo my make up so we won't be going out after all'
  - 'I realise you are too little to be able to do X. I need to help you get past the spitting stage as normally it is very little children who do that'
  - 'you will need to brush your teeth to get all the germy spit off your teeth. It's not good for you.' Naturally, the teeth cleaning may be very long and boring. This also helps where there are sensory issues. (It's important that you

don't get into a situation where you are forcing the child to brush their teeth or wrestling with them. Use techniques explained in Defiance)

- ○ 'I won't be able to sit as close to you when we play this game'
- ○ 'I don't want to be too close to you right now'
- ○ 'you will need to think of a way to put this right. I have thought of something and will let you know later what that is.' (Use this when you can't think of anything right now, as it will stop you overreacting.)
- If the child has spat at something, or on the floor, get them to help you clear it up, using 'showing sorry' techniques, 'Looks as if you spat on the floor. Here is the spray and cloth to help clear it up.'
- Keep a 'spit bottle' or bucket handy. If the child spits, you can get them to carry the bottle round, or stay near the bucket 'in case of accidents'.
- Lemons tend to reduce saliva and make it more difficult to spit. You can put lemon juice in food or give the child a slice of lemon to suck on. You cannot force the child to put the lemon in their mouth obviously, but often our children are very happy to have a slice, especially if added to orange slices. I might say, 'I have noticed that sometimes you have too much spit and it falls out in the wrong place. Luckily these fruit slices will help you with that.'
- Use distraction. If you can see the child is about to spit, make a loud noise, clap, look past the child as if you have seen something. Then once interrupted, you can offer the spit bottle.
- If you can access an empathic feeling in the moment, you can try saying, 'Wow, it looks as if you are really angry! Do you need my help?'

Strategies after

- If a child is spitting a lot, make sure you give them positive attention when they stop! For example, 'Oh great, now you have stopped spitting we can...'

- Try 'naming the need', 'Sometimes children spit to try to keep people away from them. It happens if they get really scared or worried. I wonder if that's what you are trying to do?'

SPLITTING *(see Triangulation)*

STAYING IN BED *(see Defiance, Lateness, Moving Slowly)*

STEALING *(see also Food Issues – for stealing food)*

What it looks like

- The child steals money.
- The child takes sentimental items and may destroy or hide them.
- The child picks up items belonging to others and hides them.
- The child deliberately plans to take items/money that do not belong to them.
- The child breaks doors, windows and so on in order to gain access.

Why it might happen

- Overwhelming need to feel loved/important – seeking nurture, especially in relation to targeting the main carer.
- The need to feel in control and powerful, particularly relating to money.
- Lack of cause-and-effect thinking – the child is unable to think about the consequences of actions.
- Dysregulation – acting in the heat of the moment.
- Jealousy, specifically with regard to stealing items belonging to siblings or other children in the family who are viewed as more 'loved'.
- Recreating a familiar environment – automatic collection of useful items as an earlier learned survival strategy.
- A subconscious compulsion to break a forming attachment (with the parent), particularly in relation to taking items of a sentimental value.

- Attraction to peer-group activities, particularly in relation to stealing money or valuable items and using these to win friendships.
- Feelings of hostility or momentary hatred towards the parent.
- Fear of invisibility/being forgotten – seeking a response.
- Lack of empathy – unable to think about the effects of their behaviour on others.
- Lack of remorse – unable to feel sorry about what they have done (avoidance of shame).
- Fear of parent/carer and other adults.
- Separation anxiety, especially if taking items that are comforting.
- Dissociation – the child may be unaware of 'automatic taking'.
- Boredom.
- Comfortable to be in the wrong/self-sabotage, especially if this is a trigger for the parent/carer.
- Emotional age – the child may be behaving in an emotional stage-appropriate manner.

Reality check

Therapeutic parenting is *not* about letting the child 'get away with it'. Some parents struggle with stealing because they feel therapeutic parenting strategies are a soft option. This is not the case. We need to be very clear with our children that we know what has happened and that there will be (natural) consequences. Avoiding standard parenting traps does not mean there is no response, it just means that we incorporate cause-and-effect thinking and nurture into our response.

Preventative strategies

- Do not leave high risk (or even tempting) items lying about! This sounds straightforward but remember our children are hypervigilant and will spot the tiniest things. It is not okay to leave money in obvious places to 'test' them. We would not leave a toddler next to an open fire to see if they could resist temptation and learn a lesson!

- Use a small 'bum bag' or similar and put all the essentials in it: keys, phone, cash and cards. This can be put on first thing in the morning and worn all day. This stops the worry of trying to watch personal important items. It has the added bonus of ensuring you can leave the house quickly, should an emergency arise.

- Locking door handles can prevent casual stealing, especially where it is opportunistic and between children. These are good as the child cannot be locked in, but can easily protect their belongings from others.

- Be vigilant! When handling a high-risk item, say out loud, 'I am putting this £20 note in my purse.' This helps you to remember later where you put things, should you feel uncertain.

- Create a 'safe area'. Install an actual safe if necessary. Put a lock on your bedroom door if you need to make sure there is one room where you can keep things safe.

- Tell visitors that they need to place high-risk items such as bags and purses in your safe area when they enter the house. This might feel a little embarrassing but it saves a much more embarrassing and traumatic situation developing.

- Where you think the child might be taking things 'automatically' due to early life survival strategies, you can make them aware of this by telling them that you are going to help them get control of automatic taking. Say you are going to leave a few things round the house to see if they can spot what you have left out deliberately. Interestingly, stealing seems to reduce when parents do this. My children told me it was because if they were going to steal, just as they were about to take it they would think, 'Ah no! This is a test one. She's not going to trick me!' I had to tell them in the end that I had not actually left anything lying around! During this period, I also had children coming up to me handing over small coins and other items, informing me that they had found one of the things I had left out for them to find. Naturally, I gave a positive reaction to this.

- Try to have as many open-plan spaces as possible. This is good for a number of issues, not least helping your child to remain regulated and connected to you. Our children need a high level of supervision and open planning helps to achieve that, while reducing opportunities for stealing.

- Use time-in. If there has been a spate of stealing, tell your child that you are worried they won't be able to stop themselves and you need to keep them close to make sure they can manage with all the tempting things that are around at present.

Strategies during

- When our children steal money or personal possessions it feels personal and frustrating, but standard reactions such as making them apologise or calling the police have very little long-term impact and can even make the situation worse. When parents and carers call the police, the overwhelming message to the child is, 'We cannot manage you, you are not safe with us.' Some parents try to use the police as a threat but this can back-fire spectacularly. See False Allegations.

- When trying to keep control of your emotional reaction, it's useful to remember they are not doing it *to* you. They are just doing it. This is more difficult to relate to when a child targets a personal possession with great sentimental value. At those times, remember that the action is about getting a *reaction*. So, adjust your response accordingly if possible.

- If this is your trigger point then, if possible, reallocate this issue to another adult to deal with it.

- Be very careful not to over-punish due to your own personal feelings about what has happened. If you are too angry to think straight, tell the child that there will be a consequence for their behaviour and that you will let them know what it is later. This gives you time to calm down and to ensure you are applying natural and meaningful consequences, rather than overzealous punishments which will harm the child and your relationship, and certainly not decrease the stealing.

- Follow your instinct! If your instinct is saying that the child took the item then go with that. If you show doubt where a child *has* stolen an item this may well lead to an escalation in the situation. A good six-point plan for responding is this:

1. State that you know child took the item in a matter-of-fact way.
2. Do not enter into any negotiation, or get drawn into arguments and accusations.
3. State the consequence, 'Well, I have decided that you did take X. Therefore, you will need to pay towards a new one.'
4. Demonstrate empathy or wonder aloud, 'I wonder if you took X because you were missing me?'
5. Say, 'I will apologise later if we find out you did not take X.' This allows you to disengage and move on. Some parents struggle with the idea of accusing a child and not being completely certain. It is important to act decisively and with certainty. In 17 years, there was only one occasion when I had to apologise after discovering one of my children had indeed not taken the item. If I had given the benefit of the doubt in the many hundreds of other situations, I would have increased my children's feelings of insecurity.
6. Disengage as soon as possible. This will prevent you from over-punishing the child, especially where this is your trigger point.

Strategies after

- 'Naming the need' is a very powerful tool to use with stealing. Often our children are unaware of what they are doing, why and what it means. You can use *Charley Chatty and the Disappearing Pennies* (Naish and Jefferies 2017) to start a dialogue about the causes of this behaviour.
- Only share how the stealing has made you feel if you genuinely believe your child can take this on board and respond to it appropriately. Too many parents share their feelings with the child, only to then be reminded that the child is at a stage where they do not appear to have any empathy or remorse, increasing the carer's sense of frustration and disempowerment.

- Ensure you follow through with consequence. It's important to think carefully about the consequence to stealing as it needs to be both related to the event *and* meaningful to the child. If the child has taken £10 and you have decided they are going to pay it back from their pocket money, there is only a point to doing this if you know the child will care about this, and cause and effect will be linked, i.e. if the child thinks, 'I stole £10 therefore I have less money this week. I am sad about that, I wish I had not taken £10.' Your child may not have such sophisticated thinking, and they may not care at all about paying the money back. The important action to them was getting the item or money in the first place. It is difficult to put in inhibitors through consequences to the adrenaline rush experienced when stealing.

- Let your child know that you know they are finding it difficult to stop taking things that do not belong to them. Explain that this can happen with children who feel wobbly, but that everyone has to learn not to take things that do not belong to them. Ask them how they think you can help with this. You might be surprised at their suggestions.

Footnote: When my son was stealing a lot of money as a teen, I got to a point where I thought he would probably stand on my dead body to get a £10 note. I realised the root cause was all about lost early nurture and trying to replace that. I came to this conclusion as I noticed he was targeting my bedroom and the bedroom of the mother of a friend. It only ever happened when I went out. I used 'naming the need' to address this with him by revisiting the story from his early life of being alone, neglected and missing Mum. I linked this to his lonely feelings when I went out and wondered if the 'little boy inside' was still closely linked in to the feelings of that little boy who was abandoned by the mother figure. My son reacted very strongly to this and I realised we had hit the nail on the head. I stopped locking doors, switched off the cameras and told him he could go in my bedroom whenever he liked if he was missing me. The stealing stopped overnight. Naturally, I did have a safe by this point so I did not leave lots of money lying around. That would have been setting him up to fail.

STEALING FOOD *(see Hoarding, Hunger, Overeating)*

SUGAR ADDICTION *(see Hoarding, Hunger, Overeating)*

SWEARING *(see also Aggression, Rudeness)*

What it looks like

- The child swears in conversation.
- The child uses swearing to try to shock others.
- The child swears in an aggressive or insulting manner.
- The child uses swearing as part of everyday conversation.

Why it might happen

- The need to feel in control and powerful – swearing may be a way to try to keep people away or an effort to control them.
- Dysregulation – acting in the heat of the moment.
- Lack of cause-and-effect thinking – the child is unable to remember or accept that swearing is not tolerable.
- Fear response – swearing may be used as a reflex response when the child is scared.
- Feelings of hostility or momentary hatred towards the parent.
- Fear of invisibility/being forgotten – seeking a response.
- Recreating a familiar environment – the language may be very familiar to the child.
- Shame – avoidance of shame and deflection. If there is an incident and the child swears, the focus may shift away from the incident and on to the swearing.
- A subconscious compulsion to break a forming attachment (with the parent).
- Attraction to peer group – mimicking actions and reactions of peers.

- Lack of remorse.
- Fear of parent/carer and other adults – need to keep them at a distance.
- Emotional age – the child may be functioning at a younger age and be experimenting with words.

Preventative strategies

- Make up a word. 'Clanters' is quite good, for example, 'I couldn't clanting do it!' Say it accidentally, appear flustered about having said it, apologise and then ask the child not to say it under any circumstances. This gives them a replacement 'swear' word. It's easier to manage as it does not have the power to shock others.
- Don't react! Sometimes our children use swear words because they are a familiar language. Gradually, as they hear the words less the words disappear naturally. The one way you can guarantee they will stick around is by gasping in horror!
- Think about the emotional age of your child. What would your response be if a much younger child used a swear word?
- Use the parental reward chart (see Rudeness). Give yourself a star every time there is a swear word.

Strategies during

- Show the child that the words hold no power over you and do not provoke an emotional reaction. Say something like, 'It must feel really difficult having all those swear words inside you. Let's get them all out.' Make sure there are not any delicate bystanders when you 'get them all out'!
- Say, 'At least you didn't say "clanters". Thank goodness for that!'
- Using natural consequences, get the child to clean their teeth, 'Oh no! Those swear words are all sticking to your teeth, so we need to get them all clean again so you are nice and healthy.' Everything comes to a stop until the teeth are cleaned. The child soon gets very bored of it. This needs to be done in a nurturing way. (Note that under no circumstances should you force the child or clean their teeth for them, but you can help if invited as part of nurture connection.)

- Use an empathic response where the swear words are a bit of a red herring, and the *emotion* being expressed is more important, 'I can see you are really angry and upset about this as normally you don't need to use the words.' Sometimes it is appropriate to ignore the swear words.
- Give the child a chance to say it the right way. Say, 'Shall we try that again? Because I don't think that came out how you meant it to.' This gives the child the chance to try a different way without invoking shame.
- Use playfulness to deliberately misunderstand them. For example, child says, 'This house is shit.' You reply, 'Yes, it's wonderful, isn't it? I particularly like the shiny door handles.'
- Simply adopt a confused expression, say nothing and wait. This can be very effective as long as you don't look threatening!
- Give the child a chance to 'rest' before continuing with the conversation, 'It sounds as if you need a break before you carry on telling me the problem. I can't understand what you are saying when there are swear words mixed in to the important stuff.'

Strategies after

- If your child has been using swear words because they did not realise they were wrong or rude, after the event it's important to revisit the actual words and be clear what is and is not acceptable.
- 'Name the need' to look at where these words came from, 'Sometimes when children have felt very scared, they use unkind words to try to keep people away from them. Maybe you have heard lots of these words before?'
- After the event, it may be the time to simply state, 'We don't have those words here because it makes everyone feel sad.' In this way you are setting out clear expectations for the future at a time when the event is still fresh in everyone's mind.

T

TAKING THINGS LITERALLY *(see Joking and Teasing, and Part 1, Chapter 1)*

TAKING TURNS *(see Competitiveness)*

TANTRUMS *(see Aggression, Controlling Behaviours, Defiance, Shouting and Screaming)*

TAUNTING *(see Joking and Teasing)*

TEASING *(see Joking and Teasing)*

THERAPY *(see Triangulation, and Part 1, Chapter 3)*

TOOTH BRUSHING *(see Brushing Teeth)*

TRANSITIONS *(see also Holidays, School Issues, and Part 1, Chapter 1)*

What it looks like

- The child's behaviour escalates or changes dramatically when there is approaching change, or following the change. This might be a change of activity, contact with significant others, the beginning and end of the school day, going on holiday, brain breaks (respite), any change in routine, change of person, moving house or any other change.
- The child uses delaying tactics to prolong the current status quo.
- The child hides (or goes blank) when a change in carer occurs.

Why it might happen

- Fear of change – the child feels unsafe and works hard to prevent the change from happening.
- Emotional age – the child may be unable to manage transitions in a similar way to the functioning and understanding of a much younger child. They are unable to comprehend permanence.
- Fear of adults, especially in relation to pick up times from nursey and school.
- The need to feel in control and stop changes happening, or provoke them, by escalating behaviours to force an end of placement.
- Lack of cause-and-effect thinking – the child is unable to visualise what the change might mean. This is especially relevant where there is a linked trigger.
- A subconscious compulsion to break a forming attachment (with the parent/carer, particularly around contact transitions).
- Fear response, especially relating to times when there is a change of carer. This is a whole new person to learn and the child does not know if they will return, no matter what you say!
- A need to try to predict the environment.
- Separation anxiety.
- Overwhelming need to keep the parent close.
- Sensory issues – the child may be overwhelmed by sensory input around the conflicting changes.

Reality check

What is a transition? For us it might mean something big, like moving house or starting a new job. For our children, it can be as small as changing from playing with one toy to another, or the change from activity to bedtime routine. Our children have very high anxiety levels around change as in the past this often had a negative meaning for them. We may just be thinking about going out somewhere nice in the car. This could be a trigger for the child as they may have been taken in a car from or to a traumatic event. Everyday experiences can be terrifying and we need to remain aware of that at all times.

If everything seems to be going really well and then your child's behaviour changes out of the blue (for the worse), you need to try to look at what the possible triggers for that are. Sometimes we cannot identify them. Sometimes they are obvious. Where the child's early life was traumatic, their brain is hardwired for fear. They generally see adults as unsafe. Because of this, if there is a change in a boundary by you or by another adult, the fear/survival response kicks back in and takes over. The child reverts quickly and instantly to old negative behaviour patterns.

The least useful thing we can do in this situation is to blame the child, or ask the child why. The child is either unaware, unconcerned, or deeply troubled and perplexed by their own behaviour. It is up to us, as therapeutic parents, to work out what is going on and how to fix it. An empathic response to the new (old) behaviours is our best starting point.

Preventative strategies

- Keep in mind what triggers there may be for your child. Sometimes these are not obvious and we can only identify them by the child's reactions to a specific change.
- Give advance warning of activity changes even if it is something that happens at the same time every day. My son used to always be surprised that it was 'suddenly' shower time!

- Use timers, such as sand timers, where the child can see how much time they have left. On computers and tablets, you can use a countdown alert as well.
- Set alarms. These can be fun songs or upbeat songs, relevant to the activity. It is less triggering for a child to have an alarm that informs them it is time for an activity change, than a parent telling them!
- As part of self-care, therapeutic parents need to take brain breaks for recovery. This needs to be handled sensitively. The best way of minimising disruption to all is for respite carers to be trained in therapeutic parenting and to come to look after the child in their own home. This can also be reassuring for the child, and they get a little break from the hard work of attaching to their new parent.
- Pause and reflect whenever you see a reaction. Think about what has just happened, or what is about to happen. This can help you to avoid or minimise reactions in the future.
- Think about the timings of when you tell children about any major events such as contact, holidays and house moves. Nearly all therapeutic parents find that giving the child a lot of notice about a change is not necessarily helpful! This just gives more time for anxiety to build.
- Where there is an approaching contact meeting with significant others in the child's life, this is likely to provoke anxiety, stress, guilt and feelings of loss and grief. As parents and carers, we may see anger and rejection. It's important to keep a diary of your child's reactions and responses and any deteriorations in behaviours such as bedwetting and aggression. This can help to determine later on how the contact is impacting on the child psychologically. If you feel the contact is not beneficial and you have evidence of deterioration in the child's behaviours and emotional well-being, this needs to be shared in a practical, fact-based manner.
- Be proactive around contact arrangements. If the child is expected to travel for hours in a car each way for a contact session with

able-bodied adults, this is not acceptable. Try to ensure that the transition is as short and undisruptive for the child as possible, especially concerning travelling to and from the contact.

- Having a planner on the wall with normal routines and small events can help the child to have visibility and feel secure about what is happening when (see Holidays).
- Use now, next, later boards (see below) or a daily planner that the child can carry around with them. It can be very reassuring for our children to have visibility about what the sequence of events is.

Here is an example of a planner:

What I do after school

| Empty school bag | Put away shoes | Have snack | Play with Lego |

- Use transitional objects. This might be something with a familiar scent which the child can keep close, such as a cloth or favourite toy.
- Avoid surprises! Don't be tempted to even use the word 'surprise' unless your child is very well established with you and secure.

Strategies during

- If your child hides (or goes blank emotionally) at pick up time, bear in mind that this is a survival strategy based in fear and the child is not doing it on purpose to annoy you. The child may be unsure that you are still safe, that you are not angry, or that you have not changed in anyway. This may be particularly prevalent where the child has been exposed to a parent who was unreliable in their response. Just carry on as normal, if possible speak to another adult and perhaps wonder aloud where the child might be, without showing any anger. If there are no other adults around you can use 'the phone strategy' and speak to an imaginary friend on the phone, using empathic commentary to lower the child's fear response.

- Reassure the child that you will be with them for the transition, or name the person who will be.
- Use wondering aloud to keep up a narrative, explaining what you think is happening for the child, 'I wonder if you are hiding under the bed because you are worried about what will happen when we leave the house? How can I help you feel less wobbly?'
- Talk about how you will return to the same place. Sometimes our children cannot visualise this, 'Once we get in the car I am going to drive to town and park in the shop car park. Then we will go to the supermarket and buy our dinner. After that we will get in the car and come home.'
- Let the child know when they can return to the activity.
- If a child is demonstrating sabotaging behaviours when approaching a significant contact, first of all try to tell the child about the contact as close as possible to the actual meeting. Let the child know that you know what is going on, 'I can see that you are very wobbly at the moment. This might be because you are due to see X tomorrow. What is going to happen is...' Give detailed information about where you are going, who will be there, how long for and where the child will go next. It is essential that the child takes a transitional object to 'return home' with.

Strategies after

- If the transitions around contact are too difficult for the child to manage, you need to follow your instincts here. All too often contact is set up with adults who have been the cause of the child's trauma, in order to *meet the adult's needs*, not the child's! Sometimes it is difficult for the child to let us know that the contact is too difficult or frightening for them, so they tell us through their behaviours.

- Following contact, our children often have conflicting loyalties and confused feelings. Avoid planning exciting or distracting activities and allow for some quiet 'down time' for reflection and reintegration.
- Use 'naming the need' and empathic reflection to help the child to explore their feelings around the contact or other transition, 'I think you might be very cross with me because you saw your Dad today and you are missing him. That must feel really sad.'

TRIANGULATION *(see also Charming, False Allegations, Lying, Overreacting)*

What it looks like

- A supporting professional, friend, family member or other adult is misled, or misinterprets an event or action after an interaction with the child.
- The child tells two (or more) different versions of an event to different people.
- The child exploits poor communication between parents and other adults to gain sympathy, empathy and additional nurture and/or to avoid a consequence.

Why it might happen

- Fear of invisibility/being forgotten – seeking attention/ attachment.
- The child needs to feel in control and safe, especially in relation to seeking nurture from 'the sympathetic face'.
- The other adult the child is interacting with does not understand therapeutic parenting or the effects of trauma.

- The child believes different versions of the same event, especially where there has been abuse. The child may not place the event in the correct time and space. This sometimes occurs when the child has real fear that the event *might* happen and is unable to distinguish between thought and actuality.
- Lack of cause-and-effect thinking – the child does not forward think about what might happen as a result of what they are saying.
- Dysregulation – the child may not be thinking clearly if dysregulated and will be mainly focused on staying safe.
- Shame, especially where the child may be 'in trouble', for example being late for school – the child deflects shame by engaging the adult in an alternative version of reality.
- Fear or fearful anticipation of a negative response from the adult they are interacting with.
- Feelings of hostility or momentary hatred towards the parent or primary caregiver.
- A need to try to draw another adult close (see 'the sympathetic face' explanation in Part 1, Chapter 6).
- Fear of change/transitions.
- Dissociation, leading to a lack of clarity about an event.
- A desire to avoid an activity or event, for example a child claims the parent has lost their PE kit in order to avoid doing PE.
- Sensory issues – the child may misinterpret a touch or a feeling, such as hunger.
- Overwhelming need to feel loved/important.
- Avoidance, especially in therapy where the child does not wish to engage with the therapist.

What *is* triangulation?

Take this example. The child is out at the cinema. You have arranged to collect her afterwards. She comes out five minutes early. You are on your way. While waiting, a supporting professional happens to pass by. Unfortunately, the supporting professional is not very skilled. The child sees her 'sympathetic face' and is driven to elicit nurture. The conversation might go like this:

SP: What are you doing out here all by yourself?!

Child: Mum hasn't come to pick me up. I have been waiting ages!

SP: How are you going to get home?

Child: I don't know. I haven't got any money! (sad face)

SP: Okay, well, here is some money. I will get it back from Mum when I see her.

The child happily goes off and spends the money, then quickly returns to meeting place. The carer is waiting and asks where she was. The child says she went to the toilet. Later that day the supporting professional contacts the carer to share her consternation that the child was in town with no means of getting home.

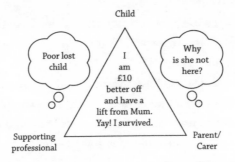

Reality check

If the child manages to elicit an additional nurture response from another adult, it's important to first of all separate out the *actual* situation (where they were, the precursor, what they said/did) from their *need* (survival driven), and your *feeling* about it (they lied! They got away with it, they manipulated the other person! They made me look bad). In the example above, it might look like this:

Situation: The child finds herself unexpectedly alone, triggering early trauma and a fear of abandonment.

Need: The child's driving need – 'Get the supporting professional to show me care and nurture. They are powerful so I need to ensure I am safe.'

Parent feels: Undermined, criticised, angry with the child for lying, angry with the supporting professional for failing to check the story.

Preventative strategies

- Agreement on boundaries is key, especially ensuring that the significant adults in your child's life are aware of therapeutic parenting strategies and the effects of childhood trauma, including what makes triangulation more likely, and the importance of secure group boundaries.

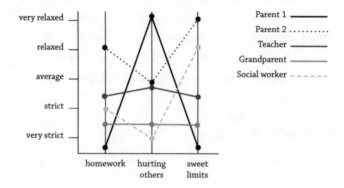

In the figure above there is plenty of opportunity for triangulation to occur. Clearly, communication is poor between the adults in the team around the child. Different boundaries lead to insecurity and triangulation. Here, for example, the child would probably be able to target which adult would be most likely to allow certain behaviours, creating conflict and mistrust between the adults.

- If there is an incident, a change in boundary, or a particular issue that surfaces (no matter how insignificant it may seem), pass the information on directly to the next adult the child is spending time with. This should be done out of the child's earshot.

- Educate those who have interactions with your child about 'the sympathetic face' and how your child may be hardwired to recognise this and react in any way they can to align themselves with others, and to keep themselves safe from a perceived threat.
- Where your child has therapy, I have found that removing the possibility for triangulation is by far the best preventer. This means finding therapists who are trained in dyadic developmental psychotherapy, an attachment or filial therapist, or practitioners using Theraplay®. All of these therapies use the relationship with the primary carer as the main focus and the parent is almost always present during therapy. This also helps the child to distinguish between fact and fiction, or confusing memories.
- You know your child best. If there is an event coming up that you know the child wishes to avoid, let them know that you are prepared, and have prepared others in order to avoid triangulation. You might say something like, 'I know you don't like PE, so I reminded your teacher that you may feel a bit wobbly when it's time to do it.'

Strategies during

- If you discover a very minor issue where the child has managed to undermine you, break a boundary or avoid a consequence, due to triangulation, it is sometimes useful to pretend you knew all about it. You might say, 'Oh yes, I spoke to Mr Smith about that already.' It's your call to decide how important the issue is, but for minor triangulations this can save some confrontation. Just ensure it cannot happen again, and speak to the other party involved!
- Normally, a therapeutic parent would let the child know that *they* knew what had happened. If I discovered that my child had managed to gain an extra lunch from unsuspecting grandparents I might say, 'I expect you wanted to check that Granny would feed you, so you played a little trick to get an extra lunch. I will have a chat to Granny so she can help you to check with me first next time.'

Strategies after

- You can use 'naming the need' to help the child link cause and effect, 'I think when you were waiting outside the cinema, a tiny part of you was a bit worried about being on your own so when X came along you needed to make sure they looked after you.'
- Let the child know that you know what has happened and the effect of their actions, without blaming them, 'I know that last week you told your teacher I had lost your PE kit. This week I have given a spare set to the teacher just in case, as I know you would not want the teacher to think that I didn't care about you.'
- Don't reveal your sources! When you discover there has been triangulation, do not let the child know the source of your information or be tempted to blame the other adult. As the unassailable safe base, you need to be clear that you 'know everything' and talk to 'lots of people' so you 'always find out what is going on in the end'.
- Allow natural consequences to occur for both the child and the adult who has been taken in. Sometimes, the other person will be resistant to believing that they have been tricked.

Footnote: In the example regarding the supporting professional and the cinema, the professional demanded that the carer repay her the money that she had given to the child. The carer explained she was unable to do this as the professional had failed to check the facts of the matter before acting. The carer let the child know that *she* knew what had happened and 'helped' the child to repay the supporting professional from her pocket money.

TRIGGERS *(see Transitions, and Part 1, Chapter 1)*

U

UNABLE TO BE ALONE *(see Anxiety, Nonsense Chatter, Separation Anxiety)*

UNABLE TO MAKE CHOICES/ DECISIONS *(see Choosing Difficulties)*

UNGRATEFULNESS *(see also Destruction, Rejection, Rudeness, Obsessions, Sabotaging, and Part 1, Chapter 1)*

What it looks like

- The child is dismissive of gifts.
- The child does not appreciate time spent, effort or presents.
- The child will not say 'thank you'.
- The child does not appreciate improvements in lifestyle, holidays and so on.
- The child spoils or destroys items, even when they have asked for them (see Damaging).

Why it might happen

- The child does not feel grateful and is of the view they have nothing to be grateful for, or is unable to feel gratitude.
- Gratitude is not appropriate.

- A subconscious compulsion to break a forming attachment (with the parent).
- Comfortable to be in the wrong/self-sabotage – the child's internal working model conflicts with their feelings about what they are 'worth'.
- Feelings around being disloyal to birth parents/former carers.
- The need to feel in control and powerful.
- Lack of empathy – unable to think about the effect this has on others.
- Dysregulation – acting in the heat of the moment.
- Shame – feeling unworthy or undeserving.
- Blocked trust, especially if they believe the positive item/time will be removed or is conditional.
- Feelings of hostility or momentary hatred towards the parent.
- Fear of invisibility/being forgotten – seeking a response.
- Recreating a familiar environment – gratitude may be an unfamiliar concept.
- Fear of change/transitions, especially relating to surprise trips out and changes in routine.
- Fear of drawing attention to self.
- Emotional age – may not have reached the emotional age to demonstrate gratitude.

Reality check

Imagine your life now. All the people who are around you, your little routines, your pets, your job and everything that makes you, *you*. Now someone is coming to your house to move you, without warning or preparation, to another town far away. Your phone and money are taken away. You have to live with a new partner, and you cannot contact your friends. On top of this you have different children to look after and you cannot see your own. You plead and beg with anyone who will listen to let you go back home. You miss your partner, your children, your pets, your bed. No one can help you. You are not even totally sure where you are living.

Two days later you are expected to start a new job. Everyone is different there and the rules have changed. Everything you thought you knew about your job is gone and you now realise you have to start from scratch. Your head is spinning. You can't concentrate. You feel ill with worry about where your family is and how they may be feeling about your disappearance. Your new boss is cross with you for not completing your work.

You go back to the new house, thinking and worrying about what on earth you can do. When you walk in the door, the person who everyone says is your 'new partner' is standing there. They have made a dinner. They tell you it's a lovely dinner and they have spent a long time preparing it. You cannot even look at it. It smells disgusting to you and you feel sick. You do not like this person and do not understand why you cannot go back home. You say you are not hungry.

They say, 'You are so ungrateful!'

Preventative strategies

- Our children often do not have anything to be grateful for. If you feel that they do, you need to look at this again from their perspective and take into account their knowledge, understanding, trauma history and emotional age. The first stage in feeling better about ungratefulness is getting to grips with how realistic our expectations are.
- Try to model thankfulness and giving, 'Oh, I'm so thankful someone invented the washing machine; otherwise I would be washing those clothes still by hand, and would not have time to sit down and play this game with you.' Or, 'I'm so grateful to have this warm coat on this freezing cold day. I bet it would be hard to be outside if I didn't own a coat.'
- Say 'thank you' as a natural part of conversation, but do not insist the child says it. Children often repeat, habitually, what they hear. Remember to say thank you to the child for small things and completed tasks.

- Don't set the child up to fail. If you have planned a surprise or event that you know the child is going to love, be satisfied with knowing that, and think of ways you will feel rewarded by the child taking pleasure in the surprise.

Strategies during

- If a child does not say thank you, it's useful to get another person to model the thanks. For example, you give the child a gift; the child accepts the gift and says nothing. The other person says, 'If X were able to he'd probably say, "Thanks for this present. I will love playing with it".' Sometimes, our children do not know what to say.
- Where a child receives something from a friend or relative, or perhaps has been to a party, do not make a big thing of telling the child to say thank you to the person. Instead, simply say within the child's earshot, 'X had a really lovely time, thank you so much.' This is usually sufficient.
- Be aware of your triggers! If the child knows that saying thank you is a 'big thing' for you, you are guaranteed a long wait. Better to disengage and move on, letting the child know that you know they are pleased with X and that you are sure they will find a way of showing that at some point.
- Making up a little happy song with the words 'you're welcome' in can help diffuse tension. Some therapeutic parents use the song from the Disney film *Moana* to great effect!

Strategies after

- Don't be tempted to remove an item due to a lack of thanks. Be aware that when our children feel unworthy of nice things they will sabotage them in order that their feeling of unworthiness is reinforced. I would say something like, 'I wonder if you feel you didn't deserve X. It's hard to feel thankful for something you feel you don't deserve. I decided that you did deserve X because... (give concrete examples of positives).'

UNTIDY BEDROOMS *(see Messy Bedrooms)*

URINATING *(see also Bedwetting, Messy Bedrooms, Poo Issues)*

What it looks like

- The child wets themselves and appears unaware.
- The child wets themselves and is aware but unconcerned.
- The child states their intention to wet themselves and then does so (see also Controlling Behaviours, and Defiance).
- The child urinates in different areas of the house or outside (see also Messy Bedrooms).
- The child is very late in potty training or regresses (see also Immaturity).

Why it might happen

- Sensory issues – the child may lack feeling and be unaware of the usual impulses.
- Immaturity and emotional age – the child is simply at a much younger developmental stage than they are at chronologically.
- Trauma-related issues, particularly around neglect and sexual abuse.
- Rewards the child with a reaction – trigger for the parent.
- Recreating a familiar environment (may be normal past entrenched behaviour). The smell of urine is a familiar babyhood smell. This is subconscious.
- Comfortable to be in the wrong – the internal working model of the child means they are comfortable and at ease with being seen to be 'dirty' or 'smelly'.
- Medical issues, particularly in relation to sensation and bladder control.
- Fear response – the child may wet themselves in fear or may be frightened to ask to go to the toilet, or frightened of the toilet.
- Blocked trust – the child cannot trust others enough to 'let their wee go'.

- The need to feel in control and powerful – the child at least has ultimate control over bodily functions.
- Lack of cause-and-effect thinking – the child is unlikely to link 'I will wet myself' to 'I will be wet.'
- Feelings of hostility or momentary hatred towards the parent, especially where the child announces their intention to wet themselves.
- Fear of invisibility/being forgotten – seeking a response.
- Fear of parent/carer and other adults.
- Fear of change/transitions.
- Separation anxiety.
- Fear of drawing attention to self, for example being afraid to ask to go to the toilet.
- Dissociation, especially where it appears the child is unaware (see also Absences).
- Overwhelming need to keep the parent close, especially to involve them in personal care.

Reality check

If you find yourself thinking, 'He just doesn't care' or, 'She did that on purpose', you need to reframe your thinking. This is *not* personal. It may be about control but it's not about 'doing it to us' as parents. It's often around the fact that our children have so little left in their life that they can control. Where there are early life histories centring around abuse and neglect, entrenched patterns of behaviour regarding wetting and soiling can take years to unpick.

The key here is to find strategies that take the pressure off both the child and ourselves. Throw out all the expectations of others and the unhelpful suggestions and comparisons such as, 'He should be dry by now.' This is not a logical problem that can be easily overcome using standard parenting techniques.

Often there are associated emotional traumas running alongside and the urinating is merely an expression of the inner turbulence. Some children describe the sensation of wetting themselves or wetting the bed as 'feeling a warm hug'. This is a stark reminder that the sensation of warm urine may have been the only comforting sensation some of our children experienced in very neglectful situations.

Preventative strategies

- Where you have a child stating a deliberate intention to wet themselves and then doing so, you can be pretty sure that this is mainly around gauging your reaction and investing in interaction (attachment seeking). You are likely to find the responses in Defiance or Controlling Behaviours most helpful for this type of urinating.
- Where the child seems unaware of the sensations of feeling wet, try looking into sensory integration therapy.
- When using pull-ups, try putting normal pants on underneath so the child feels the sensation of wetness, but be aware that sensory issues may confuse this.
- As a therapeutic parent, you will have a strong routine. Build in 'toilet time' to that routine. Think along the same lines as you would for a very young child in the early stages of potty training. Everyone nips to the loo before meals, or just before TV time, for example.
- If a child is urinating in different parts of the house, especially the bedroom, try providing a bowl or potty for them to wee in. This can be particularly helpful where the child is struggling to 'let go' of their bodily fluids. Sarah Dillon (an attachment therapist and former child in care) describes this as 'sad wee' and 'happy wee'. The happy wee goes down the toilet and the sad wee goes in the bowl. There may be a facilitated discussion around the 'sad wee'.
- Don't be afraid to regularly review your beliefs about what stage the child is at. For example, the child may be five years old and have come to you in pull-ups, with a label of 'not being potty trained'. We do find, however, that often parents simply move forwards and see what happens. A simple suggestion, with no pressure, about new pants can do the trick. Similarly, transitions often trigger regression, so it's very normal for a child who has

just moved to regress. It's important to allow the child to regress and start from scratch if necessary. I normally recommend a minimum period of six months in a new placement before even attempting to start to address potty training and related issues.

- If you are attending an event where there are likely to be high levels of dysregulation and excitement, consider putting on pull-ups just for that event. This avoids increasing shame. Constant stressed reminders about 'using the toilet' are likely to invoke feelings of shame and increase the chances of an accident.
- It may seem obvious but make sure school has spare clothing – as many sets as necessary, including PE kit. It can be shaming for the child to have to wear the school's own supply of spare clothing.

Strategies during

- Think about your reaction. If you have just discovered a new pool of wee, or the child has just wet themselves for the tenth time that day, take a deep breath before responding.
- When potty training, avoid asking the child if they need the toilet as they often do not know, due to sensory issues. Instead just say, 'Toilet time now'.
- Where there is a lack of awareness, ensure you point out sensitively what has happened, maybe with a code word that the child knows means, 'You have had an accident.' We used to say, 'It looks like you need some help.'
- Where you find a puddle of urine, state out loud factually what you have found without invoking shame. You might say, 'Oh, I can see there's some wee here.' Rather than, 'Did you do this?' Asking the child if they did it is merely inviting them to tell a lie to cover their shame.
- Wondering aloud can help in different situations:
  - 'I wonder if you wet yourself because you thought I had forgotten you?'
  - 'I wonder if you did a wee in the corner of your room because you were saving up your sad wee?'
  - 'I wonder if you wet yourself because you were so worried about seeing X today?'

Strategies after

- A knee-jerk reaction might be to tell the child to clean it up. Parents get very stressed about urinating. The smell is pervasive and unpleasant. This can become a trigger for some parents (I was one of them), and then we have to be really careful about overreacting. When we tell a child they have to clean it up, it's a bit like telling a two-year-old that you find their bodily functions disgusting, therefore they are disgusting. This may then reinforce the child's view of themselves as 'bad'. However, the therapeutic parenting strategy of natural consequences, linking cause and effect, can be used so the child *helps* to clear it up. This is best done in a nurturing way, 'Oh, I see there's some wee here. Help me clear it up using this. Let's do it quickly together then we can go and...' (We used to keep handy a mixture of bicarbonate of soda and vinegar, which was quite effective.) This keeps the child out of toxic shame and also enables them to 'put it right'. Our children often want to find a way to do this.
- Where you are using bowls for 'sad wee' help the child to empty them down the toilet, maybe facilitating speculation about the sadness. 'Naming the need' is useful here, 'I wonder if there's lots of wee in this bowl because you were sad yesterday about...'

Footnote: You may find it comforting to remember that toilet issues nearly always resolve over time. It can be extremely difficult to stay focused on a positive future, while worrying about when it will end. Be kind to yourself and allow yourself to indulge in measures that help to prevent the smell, such as laminate flooring or lino with washable rugs, pull-ups when necessary to relieve stress, and stepping away from the competitive parents 'side show' around these issues.

Further resources

ERIC – a charity supporting parents dealing with bowel and bladder problems: www.eric.org.uk.

VACATIONS *(see Holiday Issues)*

VICARIOUS TRAUMA *(see Compassion Fatigue, and Part 1, Chapter 7)*

VIOLENCE *(see Aggression)*

W

WAKING ANGRY *(see Sleep Issues)*

WAKING EARLY *(see Sleep Issues)*

WEE *(see Bedwetting, Urinating)*

WETTING SELVES *(see Bedwetting, Urinating)*

WHINING *(see also Arguing, Nonsense Chatter)*

What it looks like

- The child complains about everyday expectations.
- The child moans about having to complete tasks.
- The child moans, whines and complains at a low level nearly all the time.
- The child complains about minor health issues or imagined health issues (see also Hypochondria).
- The child complies but often states that expectations are unfair.
- The child complains that others are treated more favourably (see also Sibling Rivalry).

Why it might happen

- Recreating a familiar environment – the child may have experienced others complaining all the time.
- Impulsivity – the child is unable to wait for 'the next thing'.
- Fear of invisibility/being forgotten – seeking a response.
- A need to try to predict the environment – the child might be seeking information.
- Fear of change/transitions – whining may be used as a delay tactic.
- Separation anxiety.
- Overwhelming need to keep the parent close.
- Overwhelming need to feel loved/important.
- Emotional age – the child may be functioning at a younger age and simply presenting needs appropriate to that age/stage.

Preventative strategies

- Think carefully how you respond to the whining. If you are saying things like 'Stop whining!' you are handing the child a reward and reinforcing the behaviour.
- Supply the child with a notebook and pen to write down all their complaints. You can even name it 'complaints book'.
- Allocate a time to hear any complaint. Build it in to a daily or weekly routine. That way, when the child is complaining you can remind them to hold on until it's 'complaints time'.
- Remember that often the child is not aware of what they are saying. What happens if you do not answer?
- Our response is the best preventative strategy, so use some of the strategies below to reduce whining and moaning.

Strategies during

- Refer the child to the 'complaints book'. Let them know you will be happy to read it later. The child will rarely go and write it down as this uses a different part of their brain. This strategy is good for helping the child to become more aware and focused about what they are actually thinking and saying. It's important not to force the child to write the complaint down as it is not meant to be some kind of punishment.

- Don't be distracted and pulled in to the moan! Keep moving forwards with what you were doing and saying previously. You don't need to respond to the moaning. You can just say, 'Oh dear, that's a shame' and keep going. You can also use phrases such as, 'That's an interesting point of view' or, 'You are probably right', much as we do when dealing with arguing. A neutral, non-engaging response can be very effective.

- Respond with a happy smile and a positive comment, 'Brilliant! I am so happy you are whining about that! Well done!' This again helps the child to stop and think about what they are saying.

- Give the child what they want in an 'imaginary' way. Acknowledge the desire and then use playfulness, 'So, you really, really want some biscuits?' (Child agrees.) 'I expect you would like ten packets!' (Child looks irritated but engages.) 'How great would it be to fill up the whole bathroom with biscuits!' Usually this interrupts the cycle and the child either starts laughing or joins in.

- When a child is whining, you can use empathic commentary, relating to what the child is actually moaning about, 'I hear what you are saying. You really, really want those biscuits.' Sometimes this can make things worse – it depends on how your child responds. I used empathic commentary to reflect on the *actual* whining, 'It must be tough to feel like you need to moan all the time to get my attention. I wonder if you were worried I had forgotten about you?'

- Use headphones to disengage. Where the whining has become pretty entrenched and you are struggling to connect, put on a happy face and say, 'My ears need a bit of a rest from all the moaning so I get to refresh them by listening to my favourite song.' You can still stay engaged with the child (if you want), do singing, and use some playfulness, but you can't hear the moaning. (Note that it is up to you whether or not you actually have the music playing. But your face will look engaged and happy.

Therefore, the whining loses its main aim – a trigger for negative interaction – and it will decrease quickly.) Therapeutic parents have had very good results using this strategy and often report that they only need to reach for the headphones and the child stops moaning. This is powerful and positive for our children as they are connected to what they are saying and the effect of that behaviour on others. If there are other adults or children who may also have been drawing away, due to the moaning, they will be more likely to re-engage.

- Use playfulness to make a big, funny drama. For example, the child is complaining that someone got the shiniest apple. I would throw myself on the floor, pretend to cry and generally berate myself for being such a dreadful mother that I lacked vigilance around the shininess of the apples. This can also be quite cathartic!

- State that you can see there is a little pity party that is happening, but normally we only have one person attending those. Let the child know that you will be available when the pity party has ended. You can sit them at the table and even give them a drink and snack for the party, then get on with your busy jobs. Ask them to let you know when they have finished.

- Use natural consequences, for example, 'I can see you are worried about the apples not being shiny enough. I have noticed that you often complain about how food looks, so this can be a nice job for you, then you won't need to worry. I will just fill up the bowl so you can wash all the fruit.'

- Be alert for any reoccurring themes (hidden with the general moaning), in case they need to be addressed properly and are masking more serious issues.

Strategies after

- Where there are gaps in the moaning and complaining, be sure to use the strategies explained in Sibling Rivalry around keeping a list of what is most unfair. You can then refer to this when needed.

- Use 'naming the need' to explore what your child is actually trying to achieve. Is this really about a deep-seated loneliness? A fear that they may be forgotten?
- Put down some boundaries about what you will and will not engage with. That way, the next time it happens you can refer the child back to this statement. It may even be helpful to have answers written up on a board ready to point the child to. For example, 'I thought about what you said earlier about the apples. Well, I have decided that as I am in charge of food and always check it is good enough and right for us to eat, I won't be talking about that anymore.'

XENOPHOBIA *(see also Rudeness)*

What it looks like

- The child is critical and rejecting of different cultures.
- The child often demonstrates defensiveness and is rude to people from other cultures.
- The child makes sweeping statements often using insults relating to other cultures.
- The child uses racist, homophobic or other discriminatory language.

Why it might happen

- Fear of the unknown – different cultures that are unfamiliar to the child are likely to provoke a hostile response, based in fear. The child may feel compelled to reject people from other cultures and work hard to keep them at a safe distance.
- Fear of different clothing, costumes, especially if the face is hidden.
- Blocked trust – the child is naturally suspicious of anything outside their immediate boundary of knowledge and experience.
- Dysregulation – acting in the heat of the moment.
- A subconscious compulsion to break a forming attachment (with the parent).

- Attraction to peer group – mimicking actions and reactions of peers.
- Fear response.
- Feelings of hostility towards a particular culture.
- Fear of invisibility/being forgotten – seeking a response through making xenophobic or racist comments.
- Recreating a familiar environment – the child may be replaying learned patterns of xenophobia. They may be unaware of the implications of their behaviour.
- Lack of empathy – the child is unable to empathise with how this action may impact on others, as well as lack of empathy for future self.
- Lack of remorse.
- A need to try to predict the environment – this is more difficult where customs and dress may be different.
- Fear of change/transitions – xenophobia may manifest as a reaction to going on holiday.
- Comfortable to be in the wrong – the child's internal working model dictates that they are unworthy of nice things so rudeness is the protective shell.
- Emotional age – the child may be functioning at a younger age and say inappropriate things.
- Loyalty to birth parents/former carers – resisting attachment to new carers/parents, especially where there are differing cultures within carer/parent group.

Preventative strategies

- Prepare children for holidays, especially where there are going to be obvious differences in language and culture.
- Ensure exposure to different languages, cultures and religions in a non-threatening environment and in a matter-of-fact way, through films and stories.
- Do not set yourself up to fail! If you reveal your fear they will not disappoint you. I once said, 'In America people do speak English but they have a different accent, so I don't want any

rude comments.' We were not even out of the airport before they were exclaiming loudly about how no one could speak 'proper English'.

- Distract and prepare children with interesting details, for example, 'The lady who is going to be our guide is an Indian lady, and she wears a sari which is really beautiful. It's more sparkly than our clothes.'

Strategies during

- Be aware of your triggers. If you feel the child is making offensive remarks and comments in order to draw a negative, emotional response from you, make it clear to the child that their attitude and comments are offensive, without showing that you are *personally* hurt or upset by the behaviour, 'That's an offensive thing to say. People who don't understand you so well may have a problem with you speaking like that.'
- If the child makes a racist comment consider if they actually understand what they are saying. What would your response be if a much younger child said the same thing?
- Avoid confrontational and punitive language or long discussions around remorse and meaning, history lessons and so on. Instead, use an empathic response to explore feelings behind strong statements. For example, the child says, 'I hate white people...!' Your response, 'Goodness me! That is *such* a lot of people to hate. It must be scary to have so much hate inside you.'
- Allow for second attempts (without planting your feet in the sand and insisting they apologise), 'Shall we have another go? Because I don't think that came out how you meant it to. What might be a better way of saying that?'
- Deliberately misunderstand what the child has said. Look confused and wait.

Strategies after

- It works well to involve natural consequences, so for example if one of my children said, 'I hate Muslims,' I might decide that the topic for dinner that night would be 'The Muslim religion'. No one was allowed to speak unless they had something to add to that discussion in an informative way. Handouts were provided. This works especially well with children who like to be the centre of attention and don't like having to be quiet for any length of time!

- Express sadness for hurtful feelings within the child, which must exist in order for them to hold these views. This happens a little after the event, using some time for reflection. Say something like, 'I can see you have some questions about the people who live in the country where we are going on holiday, but I think earlier you were feeling wobbly about going on holiday and your words came out wrong.'

- 'Name the need' to look at where these words came from, 'Sometimes when children have had scary things happen to them, they get even more wobbly when they see people who look and act differently from them. Let's look at some of the differences.'

Y

YELLING *(see Shouting and Screaming)*

Z

ZZZZ *(see Sleep Issues)*

References,

Further Reading and Websites

Publication references

Baylin, J. and Hughes, D. (2016) *The Neurobiology of Attachment-Focused Therapy: Enhancing Connection and Trust in the Treatment of Children and Adolescents* (Norton Series on Interpersonal Neurobiology). New York, NY: W.W. Norton & Company.

Bomber, L. (2011) *What About Me? Inclusive Strategies to Support Pupils with Attachment Difficulties*. London: Worth Publishing.

Brown, B. (2012) TED Talk: 'Listening to Shame.' 16 March. Available at: www.ted.com/talks/brene_brown_listening_to_shame, accesssed on 5 December 2017.

Colley, D. (2017) *Attachment and Emotional Development in the Classroom*. London: Jessica Kingsley Publishers.

Golding, K. (2017) *Everyday Parenting with Security and Love*. London: Jessica Kingsley Publishers.

Harris, R. (2010) *Let's Talk About Sex*. London: Walker Books.

Hughes, D. (2016) *Parenting a Child Who Has Experienced Trauma*. London: CoramBAAF.

Hughes, D. and Baylin, J. (2012) *Brain-Based Parenting: The Neuroscience of Caregiving for Healthy Attachment*. New York, NY: W.W. Norton & Company.

Hughes, D. and Golding, K. (2012) *Creating Loving Attachments: Parenting with PACE to Nurture Confidence and Security in the Troubled Child*. London: Jessica Kingsley Publishers.

Karst, P. (2000) *The Invisible String*. Camarillo, CA: DeVorss & Co.

Naish, S. (2016) *Therapeutic Parenting in a Nutshell: Positives and Pitfalls*. Amazon CreateSpace.

Naish, S. and Jefferies, R. (2016) *Rosie Rudey and the Very Annoying Parent*. London: Jessica Kingsley Publishers.

Naish, S. and Jefferies, R. (2016) *William Wobbly and the Very Bad Day*. London: Jessica Kingsley Publishers.

Naish, S. and Jefferies, R. (2016) *Charley Chatty and the Wiggly Worry Worm*. London: Jessica Kingsley Publishers.

Naish, S. and Jefferies, R. (2016) *Sophie Spikey has a Very Big Problem*. London: Jessica Kingsley Publishers.

Naish, S. and Jefferies, R. (2017) *Rosie Rudey and the Enormous Chocolate Mountain.* London: Jessica Kingsley Publishers.

Naish, S. and Jefferies, R. (2017) *William Wobbly and the Mysterious Holey Jumper.* London: Jessica Kingsley Publishers.

Naish, S. and Jefferies, R. (2017) *Callum Kindly and the Very Weird Child.* London: Jessica Kingsley Publishers.

Naish, S. and Jefferies, R. (2017) *Katie Careful and the Very Sad Smile.* London: Jessica Kingsley Publishers.

Naish, S. and Jefferies, R. (2017) *Charley Chatty and the Disappearing Pennies.* London: Jessica Kingsley Publishers.

Oakwater, H. (2012) *Bubble Wrapped Children: How Social Networking is Transforming the Face of 21st Century Adoption.* London: MX Publishing.

Ottoway, H. and Selwyn, J. (2016) *No One Told Us It Would Be Like This: Compassion Fatigue and Foster Care.* Bristol: The Hadley Centre, University of Bristol.

Rodwell, H. and Norris, V. (2017) *Parenting with Theraplay®.* London: Jessica Kingsley Publishers.

Rowell, K. (2012) *Love Me, Feed Me: The Adoptive Parent's Guide to Ending the Worry About Weight, Picky Eating, Power Struggles and More.* Family Feeding Dynamics.

Smith, J. (2012) *The Parent's Guide to Self-Harm.* Oxford: Lion Books.

Van der Kolk, B. (2015) *The Body Keeps the Score: Mind, Brain and Body in the Transformation of Trauma.* New York, NY: Penguin Books Ltd.

Wilson, G. (2015) *Your Brain on Porn: Internet Pornography and the Emerging Science of Addiction.* Margate: Commonwealth Publishing.

Further reading

Flores, P.J. (2011) *Addiction as an Attachment Disorder.* New York, NY: Jason Aronson Inc.

Heegaard, M. (1993) *When a Family is in Trouble.* Mineapolis, MN: Woodland Press.

O'Connor, D. (2009) *I Can Be Me: A Helping Book for Children of Alcoholic Parents.* Bloomington, IN: AuthorHouse

Seigal, D.J. (2014) *Brainstorm: The Power and Purpose of the Teenage Brain.* New York, NY: Tarcher.

Shawe, B.F. (2005) *Addiction and Recovery for Dummies.* New York, NY: John Wiley and Sons.

Spinney, C.J. (2016) *Heroin Addiction: The Addiction Guide for the Amateur.* Amazon CreateSpace.

Websites

Dr Bruce Perry http://childtrauma.org

Dr Bessel Van der Kolk: http://besselvanderkolk.net/index.html

ERIC – a charity supporting parents dealing with bowel and bladder problems: www.eric.org.uk

Family Lives – information on drugs and alcohol with adolescents, includes talking to teens about drugs: www.familylives.org.uk

Frank – for young people to access information and support: www.talktofrank.com

Functional Neurological Disorder (non-epileptic seizures) support and information group: www.fndaction.org.uk

National Association of Therapeutic Parents (NATP): www.naotp.com

National Society for the Prevention of Cruelty to Children (NSPCC): www.nspcc.org.uk/preventing-abuse

Parents Protect – for up-to-date information and top tips on keeping your children safe online: www.parentsprotect.org

Recovery.org.uk – drugs and alcohol rehabilitation and other related help: www.recovery.org.uk

Stop it Now! – to talk through your concerns about a child's sexualised behaviour: www.stopitnow.org.uk/concerned_about_a_childs_behaviour.htm

XXXAware – this site gives step-by-step instructions on how to set up parental controls on a range of broadband providers and tech products and is very user friendly. It's a one-stop shop for parental controls: www.xxxaware.co.uk